The Winning Combination

21 Keys to Coaching and Leadership Greatness

Pat Williams with Jim Denney

ISBN: 978-1-60679-106-6
Library of Congress Control Number: 2010926644
Cover design: Brenden Murphy
Book layout: Studio J Art & Design

Coaches Choice
P.O. Box 1828
Monterey, CA 93942
www.coacheschoice.com

Dedication

I served as the general manager of the Philadelphia 76ers from 1974 to 1986. I dedicate this book to four sports leaders of that era, whom I greatly admire: Billy Cunningham, coach of the 76ers; Dick Vermeil, coach of the Eagles; Dallas Green, manager of the Phillies; and the late Fred Shero, coach of the Flyers.

Acknowledgments

With deep appreciation, I acknowledge the support and guidance of the following people who helped make this book possible:

Special thanks to Bob Vander Weide, Rich DeVos, and Alex Martins of the Orlando Magic for their encouragement.

Hats off to my associates Andrew Herdliska and Latria Leak; my proofreader, Ken Hussar; and my ace typist, Fran Thomas.

Thanks also to my writing partner, Jim Denney, for his superb contributions in shaping this manuscript.

Hearty thanks also go to my publisher Jim Peterson and my editors Kristi Huelsing and Angie Perry. Thank you for believing that we had something important to share, and for providing the support and the forum to say it.

And, finally, special thanks and appreciation go to my wife, Ruth, and to my wonderful and supportive family. They are truly the backbone of my life.

Contents

Foreword

Having just published my first (and probably last) book, I am amazed at what Pat Williams has done through the years. It is hard work to write a book, something I maybe didn't realize until I was in the middle of my own.

However, I sure wish he had gotten around to this one about 37 years ago. He could have saved me from the trial and error method I've used over the years of my coaching career to form a list that is pretty much exactly what Pat has presented in this book. But that's not really such a surprise. In addition to using me as an example more times than he should have, he has related stories about some of my very own coaching mentors. You can't go wrong taking your cue from people like Coach Dean Smith, John Wooden, Bob Knight, Pat Summitt, Bear Bryant, and many other people I have had the privilege to know and study, just like Pat. All of them have set records (Chapter 21) in their coaching careers. The stories Pat relates can now guide anyone toward coaching and leadership greatness.

Not one of us is ever too good to keep learning (Chapters 9 and 20). Each year I try to watch some other coach conduct practice. I choose someone who does a great job teaching an aspect of the game that I need to be better at teaching. When looking for players, talent (Chapter 16) is my first requirement, but character (Chapter 2) is my second. I titled my book, *Hard Work* (Chapter 3). As a basketball coach, I have said that Coach Smith was the innovator; I'm the copier. But I also say that I'd be fired as a football coach, because all I'd want to run were dippsy-doodle plays—double reverses, shoestring plays, and the Statue of Liberty. That's bold and confident (Chapter 8). As it is, I probably scare people with our fast style of play.

Our practices are about discipline (Chapter 5), preparation (Chapter 6), taking care of the little things (Chapter 12) and not being the team to give in to fatigue (Chapter 4). On the court, it's all about the team (Chapter 18), and getting the most out of players (Chapters 14 and 15), but off the court, it's about the individual (Chapter 10). If things are not going well, maybe I'm not communicating well (Chapter 19) or we just need some perspective, so we'll take a day off and do something fun and silly (Chapter 11).

I've been fortunate to have great assistant coaches, and my current staff of four has been with me a total of 54 years (Chapter 13). And I'm still working on a couple of Pat's principles. The media and the other critics in the Internet age still drive me crazy

(Chapter 17), and I haven't always handled them as well as I could have. My wife thinks I still need to work on maintaining balance (Chapter 7).

Whether you're just starting out, or you've been doing your job for a while, you couldn't spend any more productive time than reading Pat's book, all 21 chapters, over the next 21 days, as he suggests.

—Roy Williams
Head Men's Basketball Coach
University of North Carolina

Introduction

What Do I Do Now?

My life changed in June 1962.

Within the space of a few days, I graduated from Wake Forest University, my dad was killed in an automobile accident, and I embarked on a career in professional sports—a career which, in one way or another, continues to this day. After my father's funeral in Wilmington, Delaware, one of Dad's friends, Philadelphia Phillies owner Bob Carpenter, gave me a piece of advice that has served me well throughout my career: "Keep your eyes and ears open, Pat, both on the field and off."

Armed with Mr. Carpenter's advice, I drove to Miami, where I would spend the next two years catching for the Class D Miami Marlins, a Phillies farm club. I reported to the manager, Andy Seminick, who had been my idol as a Phillies catcher in the late 1940s and early '50s. He was one of the "Whiz Kids" of the NL pennant-winning Phillies of 1950, and I had gotten to know him while hanging around Shibe Park throughout my teen years. I was honored to have Andy as my first manager in the pros, and he became a mentor to me.

One of our pitchers was Ferguson Jenkins, who would go on to win the National League Cy Young Award in 1971 and become the first pitcher in the majors to achieve 3,000 strikeouts with fewer than 1,000 walks. I caught five of his seven victories in the 1962 season.

One Sunday night in July 1962, we were playing at home against the Kansas City A's farm club from Daytona Beach. Daytona had a runner at second, Fergie was pitching, and I was catching. The batter knocked a base hit to the outfield, the throw came to the plate, and I had it in time. As the runner rounded third, he saw I had the ball—and he knew he had to knock me over or he was out. So he came at me, shoulder down, and knocked me base over apex. I rolled back onto my feet with the ball firmly grasped in my hand. He was outta there!

Next day, the *Miami News* ran a five-frame sequence of that play, showing the runner bowling me over at the plate. That baserunner was 17 years old at the time, signed right out of high school. His name was Tony La Russa; he was called up to the majors the very next year and went on to become one of the most successful managers in MLB history.

My Coaches and Mentors

Throughout my two years as a minor league player, I remembered Bob Carpenter's advice: "Keep your eyes and ears open, Pat, both on the field and off." I absorbed everything I could about the game—on the field, in the locker room, and in the front office.

I was mentored by the team's general manager, Bill Durney, who had worked for the legendary baseball owner-promoter Bill Veeck in the early 1950s. Durney introduced me to Veeck, who had retired to Easton, Maryland. Bill Veeck's Cleveland Indians had won the World Series in 1948 and his White Sox had taken the American League pennant in 1959. Most important of all, Bill Veeck was a consummate showman, and every baseball fan knew that, win or lose, you always had fun at one of Bill Veeck's games.

I'll never forget that sunny September day when I drove to up the tree-lined drive to Bill Veeck's home overlooking the Chesapeake Bay. He was sitting on the front steps, bare-chested, clad in tan shorts, with a book of Civil War poetry in his hands. While serving in the Marines in World War II, he'd lost a leg in an accident involving a recoiling artillery piece. He was not wearing his wooden leg when I walked up to the house to meet him, but he later strapped it on and we played a game of badminton in the backyard—and he beat me.

I was surprised to find the great baseball entrepreneur to be a gentle, soft-spoken man with a quick mind and a rich vocabulary, thanks to his extensive reading. He was a gracious host and offered me four pieces of invaluable advice, which I never forgot: "First, know somebody," he said. "It's almost impossible to get inside this game if you don't know somebody. Second, learn to type. Third, learn all you can about advertising and marketing. Fourth, get some kind of business background."

As I drove away from my first encounter with Bill Veeck, I felt I had been to the mountain and received a revelation from on high. I followed his advice, and Bill and I maintained a friendship that continued until his death in January 1986. I was keenly aware, during those first few years after the loss of my father, that I needed a lot of fatherly insight and wisdom. So, whenever I faced a major life choice or career decision, I always called upon the wisdom and experience of my mentors, including Bill Veeck.

My first two years in pro sports in Miami laid the groundwork for the rest of my career. As a minor league player, I learned what it feels like to ride the team bus on the road, to experience the highs and lows of athletic competition, to know the fears and insecurities of a professional athlete. Those early playing years gave me a valuable perspective on my job as a sports executive and a business leader. Every time I've ever had to sit down with a player and tell him he was being waived or traded, I remembered how I felt as a young player—how badly I wanted to make it in baseball. The hardest chore in sports is pouring cold water on a young athlete's dreams.

By the end of my second season in Miami, that cold water was *raining* on my dreams like a monsoon. I knew that my .295 batting average in the low minors was not going to propel me into the major leagues. So I began to think about all the insights I'd learned about coaching, managing, and promoting in pro sports—insights I'd gained from Bob Carpenter, Andy Seminick, Bill Durney, and the great Bill Veeck. The front office beckoned—and I answered the call.

"What Do I Do Now?"

After serving a front office apprenticeship in Miami, the Phillies organization gave me a minor league ballclub to operate—the Phillies of Spartanburg, South Carolina. There, in early February 1965, I met a man who literally transformed my life, team co-owner R. E. Littlejohn. Mr. Littlejohn was a courteous, soft-spoken Southern gentleman who took a fatherly interest in my career. He gave me a crash course in the business side of baseball—and I needed it, because the season would open in just two months.

There I was, a mere 24 years old, one of the youngest execs in professional sports history, living in a strange city, taking full responsibility for a pro sports team for the first time in my life. I remember visiting Spartanburg's Duncan Park for the first time—a fixer-upper of a ballpark if there ever was one. I looked at the dilapidated stands and the weed-grown field, and I tried to picture the season ahead.

"What have I gotten myself into?" I wondered. "What do I do now?"

Mr. Littlejohn turned me loose to run the team pretty much as I saw fit. Drawing on the excellent counsel I received from Bill Veeck and my other coaches and mentors, I plunged in, remodeled the ballpark, brainstormed promotional ideas, and put on a good show for the Spartanburg fans. At the end of the season, the parent organization in Philadelphia complimented my efforts and I was named Executive of the Year in the Western Carolinas League.

But I couldn't have done it without my coaches and mentors. I would have been completely lost without their sage advice—especially that word from Phillies owner Bob Carpenter: "Keep your eyes and ears open, both on the field and off." That bit of counsel opened the door to all the other wisdom and insights I received.

The years rolled by. I raised a family, moved from minor league baseball to NBA basketball, served as general manager of the Philadelphia 76ers, collected an NBA championship ring there in 1983, then moved to Florida in 1986 and helped build an NBA franchise from scratch in Orlando.

One day in January 2005, I got a phone call from my 27-year-old son Bobby. After coaching in the Cincinnati Reds farm system for five years, he had just been offered the chance to realize his dream: The Washington Nationals (formerly the Montreal Expos) wanted him to manage a farm club, the Vermont Expos, in the New York-Penn League.

"I accepted the job, Dad," he said. "But I've got to tell you, it's kinda scary. Dad, what do I do now?"

Déjà vu! It hit me that Bobby's call came *almost exactly* 40 years after I had stood in Duncan Park and wondered, "What do I do now?" And here was my son, calling me to ask the very same question.

The fact is, I'm sure every coach, every manager, every leader in every field of endeavor, must ask himself that same question many times over the course of a career. I know I faced that question whenever a new challenge was thrust upon me, whenever a big new opportunity came my way: "What do I do now?"

In other words: "Now that I have the job, how do I succeed in it? How do I rise to the challenge of leadership? What should my priorities be? How do I set goals? How do I make good decisions? How do I gain the respect of my players? How do I gain the confidence and approval of my bosses? How do I keep from falling flat on my face and making a fool of myself?"

Wisdom on a Napkin

A few days after Bobby's call, I was talking to my friend Chuck Daly (the Hall of Fame NBA coach who passed away in May 2009). I told Chuck about Bobby's question. He said, "Pat, when I got my first head coaching job at Boston College, and again when I got my first NBA head coaching job in Cleveland, my first thought was the same as Bobby's: 'What do I do now?'"

I realized that Bobby's question—and mine and Chuck's—was undoubtedly a universal question among coaches, managers, and leaders of all kinds. So, whenever I encountered anyone in the leadership profession, I would pose this question: "From your experience, what are the keys to being a successful coach?" I asked this question of leaders in every sport and leaders outside the sports profession.

In June 2005, I attended the 25th anniversary celebration of the Washington Speakers Bureau. The guest list was stellar: Lou Holtz, Rudy Giuliani, Joe Theismann, Tom Peters, Doris Kearns Goodwin, and many more. During a trip to the dessert table, I found myself within arm's reach of Gen. Colin Powell, who was picking up an éclair before leaving.

"General Powell," I said, "I'm Pat Williams of the Orlando Magic. My son Bobby just became a manager in the Washington Nationals farm system, and he's eager to do everything he can to be successful in that role. Would you have any advice for him?"

The general looked me in the eye and said, "Tell your son, 'Take care of your troops.' And tell him, 'Keep your mouth shut and do your job.'" He started to leave—then paused and added over his shoulder, "And tell him, 'Stay focused on this job—don't worry about your next job.'"

Then he was out the door.

I snatched a napkin from the dessert table, whipped out my pen, and wrote down the advice General Powell had given me—a 20-second course in effective leadership. The next day—as I did with every scrap of coaching and leadership advice I was gathering—I photocopied that napkin and all my other recent notes and mailed them to Bobby.

Collecting leadership advice for Bobby became a project—then an obsession! Soon, I was chasing every prominent coach in America. Over a five-year period, I collected advice from more than 1,500 coaches from all major sports, college and pro—insights from such legendary leaders as Red Auerbach, Phil Jackson, Marv Levy, Alvin Dark, John Wooden, Jack Ramsay, Tony Dungy, Tommy Lasorda, Scott Linehan, Marty Schottenheimer, and more. I published all of those responses word-for-word in *The Ultimate Coaches' Career Manual.*

As I collected and collated thousands of quotations and stories from hundreds of great coaches, I realized that a number of themes recurred again and again. Breaking them down into categories, I arrived at what I call *The Winning Combination: 21 Keys to Coaching and Leadership Greatness.* These 21 insights are the keys to being a great coach and bringing out the greatness of your players.

My Goal: To Change Your Life

When I saw that these insights divided neatly into 21 chapters, I thought, "That's perfect—and 21 is the perfect number of chapters!" Maxwell Maltz, in his 1960 self-help classic *Psycho-Cybernetics,* said that it takes 21 days to change a habit. If it takes 21 days to change a habit, then it takes 21 days to change your life and transform your career as a leader.

And that's what *The Winning Combination* is about. I didn't write this book merely to dump a lot of motivational platitudes on you. I designed this book to be a habit-changer and a life-changer. If you will give me just a few minutes a day for the next 21 days of your life, I think you'll find that this book will literally be a *game-changer* for you.

I wish every leader and coach could have had the advantage of my mentors and teachers. I wish you could have sat with me through the years, listening to the wisdom of Mr. Littlejohn, Bob Carpenter, Andy Seminick, Bill Durney, and the great Bill Veeck. I wish you could have stood beside me at the dessert table as Gen. Colin Powell dispensed his principles of effective leadership. I wish you could have listened in on my conversations with great coaches and managers from every major sport.

Since that's not possible, I've done the next best thing. I've distilled their insights into these pages and presented them to you between these covers—a feast for the soul; a banquet for the heart and mind of every leader. These pages answer every question of every person who has ever asked, "What do I do now?"

These 21 principles transcend the world of sports and coaching. They are truly the keys to great leadership in every field of endeavor, from sports to business to government to religion to the military. Whenever you ask yourself, "What do I do now?," come back to these pages for 21 tested, proven, authoritative answers.

I hope you'll underline this book, highlight it, dog-ear it, and scribble in the margins. And I hope you'll recommend it to friends and colleagues and give it as a gift to other leaders and coaches—especially to those people in your life who are asking themselves, "What do I do now?"

Above all, after you've read it, drop me a letter or email, or give me a call. My contact information is at the back of this book. Let me know what you think. Let me know how this book has affected your life.

I'm looking forward to hearing from you.

—Pat Williams
Senior Vice President
Orlando Magic

1

Be Yourself

©Kevin Sullivan/The Orange County Register/ZUMA Press

Who was the greatest coach of all time?

Legendary NFL coach Vince Lombardi certainly belongs near the top of anyone's list. At age 45, Lombardi took over as head coach and general manager of the Green Bay Packers. At that time, the Packers were a perennially losing team, which had not had a winning season in more than a decade. The previous season, the Packers had won one game, lost 10, and tied one.

Things changed quickly under Lombardi. During his first season with the team, the Packers immediately improved to 7-5. The next year, he coached the Packers to the 1960 NFL championship game versus the Philadelphia Eagles. The Packers nearly won that game, but Packers fullback Jim Taylor was stuffed just a few yards short of the end zone when the clock expired. Afterwards, Lombardi declared that the Packers would never again lose a postseason game under his command—and he kept that promise, winning his next nine postseason games.

Lombardi coached the Packers to three consecutive NFL championships (1965 through 1967)—a feat that has never been equaled. Indeed, Lombardi never had a losing season in the NFL. He retired as head coach of the Packers after the 1967 season, having won five league championships in his nine years at Green Bay. At that point in his career, the 55-year-old Lombardi was so popular that 1968 presidential candidate Richard M. Nixon actually short-listed Lombardi as a possible running mate.

After a one-year hiatus from coaching, Coach Lombardi accepted the post of head coach of the Washington Redskins in 1969. His first order of business was to meet one-on-one with starting quarterback Sonny Jurgensen, so that he could start building a good working relationship with him before training camp.

"Sonny," Lombardi said, "I just ask one thing of you—I want you to be yourself. Don't emulate anyone else. Don't try to be someone you're not. Just be yourself."[1]

Be yourself! That was Coach Lombardi's message to his players—and he lived by that simple dictum every day of his legendary career. Lombardi knew who he was—his own strengths and limitations, his own assets and liabilities, his own talents and deficits—and he coached his own way. He didn't try to copy other coaches or please everybody else. He knew who he was, and coached from that zone of self-confidence. "In all my years of coaching," he once said, "I have never been successful using somebody else's plays."[2]

As you lead, heed the words of Vince Lombardi. Be yourself.

Learn From the Best—But Be Yourself

Maggie Dixon was 28 years old when she interviewed for the women's basketball coach position at the United States Military Academy at West Point. The prospect of coaching at West Point was daunting, and Maggie Dixon wondered if she could fit into the regimented environment there. So she asked her brother, Jamie Dixon, head coach of the University of Pittsburgh men's basketball team, if he had any advice.

"It's Army," he told her. "It's not the traditional basketball setting. I don't know what to tell you, Maggie, except just be yourself."

Maggie Dixon took her brother's advice. She interviewed and got the job—by being herself. Though she had been an assistant coach at DePaul for four years, this was her first assignment as head coach. Jamie Dixon proudly reflects that his sister approached every challenge by "coming out of the blue, but with confidence in herself and her background." That air of total self-confidence, Jamie says, "tells you everything you want to know about Maggie Dixon."

The West Point women's basketball team finished the 2005-2006 season—its first season under Maggie Dixon's command—with a strong 20-10 record. Her players stunned the collegiate sports world by winning the Patriot League conference and securing a berth in the NCAA tournament. It was the first March Madness appearance by any Army basketball team, men's or women's.

Asked to describe her favorite moment of the entire season, Maggie Dixon cited the victory over Holy Cross in the Patriot League tournament. The game was played on West Point's home court, and Maggie recalled, "The cadets stormed the court, and these 300-pound football players hoisted me up in the air. It's one of those things you only dream of happening."

At the NCAA tournament, Maggie Dixon's team was defeated by the University of Tennessee in the first round. Maggie went home to prepare to begin her second season as Army head coach. Tragically, it was not to be.

Just a few weeks later, on April 5, 2006, Maggie was sharing afternoon tea in the home of a friend when she suddenly collapsed. She was rushed to Westchester Medical Center in Valhalla, New York, where she died the following night. Maggie Dixon had suffered a severe cardiac arrhythmia related to a previously undiagnosed enlarged heart. She was 28 years old.

Maggie Dixon was buried at West Point Cemetery, and the Women's Basketball Coaches Association created the annual Maggie Dixon Award to recognize rookie coaches who, like Maggie, achieved outstanding achievements during their first season. It's a tribute to a young woman who packed a lot of accomplishment and leadership influence into a brief span of life—by being herself.[3]

Before becoming a basketball analyst for ESPN, Jay Bilas was a four-year starter with the Duke University men's basketball team. Coached by the brilliant hardwood strategist Mike Krzyzewski, Bilas helped Duke reach the Final Four and the National Championship game in 1986. In an ESPN article "Learn From the Best, But Be Yourself," Bilas recalls:

> In 1981, I chose to play for a little known coach named Mike Krzyzewski, who had been named the head coach at Duke two years prior. I played for Krzyzewski from 1982 -1986, and was later an assistant coach on his staff for three years. ... Krzyzewski would tell the assistants, "When you have your own programs, don't just blindly do things like we do it here. There is more than just one way to do things, we just believe that this is the best way for us."
>
> When preparing for an opponent, Krzyzewski often would point out how much he admired the way another coach did things, but that the particular style just didn't work for him. He said many times that there were many different ways to be successful in the game, and a lot of diverse ways to play and win, and not to be fooled into thinking that his way was the only way. Krzyzewski spoke often of belief in yourself and your system, but having the guts to be flexible and to change when change was called for.[4]

Hall of Fame NBA coach and TV analyst Hubie Brown says that "Be yourself" is the most fundamental principle of good coaching and sound leadership. "If there is one piece of advice I give to coaches," he said, "it is to stay within your own personality. That is what the great ones do. Even at the NBA level, you find coaches who try to be someone else. The players look right through those guys. Your presence is key. You have to be honest with yourself and the players."[5] Or, as former college football and NFL coach Gene Stallings said so succinctly, "You've got to coach your own personality."[6]

Some coaches are screamers and butt-kickers. Others get the same results by speaking softly and reasonably to their players. Neither approach is necessarily the "right" or "wrong" way to coach. You have to do what works for *you*, not what works for some other coach.

As one former baseball manager told me, "If your son Bobby has a personality like Billy Martin—feisty and intense—tell him to manage like Billy Martin. If he has a personality like Walter Alston—calm and controlled at all times—tell him to manage like Walter Alston. He should study a lot of different management styles, but ultimately he's got to work within his own personality and develop his own style."

Soon after retiring from the NFL, former Indianapolis Colts head coach Tony Dungy—the only NFL coach to take his team to 10 consecutive playoff appearances—sat for an interview with David Asman on the Fox Business Channel. "Tony Dungy," Asman said, "you're not one of those screaming coaches that people are in fear of. And that's your message. You don't have to scream to motivate your players."

"That's true," Dungy said. "There's no one right way to coach. You have to be yourself. You have to coach within your own personality. Everybody has a certain way to do it, but the big thing is that you have to communicate information. I always felt that the best way to communicate information is in a steady manner, and guys would hear you. That's just my style. It doesn't mean it's the best way, but it's my way."[7]

Paul "Bear" Bryant, the late, great Alabama football coach, agreed. "To be a good coach," he once said, "you have to be yourself. You have to be your own coach. We all have personalities and different ideas of our own, and you will have your own plan. Your plan won't be like mine, but you will have a plan, and you will be able to sell it to your team and staff."[8]

The Courage of Your Convictions

Ralph Waldo Emerson may not have been a great coach, but he was a great leader among transcendentalist poets and philosophers—and at times he dispensed brilliant coaching advice. "To be yourself," he said, "in a world that is constantly trying to make you something else is the greatest accomplishment."[9]

It takes a lot of courage to boldly be yourself, to stand up for your convictions, to do what you believe is right when the world around you is trying to make you into something else. One person I admire for courageously being himself is my friend, former MLB manager George "Sparky" Anderson. My friendship with Sparky goes back almost 45 years. I met him in 1965, my first year in Spartanburg, when he was managing the Cardinals of Rock Hill, South Carolina. We saw a lot of each other that summer.

Sparky went on to the big leagues and managed the Cincinnati Reds to the 1975 and 1976 World Series victories, and then managed the Detroit Tigers to a World Series title in 1984. He's a leader who lives, breathes, and exemplifies what it means to be yourself, no matter what the situation, no matter how much pressure and opposition you face.

Sparky Anderson changed the game of baseball forever. There have been a number of game-changers in baseball history—Jackie Robinson, who broke the color barrier;

Roger Craig, the innovator of the split-finger fastball; and Curt Flood, who created free agency by refusing to be traded. But Sparky Anderson changed the game by inventing the modern bullpen.

Prior to the Sparky Era, it was unusual for a starting pitcher *not* to go all nine (or more) innings. As a result, pitchers would sometimes blow out their pitching arms in long, hotly-contested games, sometimes even ruining their careers. For example, promising 25-year-old pitcher Steve Busby of the Kansas City Royals pitched 12 innings in Angel Stadium in Anaheim on June 25, 1975. Busby went into that game with a record of 52-35 and two no-hitters, and the Royals beat the Angels 6-2 in a hard-fought duel. Soon after that game, however, Busby was diagnosed with a torn rotator cuff. In spite of surgery and therapy, he never fulfilled his early promise, and his career sputtered to an early end in 1980.

Around that time, in the mid-1970s, Cincinnati Reds manager Sparky Anderson was concerned about extending the careers of his pitchers. He kept a close watch on his pitchers—and frequently, after five or six innings, he sent in a reliever. In fact, in 1975, the Reds caused a sensation by playing 45 games in a row in which the starting pitcher didn't finish the game. Today, of course, relief pitchers are the norm in baseball—but it was a different game in Sparky's day.

Sparky wasn't very popular with his pitchers, who hated to see Sparky come out of the dugout and approach the mound. And even though the Reds were leading their division, Cincinnati fans *despised* him—and gave him the nickname "Captain Hook." They longed for the old-school baseball drama of two pitchers dueling it out for nine or more solid innings, and they thought the Reds' manager was hurting the game.

But Sparky endured the jeers, the boos, and the flying bric-a-brac. He stuck to his principles, and in the process, he extended quite a few pitching careers. Most importantly, the entire league eventually came around to Sparky's way of thinking.

As a result, Sparky Anderson forever changed the game of baseball because he was determined to be himself, do what was right, and let the chips fall where they may. Baseball writer Bill James reflected, "I always admire people who have the courage to confront the conventional wisdom. … It's easy for us [outside the game] to say whatever we think, because there are no consequences to it. It's much harder to say, 'I think the conventional wisdom is full of beans, and I'm not going to go along with it,' when you're inside the system and exposed to the possibility of actual failure. I think the people who do this drive the world to get better."[10]

Be yourself—that's good advice, not just for coaches and managers, but for leaders in every arena, from the ballfield to the battlefield, from the locker room to the board room. That's why *BusinessWeek* magazine once went to Sparky Anderson for his leadership insight, asking, "What one piece of advice would you give to a CEO about to take over a company for the first time?" Sparky replied:

> You are who you are. … Always be yourself. …
>
> Biggest trouble I see guys getting into is when they try to get in with the right side and the right people. They play both ends, see which end has the most power, and latch on with them. Be straight up. …
>
> You can't learn to manage by copying [other leaders]. Take [former Miami Dolphins coach] Don Shula. He's the greatest coach. Shula is Shula. It's his way. It's not your way or my way.
>
> You've got to do it your own way.[11]

And as a leader, always lead from within your personality and your own unique set of skills. Learn from others, but don't be a slave to the leadership style of anyone else. Lead according to your strengths and abilities. Lead according to your principles and values and best judgment. Don't give in to pressure or popular opinion or the boos of the fans.

Do it your own way. Be yourself.

Let Your Players Be Themselves

Not only should you strive to be yourself as a coach and a leader, but you should encourage your players to be themselves as well. Bear Bryant was one of college football's winningest coaches—323 victories, 13 conference titles, and six national championships. Bryant always stressed that great teams are made of unique individuals, each with a singular set of skills, talents, and character qualities. Don't mass-produce players with a cookie-cutter. Instead, coach and mentor your players in such a way that they can discover and display their own uniqueness. "Don't make them in your image," Bryant once said. "Don't even try. You don't strive for sameness. You strive for balance."[12]

John Wooden—unquestionably the greatest college basketball coach of all time—is also one of the greatest practitioners of the leadership advice, "Be yourself." From 1966 to 1969, the star center of Coach Wooden's UCLA Bruins was a 7'2" African-American from New York City named Lew Alcindor (years later, after converting to Islam, Alcindor changed his name to Kareem Abdul-Jabbar). Once, during a road trip, the UCLA team bus stopped at a restaurant for a dinner break. While the lanky center was sitting at a table with Coach Wooden and the team, he heard someone in the diner whisper loudly, "Look at that black freak!"

Coach Wooden saw that the young man had heard the comment, and was hurt by it. Tears brimmed in Alcindor's eyes. Wooden leaned toward his star player and said, "Lewis, people hate what they don't know, and what they are afraid of. But don't ever stop being yourself."

The young man (who would go on to score a record-setting 38,387 points in a two-decade-long NBA career) grinned at his coach—and he never forgot that advice.[13] It's the same fatherly advice Polonius gave his son Laertes in Shakespeare's *Hamlet,* Act I, Scene iii:

> This above all: to thine own self be true,
> And it must follow, as the night the day,
> Thou canst not then be false to any man.

So take the advice of the great coaches and leaders, the champions who have mastered and transformed the game: Encourage your players to be themselves—to be fully-functioning, unique contributors to your team. Turn them loose to do what they do best. Build your tactics and strategies around their strengths and abilities.

Above all, do what you believe is right—and always be yourself.

2

Build Character

On April 13, 2002, I went to a reception for the 106th Boston Marathon. There, I met Bob Kraft, owner of the New England Patriots—the team which had won Super Bowl XXXVI just two months earlier. I introduced myself and we chatted briefly. At the end of our conversation, I said, "It's a real pleasure to meet you, Bob."

"Likewise, Pat," he said.

As I turned to walk away, he took a step toward me and added, "You have a nice reputation."

Two days later, as I ran in the Boston Marathon on Patriot's Day, Bob Kraft's words came back to me again and again, and put a little extra spring into my step.

Of course, character and reputation are not always the same thing. A person of good character can be wrongly defamed, and a person of bad character can hide behind an undeserved reputation—at least for a while.

But for the most part, a good reputation is built upon the foundation of good character. As a coach and a leader, good character should be one of your foremost concerns. Always recruit people of good character to your team, always seek to improve the character traits of your players, and always be a role model of good character to your team.

A marathon is a microcosm of life, an allegory of what a life of leadership is all about. As a coach, you are running a race. It's not a sprint; it's a marathon. You're in it for the long haul—and marathons have a way of revealing character.

I think of the 84th Boston Marathon in 1980. In that race, the first-place woman runner, Cuban émigré Rosie Ruiz, completed the race with a women's record time of 2:31:56—or had she? Her Boston time was 25 minutes faster than her finish in the New York Marathon, six months earlier. Her explanation: "I got up with a lot of energy this morning."

Ruiz's story quickly crumbled. People came forward, claiming they saw her leave the crowd of spectators and join the runners just a mile short of the finish line. A videotape check showed that Ruiz did not appear in any footage of the first 25 miles of the race. Soon, evidence emerged that she had not only cheated in the Boston Marathon, but had taken a shortcut via the subway in the New York Marathon.

Ruiz was stripped of her medal and publicly disgraced. Unfortunately, the real winner, Jacqueline Gareau of Canada, was denied the attention she had earned by running the race honestly, because it took several days for the truth about the hoax to come out. As a result of the scandal, officials made changes to guarantee that no runner could ever perpetrate such a hoax again—changes which included video surveillance, checkpoints, transponder monitoring, and so forth.

It's unthinkable to me that anyone could enjoy a "victory" won by cheating, but some people seem to want to grab the glory without earning it. One of your jobs as coach is to focus on the character of your players and remove from your team those who would "win" by lying and cheating.

Leadership Is Influence

"My admiration for leaders is not based on their achievements," Coach John Wooden once wrote. "Rather, it is based on the quality of their leadership. Character is the most essential component of leadership." [1]

John Wooden is one of my heroes. In recent years, I've gotten to know him as a friend. In fact, I wrote a book about his life, his character, and his coaching philosophy—(written with David Wimbish, HCI, 2006). During one of my interviews with Coach Wooden, he shared a story about the importance of character in coaching. (Note, by the way, that he refers to coaching as "teaching.")

"In my third year of teaching," he said, "the co-captains and best two players on my team failed to show up for a game. The next day, they told me they had both been sick in bed. I showed them a picture taken the night of the game—a picture of these two young men having a good time at a dance. I said, 'It looks to me like that dance was more important to you than the game or the team.' Then I dismissed them from the team for the entire year.

"One of those boys, whose father was the vice principal of the school, said that his dad would have me fired. I later talked to the boy's father. He was disappointed when I told him that his son would be off the team for the whole year. But he later thanked me for taking the action I did. He said, 'That was the best thing that ever happened to that headstrong son of mine.' The incident gave me confidence in standing up for my beliefs. I was trying to do more than build a winning team; I was trying to build character. And building character is always the right thing to do."

Coach Wooden also tells the story of the time Bill Walton, his superstar center at UCLA in the early 1970s, came to his office with a question. For several months, Walton had been experiencing a great deal of pain in his knees. The pain showed on his face as he ran the length of the court.

"Coach," Walton said, "I've heard that smoking marijuana can help reduce the pain in my knees. Would it be okay with you if I used it—just for medicinal purposes, to help with the pain?"

Coach Wooden quietly replied, "Bill, I haven't heard that marijuana is a pain reliever, but I have heard that it is illegal."[2] And that was that.

Nothing was more important to John Wooden than the development of his players' character. His quiet but firm insistence on character made a profound impact on Bill Walton—and on another famous Walton. Bill's son, L.A. Lakers strong forward Luke Walton, recalls being raised as a second-generation disciple of John Wooden.

"As a kid growing up," Luke recalls, "all four of us Walton boys had John Wooden's motivational quotes posted everywhere—on our refrigerator, on the bathroom mirror, in the car. Dad would even tape Wooden sayings on our lunch pails."

Character is always under construction. It is shaped and defined by the choices you make. When you make good ethical and moral choices, you strengthen your own character and exemplify good character to others. But if you give in to your baser impulses, you chip away at the foundation of your character.

Great leaders always make character a priority. General Norman Schwarzkopf, chief strategist of Operation Desert Storm, put it this way: "Leadership is a potent combination of strategy and character. But if you must be without one, be without the strategy."[3]

Leadership is influence, the ability to inspire and motivate people to do what they might not otherwise do. I'm sure you can point to people in your early years and young adulthood who have literally changed the course of your life. You can point to a few people and say, "I wanted to be just like him," or, "I was inspired by her example."

When I was in the ninth grade at Tower Hill School in Wilmington, Delaware, I had two coaches who profoundly impacted my life. In fact, they continue to impact my life today by the way they lived their lives and by the words they said. First, was our baseball coach, Peanuts Riley. He was a former Phillies minor league farm hand, and we all loved him. Having been a pro, he really knew baseball, he taught baseball, and he was full of fascinating stories about playing pro ball. He cared about his players, and we were always welcome to go to his house and talk baseball, or call him at any time to tap into his insight.

When I was 19, I played in a summer baseball league in Nova Scotia with some very talented college players. I was probably the youngest player in the league, and the least experienced—and I was hanging on for dear life. I wasn't sure I had the ability to compete in that league. So I wrote to Peanuts Riley and laid out all my self-doubts. He wrote back, "Don't ever lose your confidence. Remember, the other fellows put their uniforms on the same way you do. Never stop swinging, and you'll be rough on all of them." That was great advice, and it sent my confidence soaring.

Before my junior year with the Wake Forest University baseball team, I expected to be the starting catcher, but when I arrived, I discovered that the coach had recruited another catcher. Suddenly, I had to *compete* for the starting position. There I was, 20 years old, and once again I wrote to my old high school coach for advice on how to handle this threat to my security. Peanuts wrote back, "Glad to hear you have someone pushing you for the catching job. That helps you and the ballclub. *Hustle a little more every day.*" I didn't want to hear that, but Peanuts was right. The competition made me a better catcher, which was good for the team.

I wrote down those two quotations from Coach Peanuts Riley, and I kept them in my wallet. I've consulted his advice again and again throughout my career. I still keep those words of advice with me to this day, almost half a century later.

The other coach who impacted my life during my freshman year in high school was Baird Brittingham. I was a 14-year-old freshman quarterback on the football team, and we were scrimmaging with Salesianum School, a Catholic school in Wilmington. The players from Salesianum were nicknamed "Sallies," and they were big, tough, and intimidating. The scrimmages were not real games, just practice sessions against players from another school. So I got to stand on the field, behind the huddle, listen to the play-calling, and watch the play unfold.

On the first snap, starting quarterback Reeves Montague called a play and it worked brilliantly. Reeves handed off to the halfback, who exploded through the line, made a cutback, and picked up a nice chunk of yardage. From my vantage point in the backfield, I saw how brilliantly it worked.

Later in the scrimmage, it was my turn to take over and call the plays. I figured, "Why tamper with something that works?" So I called the same play that Reeves had called. I handed off and the halfback blew through the line for an eight-yard pickup. Afterwards, assistant coach Baird Brittingham came up to me. He was a big bullnecked guy, a former starting center at Yale, who was very gruff and intimidating. He said, "Why did you call that play?" From the way he said it, it didn't sound like he was going to pin a medal on my chest.

I replied, "Because Reeves did." He popped me on the shoulder pads, and said, "That's exactly what I wanted you to say. That's how a quarterback thinks." In other words, he knew that I had been paying attention, I had eavesdropped on the huddle, I saw which play worked, and I filed it away for when my time would come. The play worked for me just as it worked for Reeves. And I had gotten a thump on the shoulder pads from Coach Brittingham, which, for me, was like being knighted by King Arthur with the sword Excalibur. It was at that moment that I first realized, "I'm a leader!" More than half a century later, I remember that moment as if it were yesterday.

That's the life-changing power of influence. That's the power of coaches to impact young lives—and that impact will reverberate down through the years. It will mean more than you can imagine. Young people are looking up to you just as I looked up to Coach Riley and Coach Brittingham. That's the influence *you* have. Use it wisely.

Your players are watching you and taking their lead from you. If they don't buy into your character, then you're not leading, you're not coaching. You're just bossing people around. But if they see you as a person of good character, they will be sold on your leadership. They will run through walls for you.

That's influence. Most coaches are remembered for their accomplishments, their victories, and their championships. But the greatest coaches of all are those who are remembered for their influence on others.

To Build Character, Exemplify Character

As a coach, you can't lead your players to a place you have not gone yourself. You cannot build character in others that you do not exemplify yourself. There are a number of qualities that make up character, and you must focus on setting a good example in all of these traits: honesty, integrity, responsibility, strong work ethic, courage, humility, and self-discipline, to name a few.

Hall of Famer Whitey Herzog has been a player, general manager, farm system director, and more. In his book *You're Missin' a Great Game*, he explains why the character quality of honesty is so important in coaching and managing in sports:

> Every word you speak has to be honest. If there's one rule you should never violate, it's Always Tell The Truth. … You'd be surprised how many managers lie to their players. Maybe a guy asks when he's going to be starting; the manager'll say, "sometime soon," or "just keep working at it, we'll see," when he knows perfectly well that ain't the case. Managers are just like everybody else: They might just be avoiding arguments or confrontation. Or maybe they're worried if they tell a guy he's a benchwarmer, he'll go negative and start causing problems. But players ain't stupid; they'll see the writing on the wall, and if you haven't been honest, you're *really* going to have problems. … I never once had a player resent me for telling him the truth.[4]

Another coach known for his honesty and other character qualities is Mike Holmgren. He's coached football at every level—high school, college, and the NFL. As a San Francisco 49ers assistant coach and as head coach of the Green Bay Packers and the Seattle Seahawks, Holmgren has shaped the careers of such quarterbacks as Joe

Montana, Steve Young, Brett Favre, and Matt Hasselbeck. Sports agent Bob LaMonte said this about Coach Holmgren:

> I've known Mike Holmgren for a long time, and you'll never meet a more straightforward guy. Everyone knows he'll always be truthful with them, and he often says, "Look, if you ask me a question, make sure you want to know the answer." One thing is certain—he will let you know where you stand with him. Sometimes you might not like the answer he gives you, but he'll be honest with you. I've never known him to tell a lie. For instance, if a player says, "Coach, why aren't I starting?" he'll give him specific reasons. If a player asks why he got cut, he'll tell him exactly why. He doesn't mince words. He doesn't do it in a harsh way, and it's not personal. The bottom line is that the players respect him because he will tell the truth.

LaMonte tells the story of a free agent wide receiver who was recruited by Mike Holmgren and the Seahawks. This player was distrustful because he felt his previous coach had deceived him. So, before he would sign with the Seahawks, he wanted to know if Holmgren would be straight with him.

"Look," Mike Holmgren said, "we want you here. We have a role for you on our team, but you're not going to be a starter. We have two young players that we plan on giving every opportunity to be the starters. Now, if one of them gets hurt, or he can't do it, then yes, absolutely, you'll get an opportunity to start. But I'm not going to tell you what you want to hear so you'll sign."

The player respected Holmgren's candor—and he signed a one-year contract. He turned out to be a good match for the Seahawks, and often started in games with three-wide-receiver formations. He went on to re-sign for additional years and had a successful career with the Seahawks.

"I never lied to a player or coach," Holmgren says, "not even to the press. My philosophy is that honesty has to permeate your entire existence. You must live your life this way, at the office and away from the office. This is where you start because if you lose trust, you can't teach. You can't communicate. Your people won't listen to you and you'll never be able to get them to do what needs to be done."[5]

After six seasons with the Detroit Pistons, Grant Hill joined the Orlando Magic, and I got to know him as not only a gifted player, but a leader of exemplary character. Before entering the NBA, Grant had played for Coach Mike Krzyzewski at Duke. Grant once told me about an experience he had at Duke that taught him the importance of good character and setting a good example.

"When I was a freshman," he said, "I got my nose broken. It was in December and Coach K invited me to stay in his home for three days over the Christmas break. Because of the pain from the broken nose, I had trouble sleeping. I'd wake up, and I couldn't get back to sleep, so I'd get up at four or five in the morning—and Coach was already up! He got up early every morning and watched game films. That taught me a lot about the way Coach K approached this game. It told me that being a leader means sacrificing sleep and being prepared. Whenever I'm tempted to slack off, I remember Coach K watching game film at five in the morning."

Character for Times of Adversity

It's hard to inspire players to improve their character if they aren't already people of character to begin with. People of good character want to improve themselves, but people of low character simply can't be motivated to improve themselves, no matter what you do.

So, if you want to build a team of good-character players, then you need to recruit players of good character. Dean Smith, former head basketball coach at the University of North Carolina, explains in his book *The Carolina Way:*

> Putting together a basketball team at North Carolina began of course with recruiting the players. This was always a careful, tedious, and unending process. And no matter how much work we put into it—and that was considerable—we knew that recruiting was an inexact science. In fact much of it was dumb luck.
>
> It's possible to cross every *t*, dot every *i*, do all the work, and still have the prospect decide to go to another school. Finishing second in a recruiting competition is no better than finishing last. It's also possible to sign a player who doesn't fit in with your program. It's the nature of the business. Fortunately we didn't make a great many recruiting mistakes at North Carolina. Our coaches were good judges of talent, and we were careful to seek young men who were good students and of high character.[6]

North Carolina men's basketball coach Roy Williams played under, and was mentored by, Coach Smith. Roy Williams once said, "You've got to recruit character. Then you mold [your players] into a team with clear expectations. You help them learn how to enjoy a teammate's success. But I simply won't recruit a kid from this generation who won't play team basketball or who has a bad attitude. I think that's the same for all generations."[7]

Always recruit for character. As Sparky Anderson once told me, "You can win a battle or two with people who lack character—but you won't win the war! Winning is the result of your effort, perseverance, and the choices you make. Sooner or later, every team faces adversity. In times of adversity, character is the only thing that can pull you through. Winning is the result of *who you are*—and who you are is your *character*."

Players and coaches who lack character traits of integrity and honesty will fail the test of temptation. If they lack traits of courage and perseverance, they'll fold in the face of obstacles and opposition. If they lack self-discipline, they won't be prepared when testing comes. If they lack poise under pressure, they'll panic when the going gets tough.

Jim Tooley, vice president of operations at USA Basketball, once told me about a lesson he learned about the importance of character in times of adversity. "Early in my career in sports leadership," Jim said, "I had an experience that profoundly affected my perspective on life. I was promoted to director of operations for the Continental Basketball Association at the age of 23 by then-commissioner Jay Ramsdell. Jay was only 25 and one of the youngest to reach his position at the time. The job was hectic and all-consuming, and involved preparing league schedules and dealing with the players and coaches on transactions, fines, suspensions, and so forth.

"On July 19, 1989, less than a year after I was promoted, I received the news that Jay had been killed aboard United Flight 232, which crashed in Sioux City, Iowa. It was a terrible shock—and my first real dose of life-and-death 'perspective.' It hit me that living this life is serious business, and the things that seem so important to us one moment can all disappear in an instant. There are more important things in life than schedules and transactions. There are issues like relationships and spending time on things that matter and making sure we are becoming the right kind of people—people of good character. After Jay was killed, I focused more on keeping balance in my life and becoming a person of high character."

How to Build Character in Your Players

Lou Holtz is the only football coach in the history of the NCAA to take six different schools to bowl games. He has coached teams from four different schools to top 20 rankings. From 1988 to 1993, Lou Holtz's Notre Dame teams racked up an overall record of 64-9-1, and Holtz coached the Irish to bowl games in nine consecutive seasons.

When Holtz took over as head coach of the floundering Fighting Irish in 1986, his first official act was to remove the names from the players' jerseys. He diagnosed the team's problem as a fundamental character issue: his players were too focused on their own egos, their own glory, and were not playing together as a team. He told his players that the only name that mattered was the name on the *front* of the jersey: Notre Dame. By teaching his players humility, he molded the team into a unified force that began winning games. Except for two bowl games in 1988 and 2008, players' names have not appeared on Fighting Irish jerseys since.

Holtz is known for his character-based approach to coaching, and especially for his "Lou Holtz Rules." He says, "I ask our players to follow three basic rules: Do what is right. Do your very best. Treat others like you'd like to be treated. Those rules answer the three basic questions we ask of every player, and every player asks of us. The questions are: Can I trust you? Are you committed? Do you care about me? People might think this is corny, but I don't care. This is what I believe."[8]

In his book *The Fighting Spirit*, Coach Holtz explained the rationale behind his character-building rules:

> 1. *Do what is right.* You know the difference, and if you have any doubt, get out the Bible. It's right to be on time, polite, honest, to remain free from drugs.
>
> 2. *Do your best.* We do not help people at all by accepting mediocrity when they are capable of being better. Don't worry about being popular. Many times, we don't encourage others to do their best because we are more concerned with our players' appraisal of our efforts than we are with them.
>
> 3. *Treat others as you'd like to be treated* (the Golden Rule). I have never seen a team, a family, or a business that can't become better by emphasizing love and understanding.[9]

Of course, rules don't build character—and Coach Holtz would be the first to tell you so. Building character is a full-time, multi-faceted job. But a set of simple, character-based rules is a good place to start.

To the foundation of character-based rules, add the strong, inspiring example of integrity and character that you yourself set as a coach. Be a 24/7 role model of integrity—especially at times when you think no one is watching. You can never take a vacation from being an example of character. Either you have good character all the time or you don't.

You can't impart to others what you yourself don't have. You can't preach what you don't practice. You never know when your players might catch you in the act of being yourself, so make sure that wherever you are—in your office, on the practice field, in your car, at the store, or even in the privacy of your own home—you never compromise your character.

Get into the practice of praising your players not only on the basis of their achievements and skills, but on the basis of character. Praise them when they demonstrate honesty, integrity, effort, discipline, and responsibility. When they fail, discipline them on the basis of character. Point out to them that this failure was a *character* lapse—a failure to persevere, or a failure of self-discipline, or a failure of humility and the need to "think team." Show them they can recover from this failure by demonstrating greater character depth in the future.

Allow your players to experience the consequences of poor choices. Make certain they know there's a price to pay for poor ethical decisions, which arise from poor character. Always be fair and evenhanded, making sure that your starters suffer the same consequences as your benchwarmers; never show favoritism on the basis of ability. If you do, you'll lose control over your team and you'll send the message that star players don't need good character and don't suffer the consequences of bad choices.

Post quotations around your facility that emphasize the importance of character. The following are some examples of such quotations:

> *"Character is manifested in the great moments*
> *but it is made in the small ones."*
> —Phillip Brooks

> *"Character is higher than intellect."*
> —Ralph Waldo Emerson

> *"Character is simply habit long continued."*
> —Plutarch

> *"When wealth is lost, nothing is lost; when health is lost,*
> *something is lost; when character is lost, all is lost."*
> —Author Unknown

Such reminders may resonate in the lives of your players for years to come.

Character First

One of the most universally admired coaches in the world of sports is retired NFL coach Tony Dungy. The former head coach of the Tampa Bay Buccaneers and the Indianapolis Colts credits his father for instilling in him such character qualities as a strong work ethic, integrity, and humility. His dad, Wilbur Dungy, was a highly respected professor at Jackson Community College in Michigan. Wilbur Dungy was such a model of humility that he never spoke of his exploits and achievements as a pilot in World War II. Tony didn't know that his father was one of the famed Tuskegee Airmen until he heard about it at his father's funeral in 2004.

Tony himself is a quiet, humble man who never talks about himself or his achievements. Unlike many players and coaches, Dungy never wears the two Super Bowl rings he won as a Pittsburgh Steelers defensive back and as head coach of the Colts.

During his tenure with the Buccaneers, he joined Tampa's Idlewild Baptist Church. The pastor, Ken Whitten, got to know Coach Dungy very well. "He's the kind of coach every pastor would love to say they're the pastor of," Whitten says. "Tony's a guy who recruits by character. [He] hires coaches that have character."[10]

As a coach, as a leader, make character one of your first priorities. Recruit players for their character. Teach character constantly. Exemplify the principles of good character in your own life.

Leadership is influence. Always influence your players to be people of good character.

3

Build a Strong Work Ethic

©Dilip Vishwanat/Sporting News/ZUMA Press

My writing partner, Jim Denney, once worked with Green Bay Packers defensive lineman Reggie White on his autobiography, *In the Trenches*. Reggie told Jim how he made the decision to step up his work ethic:

"While I was at the University of Tennessee," Reggie said, "I wanted to make All-American. Problem was, I wasn't focused on the hard work and conditioning I needed to achieve those goals. I wasn't working out like I should. I got a sprung ankle in the game against Duke, then I sprung the other ankle playing Alabama. Then I injured my elbow, and after that, I got a pinched nerve in my neck. The local press started saying that Reggie White lacked toughness—and that made me mad!

"So I spent more time in the weight room to build my strength. I increased my speed with sprinting, and built up my endurance by running the track. As a result, my senior year was a great year. My power and durability increased, I stepped up my game a notch, and I played without injury.

"Later, when I began playing pro ball, I let my work ethic slide a bit—and it showed. My first pro season, I got a sprung ankle and a broken rib. In 1985, I was watching *Monday Night Football*, the Redskins versus the Giants. That was the game where [Giants' outside linebacker] Lawrence Taylor sacked Joe Theismann, sending him out of the game with a broken leg. Theismann's career was over, just like that.

"I thought, 'Man, my career could be ended in a whiff, just like Joe's!' Theismann was in pretty good shape, but his leg was shattered like a matchstick. I knew that if I wanted a long career in this game, I needed to step up my work ethic again. I decided I was going to be in better shape than anyone else in the game. From then on, I worked out every day, even in the off-season. That's why I was able to avoid injuries most of my career."

Jim Denney saw Reggie's work ethic in action. "I met with Reggie at his home in Knoxville in May 1996," Jim recalls. "I saw him work out in the gym behind his home every day, even though it was the middle of the off-season. He had a work ethic that just wouldn't quit. That's why he had one of the longest consecutive-start-streaks in the history of the NFL.

"I was stunned when I turned on the news the day after Christmas 2004 and heard that Reggie had died of a respiratory ailment. He was the most physically powerful human being I have ever met. He seemed indestructible, like Superman. As it turned out, Reggie was no match for a disease called pulmonary sarcoidosis.

"But when he was on the football field, quarterbacks feared him and it usually took two or three offensive linemen to stop him. Reggie had a work ethic that wouldn't quit, and that was the key to his greatness."

Hardworking Coaches Build Hardworking Teams

Pat Summitt is head basketball coach of the University of Tennessee's Lady Volunteers. She is not only one of the most successful *women's* coaches, but truly one of the most successful coaches in sports history, period. She has collected eight NCAA titles (1987, 1989, 1991, 1996, 1997, 1998, 2007, and 2008)—an achievement eclipsed only by John Wooden's 10 NCAA championships at UCLA. Summitt coached the Lady Vols to an undefeated season in 1997-1998.

Before she entered coaching, she won All-American honors as a college basketball player for the University of Tennessee-Martin and earned a silver medal with the USA team at the 1976 Summer Olympics in Montreal. Eight years later, she returned to the Olympics, this time as coach of the USA women's basketball team—and her team brought home the gold.

Raised on a farm outside of Henrietta, Tennessee, she learned the value of hard work early in life. The youngest of four children, she developed toughness and a competitive spirit in order to hold her own against three older brothers. Her parents assigned her a share of the chores—and her reward for a job well done was a chance to play two-on-two basketball with her brothers.

Pat's mom and dad supported her love of basketball. When they discovered that the local school district didn't offer girls' basketball, her dad moved the family to the next county, where girls' basketball was offered.

Coach Summitt has been head coach of the Lady Vols since she was just 22 years old (she had only recently graduated and served a brief apprenticeship as assistant coach). When she got the head coaching job, she had never coached a game before. At the same time, she was also working on a master's degree, teaching phys ed courses, and undergoing knee therapy and training for the 1976 Olympics. Her farm girl self-discipline and tough work ethic served her well during that grueling first season.

As a coach, Pat Summitt preaches the same hard-nosed work ethic she learned as a farm girl, saying, "I tell kids, 'If you're lazy, stay as far away from me and our program as you can because you'll be miserable. We work hard.'"[1]

Another coach famed for his work ethic was longtime Alabama football icon Paul "Bear" Bryant. He may have been the most driven and work-obsessed coach in the history of collegiate football. His work ethic was rooted in his belief that every day is a gift from God, and that we must be productive in order to fulfill the promise of the gifts God has given us. In his office, he kept a framed plaque which read:

What have you traded for what
God has given you today?

And on the wall of his home, another framed plaque read:

Ask God to bless your work.
Do not ask Him to do it for you.[2]

A coach with a strong work ethic will produce a team with a strong work ethic. Vince Dooley, the longtime head football coach and athletic director at the University of Georgia, knew Bear Bryant very well as an opponent. "Coach Bryant changed football in the SEC in two pretty fundamental ways," Dooley said. "One, he elevated the work ethic. He was the hardest-working guy you've ever seen, and that meant the rest of us had to work harder coaching, scouting, recruiting, the whole bit. Two, his teams just played harder, and that meant our teams had to play harder to compete."[3]

David Chadwick played basketball for Coach Dean Smith at the University of North Carolina from 1967 to 1971, and is the author of *The Twelve Leadership Principles of Dean Smith*. David told me the following story from his playing days at UNC:

"Right after my sophomore year at UNC, I had the annual meeting with Coach Smith about the next year. I hadn't played a lot and I really wanted to play more the next year. Knowing Coach Smith's penchant for team play, I rehearsed in my mind what I needed to say to him to impress him for more playing time. I knew I had to emphasize the team.

"I went into his office and began my speech. 'Coach,' I said, 'I really want to help the team. You know how much I value the team. The team is all important. So, as I go home this summer, how can I help the team next year?'

"He paused for a moment, then asked, 'David, you really want to help our team next year?'

"'Yes sir, more than anything else,' I said.

"He leaned across his desk, looked me in the eye, and said, 'David, if you really want to help this team next season, go home this summer and become a better player.' Then he outlined the things I needed to do to improve. I went home that summer and did exactly as he said. I worked hard and became a better player, and just as Coach Smith said, I got significantly more playing time for the next season—and the team had a successful season.

"Coach Smith knew that a team is only as strong as its weakest link. He also was emphasizing personal responsibility. My hard work, my own personal work ethic would contribute to making UNC a much better team! The success of the team is connected to the hard work of the individual."

Setting a Hardworking Example

As player, scout, coach, and manager, Andy Seminick spent most of his career with the Philadelphia Phillies organization. I met Andy when I was a young Phillies fan, hanging around Shibe Park. Years later, I got to play for Andy during my brief career in the minors with the Miami Marlins. Ninety of the players Andy managed or coached eventually made it to the major leagues, including Ferguson Jenkins, Greg Luzinski, Bob Boone, Mike Schmidt, and John Vukovich.

I got to know John Vukovich in 1967 soon after I began running the Spartanburg Phillies. Later, Vuke played for Andy in the Triple-A Pacific Coast League, and he and I talked a number of times, comparing notes on what it was like to play for the great Andy Seminick.

"Andy was old-school," Vuke once told me. "He had a cast iron work ethic, and he expected everyone to keep up with him. When I played for him in the PCL, we'd play a game in Hawaii, then take an all-night flight back to Portland, Oregon, then take a bus to Eugene. Everybody on the team was lagged out because of the travel and the three-hour time difference. But we didn't go home. We went straight to the ballfield—Andy's orders. We put in a full day of batting practice and infield.

"Andy was older than the rest of us, and you'd think he'd want to get some sleep. Nope. He didn't need sleep, and he figured the rest of us didn't either. And you didn't hear anybody complaining. Everyone on the team knew that Andy had caught in the 1950 World Series with a broken ankle. So no one was gonna tell *that* guy, 'I'm tired.'"

Andy Seminick set an example for his players of a work ethic that just wouldn't quit. When a manager or coach demonstrates that kind of work ethic, players will be inspired to match it. If you're that kind of leader, count on it—your players will always remember you for it.

Leadership expert Henry T. Blackaby wrote about the importance of influencing others through an example of hard work:

> Leaders dramatically influence the culture of their organizations through their own work habits. Being a leader does not mean one has "made it" and is now exempt from hard work. Rather, leaders should set the pace for others. Few things discourage employees and volunteers any more than lazy leaders. Leaders should not ask their people to undertake tasks they are unwilling to perform themselves. While the role of leaders does not allow them to spend all their time laboring alongside their people, they can seek to encourage their followers by their example of hard work. Leaders should ask themselves, "If the people in my organization worked with the same intensity as I do, would they enhance the operations of this organization or would they reduce it to a crawl?[4]

Harvey Mackay, author of *Swim with the Sharks*, once said, "Believe me, any time a boss will roll up his or her sleeves and actually do some grunt work, word will reach every corner of the shop."[5] In their incisive masterpiece of leadership insight, *The Little Book of Coaching*, business guru Kenneth H. Blanchard and coaching legend Don Shula talked about the importance of a leader's work ethic:

> There is no easy walk to excellence. You and your team have to train so hard that you are almost perfect on the day of the game. The best of the best know that there is no such thing as a shortcut. All great results are built on the foundation of practice and preparation. So get overprepared and help your people do the same.[6]

A few years ago, Sparky Anderson explained his work ethic to me this way: "I was always driving myself. I competed with my players. I dared 'em to keep up! I think that's what made me successful as a manager. I didn't want it said that any player on my team worked harder than I did."

Set Your Watch Fast

Football coach Dick Vermeil, one of my favorite personalities in the sports profession, has earned the distinction of being named "Coach of the Year" at four different levels— as a high school coach, junior college coach, NCAA Division I coach, and NFL coach (Philadelphia Eagles, St. Louis Rams, and Kansas City Chiefs). He coached the Rams to an NFL championship in Super Bowl XXXIV, January 30, 2000. As sportswriter, Jack Gallagher observed:

> Vermeil is a testament to what hard work and perseverance can do in any endeavor in life. Success breeds success. It's not luck, folks. Over the years, Vermeil has outworked his opponents and inspired his teams with his superior leadership and tactics. That's why he's been named Coach of the Year on four different levels of the game. … To this day, he remains the only coach to take teams to both the Rose Bowl and the Super Bowl.[7]

Football coach Woody Hayes (1913-1987) is famed for winning five national titles and 13 Big Ten championships during his 28-year tenure as head coach at Ohio State. In a 2002 documentary aired by Ohio State University-owned radio station WOSU, former quarterback Rex Kern (who played for Woody before going on to play for the Baltimore Colts and Buffalo Bills) recalled:

> Coach Hayes had some of the greatest work habits—the greatest standards and ethics for work that I had ever been around. Coach Hayes always believed never, ever, ever give up—never quit. And Ohio State was a graveyard of coaches for a period of time before Woody got there.

So, Woody decided that, "Hey, I'm gonna get up 30 minutes earlier, and there won't be anybody who will outwork me. Now they might be smarter than I am. They may have greater football knowledge, but no one—no one—will outwork me." …

Coach Hayes would always set his watch 10 minutes fast, and my watch today still runs 10 minutes fast. And my staff in the business world knows that we start meetings on my time, which is Woody's time. Woody would always do that so he would make certain he was there on time. He would always work hard. He was relentless. He was a perfectionist. …

There was no one who worked harder than Woody.[8]

One of the great role models of a hard-nosed work ethic is Vince Lombardi. Yet Lombardi credited *another* coach for teaching him what "hard work" really means— Red Blaik. Lombardi's son, Vince Jr., recalls:

Vince Lombardi was always a hard worker. When he took the assistant coaching job at West Point under head coach Red Blaik, though, he got a new perspective on what constituted "hard work." Blaik lived and breathed football during most of his waking hours. It wasn't unusual for him to reassemble his coaching staff after dinner and to watch films and discuss strategies until midnight. Then they'd be at it again first thing in the morning.[9]

Mentored by Red Blaik, Lombardi took those hardworking habits with him when he joined the New York Giants as an assistant coach, and again when he became head coach at Green Bay and Washington. Giants head coach Jim Lee Howell recalled, "When the other coaches—the rest of us—would leave the Giant offices, there was always one light still burning, the one in Vince Lombardi's office."

Lombardi drilled his players relentlessly. He put them through the same play again and again until they could execute it flawlessly. If one player made even the smallest mistake, he would yell, "Run it again!" In fact, the words "Run it again!" became such a familiar slogan that when the players made a mistake, they yelled, "Run it again!" to save Lombardi the trouble.

Vince Lombardi Jr. offers three Lombardi-style techniques to make sure that you, as a coach, truly exemplify a strong work ethic:

Perfect your discipline: Hard work is *discipline*: focused training that develops self-control. It helps you make the hard decisions, endure pain, and stay on track despite stress, pressure, and fear.

Invest in your talent: All too often, our culture celebrates success without effort. ... You have a duty to invest in your talent, for the long-term.

Start at home: Lombardi's grueling schedule sent a message to his players. They all saw him put in more effort than they did, and therefore were motivated to put in more effort themselves.

"The harder you work, the harder it is to surrender."[10]

Former shortstop and retired MLB manager Alvin Dark played for six different teams from 1946 to 1960, and managed five different teams from 1961 to 1977. A few years ago, he shared with me his philosophy of sports management in a nutshell: "A manager," he said, "needs to be close to his players—but not *too* close. He should be friendly enough with them to know their problems. But he needs to stay out in front of them in order to provide leadership. A manager and his team are like a train—and a manager is the engine, not the caboose. An engine works hard and pulls a load. If you don't work hard, then you can't tell your players they need to work hard. The leader has to work *at least* as hard at his job as the players work at theirs."

That's sound advice from a leader who knows.

"Make 'Em a Hand"

As head of the United States Central Command, General Tommy Franks (U.S. Army, retired) was responsible for combined military operations in the Middle East and directed the War on Terror following the attacks of September 11, 2001. After his retirement, I had the privilege of interviewing General Franks by telephone. During our talk, I mentioned that my son David is a Marine and was involved in combat during the invasion of Iraq in 2003.

I heard a quaver of emotion in the general's voice as he replied, "Tell your son that someone else loves him besides you."

A few days later, I proudly passed that message along to David.

In that conversation, I learned that General Tommy Franks is a man who truly cares about his troops. I remembered that, just a few months after the 9/11 terror attacks, General Franks was interviewed by the news media, and he revealed himself as a man with a strong work ethic. A reporter asked, "Is there anything from your childhood, something you learned, that prepared you for this moment in your life?" General Franks replied:

There was something that I learned from a high school football coach, a fella by the name of Harold Garms, out in Midland, Texas. If he said it once, he said a thousand times while I knew him. He said, "You never quit." So that's the first thing.

And much more important than that, I remember when I was getting on a bus in 1967, about to go to Vietnam. I was getting on a bus in Austin, Texas, because I decided I was gonna ride across the country out to the West Coast and fly on to Vietnam because I wanted to see the country. My dad and my mother took me down to the bus station, and when I got on the bus, I said, "Well ... what kind of guidance would you give me about all this and what I'm gonna do and everything?"

And my dad said, "Well, make 'em a hand."[11]

Now, unless you're from Texas, you may be wondering what "make 'em a hand" means. The "hand" Tommy Franks' dad was talking about is a worker, like a farmhand or a field hand or a steel hand—someone who works hard at a certain trade. General Franks went on to say:

I think that's pretty good advice. It's sort of Texas-speak—"make 'em a hand." What that means is wherever you go, whatever you do, whoever you work for, be a good worker. Make 'em a hand.[12]

I agree with the general. That is great advice. Whatever you do, wherever you go, whatever role you play, whether you are an assistant coach, a head coach, a manager, or the general in charge of the entire United States Central Command, be a good worker, and set a good example of hard work for everyone around you.

Make 'em a hand.

4

Build Perseverance

They called 'em "the Junction Boys."

That's the label proudly worn by the survivors of Bear Bryant's summer football camp in Junction, Texas, in September 1954. The Junction Boys are the stuff of legend. Sportswriter Jim Dent wrote a book about them. ESPN made a movie about them. Here's the story:

In 1954, Texas A&M University hired Paul "Bear" Bryant as head football coach. When he arrived on the campus in College Station in February, Bryant found his players to be undisciplined, out of shape, and unprepared to play football. Some had a bad attitude. Others were girl crazy. So, Bryant decided to set up a camp on a 411-acre tract of land owned by the university in the dusty little town of Junction.

There would be no distractions in Junction. There was nothing to do in that little hill-country town. In fact, the region was undergoing the worst heat wave and drought in recorded history. Throughout the 10 days of the football camp, temperatures topped 100 degrees F. every day. The heat compounded the suffering inflicted by Bryant's grueling workouts. Practice began at dawn and continued throughout the day with only brief breaks for meals and team meetings.

Of course, we now know that the kind of practice Coach Bryant used can be dangerous. Every so often, we hear about football players suffering heat stroke and even death, due to exhaustion and dehydration in summer practices. In Coach Bryant's day, however, coaches often put their players through brutal practice regimens to increase their stamina and endurance.

Bear Bryant wasn't just trying to toughen up his players. He was also trying to weed out those who lacked the commitment to endure. If any of his players were going to quit on him, he wanted it to be during practice, not during a big game. It worked. Every day, fewer and fewer players showed up for practice. Many players quit the team.

No one knows for sure how many players showed up on the first day of the 10-day football camp at Junction. Some say the number might have been nearly a hundred. We do know that the number of survivors on day 10 was roughly a quarter to a third of that number. Two of the survivors, Jack Pardee and Gene Stallings, went on to coach in the NFL, and Stallings also coached college football at Texas A&M and Alabama.

Preparing for the "Fourth Quarter"

Did the Junction Boys learn a profound lesson in perseverance during those 10 days of suffering? Absolutely. Did the experience mold them into a championship team in the 1954 season? Nope. Fact is, the Junction Boys only won one game that season, and lost nine.

But that single losing season was the *only* losing season of Bear Bryant's 37-year career as a head coach. The Junction experience became the foundation for the winning seasons ahead, and the Junction Boys became the nucleus of a 1955 Texas A&M team that went 7-2-1, and a 1956 team that finished the season 9-0-1, winning the conference.

Moreover, the Junction Boys learned more from their experience than how to win football games. They learned to persevere in the game of life. Jack Pardee recalled, "Coach Bryant compared the fourth quarter to getting ready for life. ... He'd say, 'What are you going to do when you're 35 years old, you get your pink slip at work, you go home, your kids are hungry, and your wife has run off with the shoe salesman? That's the fourth quarter. Are you going to quit then? Is it going to be too tough for you? Or can people count on you?'"

Jack Pardee eventually went through some "fourth quarter" trials in his life. He relied on the lessons of his Junction days—lessons in perseverance and endurance—to get him through those trials.

He was 28 years old and enjoying a successful NFL career when he noticed a fast-growing mole on his arm. The mole turned out to be cancer. Fortunately, he caught it in time and was completely cured—but a diagnosis of cancer at such an early age gave him a more serious perspective on life. Suddenly, he realized what Bear Bryant had been trying to teach him about the "fourth quarter."[1]

Though I wouldn't recommend that you put your players through a grueling Junction experience, I hope you'll prepare your players for the "fourth quarter" experiences of life. If you prepare them to meet life's challenges with stamina, endurance, and commitment, then they'll be ready for anything they face in the future.

Perseverance is not just for football games. Perseverance is for life.

Profiles in Perseverance

Perseverance is an absolute requirement for any leader. Whether you are a Little League coach or the leader of the free world, you must have the character quality of endurance. Quitters need not apply.

While researching his biography of President Ronald Reagan, Dinesh D'Souza interviewed one of Reagan's most prominent media opponents, ABC White House correspondent Sam Donaldson. D'Souza was amazed to find that Donaldson, infamous for his highly confrontational questioning of Reagan at press conferences, looked back on Reagan with respect and fondness. The quality Donaldson admired most in Reagan was his persistence.

"Looking back on the Reagan presidency," D'Souza wrote, "Donaldson admitted to me that he has been forced to reconsider the merits of the man. 'We thought he was a lightweight, and maybe he didn't know everything, but he was a tenacious fellow who knew what he wanted. He reminds me of the Gila monster: when it grabs you, you can't get away. He came to Washington to change the world for the better, and for the most part, he did.'"[2]

Historian and leadership authority Donald T. Phillips observed that perseverance is a key quality of leadership. He wrote:

> Among people who wish to be leaders, but are unable to succeed, there exists a tendency to back off after a significant event has been accomplished. Statements often heard in such cases include: "Well, now that I've worked hard for three months, I think I'll lie back and catch up on my reading," or "I've done my job, let somebody else do something for a change," or "It's not my fault if we don't succeed, I did what I was supposed to do."
>
> However, successful leaders never sit back and rest on their laurels. Washington, Adams, Jefferson, and Madison possessed a slow and steady fire of persistence, determination, and action. It is a proven maxim of leadership that the fire of a truly great leader is always burning.[3]

Perseverance is the key to overcoming trials of adversity in every arena, whether in the political arena or the sports arena. My friend Bill Curry, head football coach at Georgia State University, puts it this way: "Perseverance is my only real strong asset. I don't have a great mind, certainly—I've proven that a million times. … But I can persevere where other people will not. I've learned that the only thing that counts is perseverance. That's what winning is. If you knock me down 77 times in a row and I still get my toe back at that line, I'm still in the fight. If I then knock you out, guess who wins. All those knockdowns don't count if I can get my toe back to the line. You just keep coming back and you keep coming back and you keep coming back until you find a way."[4]

One of the most instructive statements I've ever heard on the subject of perseverance came from Coach George Allen. When he was chairman of the President's Council on Physical Fitness, he said:

> One of the most difficult things everyone has to learn is that for your entire life you must "keep fighting" and adjusting if you hope to survive. No matter who you are or what your position, you must keep fighting for whatever it is you desire to achieve. … Health, happiness, and success depend upon the fighting spirit of each person. The big thing is not what happens to us in life—but what we *do* about what happens to us.[5]

Coach Allen practiced what he preached. As a head coach in the NFL, he took two bottom-of-the-rankings teams—the Los Angeles Rams and the Washington Redskins—and turned them into winners. In the process, he amassed a 16-year streak of winning seasons. Finally, in 1977, George Allen retired from coaching in the NFL.

Thirteen years later, the athletic department at Long Beach State University called him, begging him to rescue their ailing football program. At 72, Allen wasn't eager to return to the sidelines. "You can get another coach," he said. "You don't need me."

"If you don't take the job," said Long Beach, "our football program is finished. We'll cancel it."

"It's as bad as that?"

"Our program is the worst."

Coach Allen couldn't resist a challenge. "I'll take the job," he said.

Arriving on campus, Allen found the Long Beach 49ers football team to be an underfunded, dispirited laughingstock. The facilities were dilapidated. The challenge seemed hopeless—yet Allen boldly promised his players a winning season if they would follow his leadership.

He went right to work rebuilding the team. He began by setting an example for his players to emulate. At 72 years of age, he went out with his players, ran laps, and did sit-ups and push-ups right alongside them. He wanted his players to know that he didn't demand anything from them that he hadn't already demanded from himself.

The season began, and the 49ers dropped their first few games. So, Coach Allen sat them down and lectured them. "I see you guys losing out on the field," he said, "then I see you coming into the locker room laughing and joking. How can you do that? How can you simply accept losing that way? How can you live with yourselves after a loss like that? Where is your fighting spirit? You don't seem to want to win. Well, I intend to change that. From now on, practice is going to be twice as tough."

The longer, more intense practice sessions made his players more focused and intense about teamwork and winning. Allen noticed that their stamina was increasing, along with their mental toughness and their will to persevere. While George Allen was teaching his players persistence on the football field, he also preached persistence in the classroom. He wanted them to succeed in life, not just football.

The new intensive practice sessions paid off. In the next game, Allen's 49ers astonished top-ranked University of the Pacific, beating them 28-7. Then came the homecoming game against long-time rival, Cal State Fullerton—and the bleachers were packed with cheering fans. The 49ers staged a breathtaking comeback, winning the game with a field goal just six seconds before the final gun. It was a triumph of perseverance over adversity.

With a record of 5 and 5, the 49ers went into the final game of the season against the University of Nevada at Las Vegas. A win would give Long Beach its first winning season in years. Allen's players went out and battled their way to a 29-20 victory. At the end of the game, the fans and players all chanted, "We love George! We love George!"

The win over UNLV gave George Allen his 17th consecutive winning season. He had delivered on his promise. He had taken a football program on the verge of cancellation, and had turned it into a winning team. After that game, Allen told reporters that his season at Long Beach was the most rewarding season of his coaching career.

Tragically, it was also his last. A month and a half after the victory over UNLV, Coach Allen's wife came home from an outing and found him on the floor of the living room. He had died of a massive heart attack.

At the memorial service, Coach Allen's son, Bruce, eulogized him by reading from a "Things to Do" list the coach had written days prior:

1. Win a championship.
2. Have every player I've recruited graduate.
3. Build a stadium.
4. Then take a tougher Job.

That is a profile in perseverance.

"Just One More Time"

If there is one person whose name is synonymous with perseverance, it's the late NCAA basketball coach Jim Valvano. Every year, ESPN holds its ESPY Awards show, and the most profound and prestigious award of the evening is the Jimmy V Perseverance Award.

Jim was a friend of mine, and I interviewed him several times on my radio show. He coached the Wolfpack at North Carolina State University in the 1980s, and also coached at Johns Hopkins, Bucknell, and Iona. Over his 19 years in coaching, he amassed an enviable record of 346-212. After retiring from coaching, he became a broadcaster and motivational speaker. His favorite topic: Perseverance! His best-known catchphrase: "Don't give up, don't ever give up!"

When Jimmy was diagnosed with an aggressive form of bone cancer in mid-1992, he knew the odds were against him. True to his nature, he never surrendered to the disease. In fact, he created an organization called The V Foundation, dedicated to finding a cure for cancer. He announced the founding of The V Foundation at the ESPY Awards show in 1993, saying, "Cancer can take away all my physical abilities, but it cannot touch my mind, it cannot touch my heart, and it cannot touch my soul. And those three things are going to carry on forever."

Eight weeks later, Jimmy V was gone—but his great spirit of perseverance lives on, fighting cancer to this day through The V Foundation. And his spirit lives on in the Jimmy V Perseverance Award, awarded annually to athletes and coaches who demonstrate Jimmy's brand of endurance and persistence.

In 2007, the recipient of the Jimmy V Perseverance Award was another Wolfpack basketball coach—Kay Yow, head coach of the women's basketball team at North Carolina State from 1975 to 2009. Over a 37-year career as a college head basketball coach, she amassed a record of 729-337. She also coached the 1988 United States women's basketball team (despite having been diagnosed with breast cancer the previous year); her team won Olympic gold. In 2007, she helped establish the Kay Yow/WBCA Cancer Fund (in partnership with The V Foundation) as a charitable organization dedicated to fighting women's cancers.[6]

Nicknamed "Iron Woman" by her players because of her indomitable spirit, Yow seemed to have beaten cancer ("my formidable foe," as she called it) in the late 1980s. When her cancer returned during the 2004-2005 season, she was forced to miss a few games while undergoing treatment. She took an even more extended leave of absence during the 2006-2007 season, missing 16 games. Her return ignited the Wolfpack, which went on to win 10 of the next 11 games.

She battled cancer bravely and persistently. But in January 2009, her battle ended. She died at WakeMed Cary Hospital in Cary, North Carolina. The 66-year-old Yow had planned her own funeral, even recording a 25-minute video message, which was played at the memorial service.[7]

One of the best summations of Kay Yow's life was offered by one of her players, Annemarie Dloniak, who was a senior in 1987. "I just felt from the very first time I met her that she had a genuine interest in me—I could feel it," Dloniak said. She also remembered how hard Kay Yow pushed her players during practice in order to build their endurance. "She drove us into the ground," Dloniak said, laughing.

Asked to describe the most important quality of Coach Yow's life, Dloniak said that it was her "never quit" attitude. Anyone who ever played for Coach Yow was familiar with the phrase, "Just one more time"—a phrase Yow used to get her players to go through one more drill after everyone was ready to drop from exhaustion.

What was Kay Yow like as a coach? "Coach Yow never cursed at you," Dloniak said, "but there was a way she would look at you and that was enough." Asked to name the most important lesson Coach Yow had taught her, Dloniak replied, "Perseverance, her positive countenance—no matter what the situation."

Annemarie Dloniak will always remember one particular game during her senior year—the 1987 ACC championship game when the Wolfpack came back from a nine-point deficit to beat Virginia for the title. Dloniak's older brother, Eric, was gravely ill in a Greensboro hospital. Just before tipoff, Eric died. Dloniak's parents were at Eric's hospital bedside, and they managed to get a message to Coach Yow during the game. They asked Dloniak's coach to give her the news of her brother's death after the game, and Kay Yow agreed to do so.

The Wolfpack won. Annemarie Dloniak helped her teammates cut down the nets, and then she looked into the TV cameras and shouted, "Hey, Eric! We won!" Then she went to the locker room and saw Coach Yow waiting for her. The bad news was written on the coach's face.

That was in 1987. A few months later, Coach Yow was confronted with her own mortality when she was diagnosed for the first time with breast cancer. Annemarie Dloniak never forgot Coach Yow's compassion in giving her the news of her brother's death, or her courage in facing breast cancer, or the message of perseverance that she exemplified on and off the court. Over the next two decades, whenever Annemarie Dloniak faced a major decision in her life, she would go back to Coach Yow for wisdom and guidance. The coach's door was always open.[8]

Bear Bryant, George Allen, Jimmy Valvano, Kay Yow—these coaches have set an example of perseverance for their players to follow. More important, they have set an example for you to follow as you influence the people around you. Jimmy V's message should be our message—and the rule we live by: "Don't give up, don't ever give up!"

5

Build a Disciplined Team

©Rick Burnham/Icon SMI/ZUMA Press

Duffy Daugherty was head football coach of the Michigan State Spartans from 1954 to 1972. When I was in grad school at Indiana University, one of my professors was Duffy's older brother, Dr. Jack Daugherty. Every Monday, Dr. Daugherty would spend the first half hour of class time analyzing the Michigan State football games coached by his brother, Duffy. The more questions we asked about Duffy's games, the less time we spent listening to Dr. Daugherty's lectures.

No question, Duffy Daugherty was an outstanding football coach, having compiled a career record of 109-65-5. He was also a great storyteller. One of his favorite stories from his coaching days came from a road game against UCLA.

With the game tied at 14 and mere seconds left in regulation play, Michigan State had moved the ball into field-goal range. Coach Daugherty sent in his kicker, Dave Kaiser. The ball was snapped and Kaiser kicked it. As the ball sailed toward the end zone, Duffy noticed that his kicker wasn't even watching the ball—he was looking down at ground level, where the officials stood in the end zone. The ball split the uprights—and Michigan State won, 17-14.

As Dave Kaiser strode back to the bench, his teammates went wild—and so did his coach. "Great job, Dave!" Coach Daugherty said, slapping him on the shoulder pads. "But why didn't you watch the ball after you kicked it?"

"I was watching the officials in the end zone," Kaiser said. "I wanted to see how they'd call it. I couldn't see the ball."

Duffy was shocked. "You couldn't see the ball!"

Kaiser grinned sheepishly. "I forgot my contact lenses. They're back at the hotel. Heck, Coach, I couldn't even see the goalposts!"

At first, Duffy was angry that Dave Kaiser hadn't mentioned the problem with his contact lenses. But then he realized that Kaiser had kicked that ball through the uprights with total confidence because he was a highly disciplined kicker. He had made that kick hundreds of times in practice because he knew the angle and distance to the goal. His body and mind were programmed to kick that ball down the slot.

Dave Kaiser didn't need to see the ball. He relied on his discipline, and that was enough to win the game.[1] One of the essential keys to effective coaching is *build a disciplined team*.

Great Leaders on Discipline

All the great coaches preach the importance of discipline—especially self-discipline. John Wooden put it this way: "Discipline yourself, and others won't need to. Never lie. Never cheat. Never steal. Earn the right to be proud and confident."[2] Coach Dean Smith of the University of North Carolina said, "The really free person in society is the one who is disciplined. Players feel loved when they are disciplined."[3]

Bobby Bowden, former head football coach of the Florida State University Seminoles, defined discipline as sacrifice, a "willingness to give up something you want to do, so you can better yourself."[4] And Mike Shanahan, head coach of the Washington Redskins, said:

> People talk about discipline, but to me, there's discipline and there's self-discipline. Discipline is listening to people tell you what to do, where to be, and how to do something. Self-discipline is knowing that you are responsible for everything that happens in your life; you are the only one who can take yourself to the desired heights.[5]

This is coaching wisdom that has stood the test of time. The ancient Chinese "coach" Lao-Tzu preached the importance of self-discipline as a key to success in the 6th century B.C.: "He who controls others may be powerful, but he who has mastered himself is mightier still."[6] And over in Israel, in the 10th century B.C., "Coach" Solomon linked discipline to a love of knowledge and wisdom: "Whoever loves discipline loves knowledge, but he who hates correction is stupid."[7]

Phil Jackson, head coach of the LA Lakers, once told me how he learned the importance of self-discipline. "When I was a senior at the University of North Dakota," he said, "my coach was Bill Fitch. I was captain of the team, but at one point, I had the job taken away from me. We were playing a game in Chicago, and I went out with some friends to Rush Street. I got back to the hotel after curfew, so Bill took away my captaincy. He said, 'You won't be captain again until you prove to me you deserve it.' Bill made me prove to him that I had the self-discipline to be captain. In time, I earned my job back and we went on to a successful season. Bill Fitch gave me a lesson in discipline that has helped me throughout my life."

Teams That Discipline Themselves

My friend Chuck Daly coached the Detroit Pistons to back-to-back NBA Championships in 1989 and 1990, and also coached the Orlando Magic from 1997 to 1999. He passed away in May 2009. Chuck was a firm yet fair disciplinarian. While Chuck was coaching at the University of Pennsylvania in the 1970s, he shared his philosophy of team discipline with his assistant, Bob Weinhauer.

Bob recently shared Chuck's thoughts with me. He said, "Chuck used to tell me, 'When it comes to discipline, you've got to hear what you want to hear and see what you want to see. You can't react to everything. You can't jump on every little infraction. A coach has to learn to overlook some things. Don't go out of your way to create unnecessary confrontation.' That was Chuck's philosophy, and even though he let some of the minor stuff slide, he had good discipline on his teams. He had complete control, and his players respected him. I think they respected him because he was firm yet fair, and he knew what to see and what not to see."

I mentioned this insight to longtime NBA coach Hubie Brown, and he laughed. "I couldn't do it the way Chuck did," Hubie said. "I heard and saw *everything*! I disciplined my players for *everything*! But I'll say this: I'd have been a better coach if I could have coached Chuck's way."

Dr. Jack Ramsay is the seventh-winningest coach in NBA history, best known for leading the 1976-1977 Portland Trail Blazers to an NBA Championship over my Philadelphia 76ers, and for his work as a broadcaster for ESPN. Dr. Jack also hired me to my first position in the NBA with the 76ers in 1968. He is a big believer in the importance of discipline. He wrote:

> The best discipline is that which comes from within. Self-disciplined people know what they must do to meet their responsibilities. They set priorities in their lives and faithfully observe daily routines that equip them to reach their goals. They have a high level of determination—nothing stands in the way of accomplishing their appointed tasks.
>
> Many athletes have this kind of self-discipline. Their coach needs only to point them in the right direction and they'll do the rest. They're punctual, reliable, and responsible self-starters.[8]

Dr. Jack tells a story from his days as head coach of the Trail Blazers. He had gone to the locker room and had posted the playing stats of his team on the bulletin board. The stats helped the players see how they compared with other players on the team and other teams in the league. Players with lagging numbers knew that they had to step up their effort in order for the team to be successful.

Moments after Jack posted the stats, power forward Maurice Lucas walked into the locker room. Lucas stopped and watched his teammates checking their stats. Then, without a word, Lucas elbowed his way past his teammates, snatched the sheets off the bulletin board, and threw them in the trash can. As the players stared at Lucas in amazement, he calmly went to his locker and started dressing out for practice.

One of the players who was there that day said that he interpreted Lucas's action to mean that the team needed to focus on discipline and preparation, not stat sheets. "Luke's attitude told us it was time to lace 'em up," the player later told Dr. Jack. "We went back to our lockers, sat down, and got ourselves mentally ready to play."[9]

That is the kind of discipline every team needs—a discipline which comes from within the team, and from all of the players. You know that your team is functioning well when you see your players taking responsibility for team discipline.

Marty Schottenheimer has coached the NFL's Cleveland Browns, Kansas City Chiefs, Washington Redskins, and San Diego Chargers. He advocates making players responsible for team discipline. He once said:

> The most successful teams I've been around were those where the players drove the machine. I'm not talking about during the game. I'm talking about in the locker room, in the meeting room, and on the practice field. Certain conditions were set. And they weren't set by the coaches as much as they were by the players themselves. There was a level of expectation in terms of preparation, effort, and so forth. If certain players fell short, the other guys were quick to say, "Get with it."
>
> That direction is much more effective coming from another player than coming from a coach. Players get tired of listening to coaches. When the guy at the next locker verbally kicks a player in the butt, it makes an impression. …
>
> A coach can scream and holler about teamwork, but the teams that really have it are the ones on which the players live it and demand it every day. It comes with mutual respect and internal leadership.[10]

Pat Summitt, head basketball coach of the Lady Volunteers, does not scream or holler at her players—but she does enforce discipline. She insists that players maintain their grades and attend all practices or be cut from the team. She encourages her players to be self-disciplined in all areas of their lives—and she has set forth her rules for individual and team success:

- Being responsible sometimes means making tough, unpopular decisions.
- Admit to and make yourself accountable for mistakes. How can you improve if you're never wrong?

- Loyalty is not unilateral. You have to give it to receive it. …
- Discipline yourself, so no one else has to.
- Self-discipline helps you believe in yourself.
- Group discipline produces a unified effort toward a common goal.
- Discipline helps you finish a job, and finishing is what separates excellent work from average work.
- Do the things that aren't fun first, and do them well.
- See yourself as self-employed.
- Put the team before yourself.[11]

Successful coaches encourage players to discipline themselves, so that the coach doesn't have to. Successful teams demonstrate leadership ability and self-discipline throughout the team. The best-disciplined team is a self-disciplined team.

The Disciplined Leader

What is discipline? It's the commitment to keep working when your body needs rest. It's the commitment to keep going when everything inside you screams, "Stop!" It's the commitment to practice and prepare yourself daily, consistently, intensely, when it would be so easy to slack off. It's the commitment to stick to a healthy, lean diet when that cheesecake looks *so* good. Discipline is painful, it's unpleasant, and it's no fun. But without discipline, there can be no victories, no championships, and no gold medals.

Discipline is constant and consistent. There is never a time when you can say, "I can drop my guard now. I can let myself go. I can slack off." Don't ever think that you can take a vacation from being a disciplined person. Your commitment to disciplined living must be total.

Vince Lombardi put it this way: "In a football game, there are approximately 160 football plays. And yet there are only three or four plays that have anything to do with the outcome of the game. The only problem is that no one knows when those three or four plays are coming up. As a result, each and every player must go all-out on all 160 plays."[12]

To build a disciplined team, you *must* be a disciplined leader. You set the tone for everything your players do. If you want a disciplined team, then inspire your players through your example. "A good leader must be harder on himself than anyone else," said Vince Lombardi. "He must first discipline himself before he can discipline others. A man should not ask others to do things he would not have asked himself to do."[13]

Discipline With Consequences

Lou Holtz is the only college football coach to lead six different programs to bowl games. He has been honored multiple times as National Coach of the Year. In his book *Winning Every Day*, Coach Holtz talks about the importance of recruiting self-disciplined players and of building disciplined teams. He has often been called a tough disciplinarian—and he wears that label proudly. He writes:

> For me, a disciplinarian is someone who requires that people understand the consequences of their decisions. You use discipline to reinforce choices. Our athletes and my children knew that if they chose to misbehave, they were also choosing to pay the consequences. For a player, that could mean a benching or even a suspension. For a child, it might mean we would ground them or deny them certain privileges. In each case, I never punished anyone; the offenders chose the punishment themselves by their actions.
>
> Mature people should be able to accept this, provided you are fair, consistent, and firm. As a leader, you have an obligation to weigh all the facts, to examine any extenuating circumstances associated with the infraction before coming to a judgment. Consistency requires that you never ignore any individual's violation of your team's rules. Talent is never a mitigating factor. Your All-American running back is just as liable for bad behavior as your third-string kicker. Pick and choose which rules you will enforce with whom and you invite chaos.[14]

Coach Holtz goes on to tell the story of how, in 1988, his top-ranked Fighting Irish of Notre Dame were slated to face the second-ranked USC Trojans. Holtz was confident that his team could beat USC and secure the number one spot—until a discipline problem arose.

Two players were notoriously late to practices, team meetings, and team meals. Coach Holtz had tried everything he could think of to discipline these two players, but nothing worked. The problem was that these were two of the best players on the team—and they knew it. They thought they were invulnerable—that their talent would shield them from being harshly disciplined.

Finally, Coach Holtz sat them down and told them, "If you are late one more time for any team function, whether it's your fault, my fault, your parent's fault, or the bus driver's fault, you are going to miss the next game. I won't play either of you."

The players were stunned. They could tell that Coach Holtz really meant it. So they were on their best behavior—for about a week. The team flew from Indiana to Los Angeles. The night before the big game against USC, both players showed up *40 minutes late* for the pregame meal.

"That tore it," Holtz recalls. "I didn't want the keys to our offense to miss our biggest game of the year—but when they decided to break our rules, they also decided to miss the game."

As he saw it, the two players had made their own choice to suffer the consequences and miss the game. His job as coach was simply to enforce the choice the two young men had made. And he did.

Coach Holtz did not want the two players hanging around and causing a distraction for the rest of the team, so he put them on a plane and sent them back to Indiana. He later reflected:

> Would it have been better if I had looked the other way? From the standpoint of winning a single game, undoubtedly. One of those boys was our leading ground gainer, the other our leading pass receiver. You can just imagine how their losses could have deflated our offense. But when you are responsible for an organization you don't make any short-term decisions that can jeopardize your long-term gains. I had no option. They chose not to play in the game when they chose to arrive late. It would have been simple to show preferential treatment. After issuing the warning as I had, I would have lost the rest of the team if I had handled it any other way. Fortunately, the absence of these two stars didn't hurt us; we won our game. I like to think that the victory was a reward for doing the right thing.[15]

Even if Notre Dame had lost that game, however, I'm sure that Coach Holtz would have had no regrets. He did the right thing. He kept his word. He enforced team discipline. Winning the game just helped to underscore the point that no player, no matter how talented he or she might be, is above the rules or immune from the consequences of team discipline.

As a coach, your job is not just to win games but to shape the minds and hearts of young people. You discipline your players by letting them receive the consequences they have chosen. And you set an example of discipline by treating every player equally and fairly.

Discipline 'Em—Then Watch 'Em Work

Dwight Thomas is a recruiting specialist at Levi, Ray & Shoup, Inc., in Springfield, Illinois, providing recruiting information to football programs across the United States. But for three decades, he was Coach Dwight Thomas, one of the most renowned high school football coaches in the state of Florida—and the man who, at Escambia High School in Pensacola, coached future Hall of Fame running back Emmitt Smith. While at Escambia High, Coach Thomas won two state titles and sent 35 young men on to play college football.

Before coming to Escambia, Thomas coached football at Choctawatchee High in Fort Walton Beach. In his four seasons at Choctawatchee, he had coached the team to a 30-12 record and was about to embark on his fifth season with 15 returning starters, plus a kicker ranked number one in the state. But, before the start of the season, the principal called Thomas in and told him that, since Thomas had not won a state championship during his first four years at the school, he was out of a job.

Thomas replied that he was going to get a job coaching the worst team in Florida—then he'd bring that team to Choctawatchee High and make the principal eat his words. A few days later, Thomas signed on as coach of the Escambia High Gators—a team that had not had a winning season in 21 years. In fact, the Gators' combined record for the previous three years was a dismal 3-27.

When Coach Thomas took over the team, he began by laying down three simple rules: "Be where you're supposed to be, doing what you're supposed to be doing, when you're supposed to be doing it." He set forth a penalty that was every bit as simple as the rules. "If they break a rule," he said, "I don't run 'em and I don't whip 'em. I just toss 'em [off the team]—that day. And they know that they're gone, so I can save the other kids. I love 'em enough to chase 'em off."

The theme of that first season was *discipline*—tough, hard-nosed discipline. He began the season with 38 seniors, and ended with four. His critics called him "Gestapo" or "Dwight the Barbarian." But the Gators went 7-3 that season—and even the critics couldn't argue with that kind of turnaround.

That first season was also when Dwight Thomas discovered that he had a freshman running back with amazing potential—a fella named Emmitt Smith. The following year, the Escambia Gators won a state title. And they repeated that feat the year after that.

Coach Thomas sees the coach's role as one of building young people's bodies, minds, and souls. "We lose so many kids over the summer who run with the wrong crowd," he says. "How we raise these kids affects how they'll raise their kids. It's where discipline and character are taught. Christ strove to teach those qualities, and when His people got them, He stepped back and watched them work. That's what coaches do. We step back on Friday night and watch them work."[16]

Discipline enabled Dwight Thomas to take charge of the worst high school football program in the state and transform it into the best. But Coach Thomas doesn't teach discipline to his players merely to win games. He disciplines them so that they will win in the biggest game of all—the game of life.

6

Focus on Preparation

In 1969, Coach Don Shula took over the Miami Dolphins, a bottom-of-the-barrel expansion team with a record of 3-10-1. Upon taking the reins of the organization, Shula said, "I'm no miracle worker. … I'm about as subtle as a punch in the mouth. I'm just a guy who rolls up his sleeves and goes to work."[1] Two years later, Shula coached the Dolphins to the first of three consecutive Super Bowl appearances.

Bob Griese, quarterback of the undefeated 1972 Miami Dolphins, recalls the grueling physical preparation he and his teammates went through under Don Shula. "Shoes" (as the players called Shula) would make them work out in pads under the hot Florida sun. They'd practice from 7 a.m. till dark. The only breaks they got were for meals and team meetings. Shula would pit the offense against the defense in intensive "Oklahoma drills" and scrimmages, then put them through endless sideline-to-sideline sprints to build up their endurance.

"It was punishing, it was murderous," Griese recalled. "In the end, Shoes pared the team down to a hard-core bunch of guys who wanted to win. We knew we needed to be tougher and more dedicated than the guys on the other side of the ball."

The payoff for all that punishing preparation came in a game against the reigning Super Bowl champions, the Kansas City Chiefs, on Christmas Day 1971. The game was tied at 24 at the end of regulation play, and again at the end of the first overtime. Going into the second overtime period, Griese thought, "They can't beat us! They're tiring out, and we've still got plenty of steam left!" The game came down to a test of endurance—and the Dolphins won by simply outlasting the Chiefs.[2]

Preparation wins games, which is why preparation is one of the keys to successful coaching. Jim Caldwell, head coach of the Indianapolis Colts, appears so calm on the sidelines during a game for a reason. I once heard him say, "I'm calm on the inside, too. When you are prepared, there is no reason to sweat."

The Joy of Preparation

In any sport, there are only so many things you can control. You can't control the weather. You can't control the officiating. You can't control injuries and illnesses among your players. But you can control the level of your preparation.

Lawrence Frank is the former head coach of the NBA's New Jersey Nets, and one of the youngest coaches in the league. He once said, "You always focus on what you can control. I can't control any of the outside forces. I can only control our preparation."[3]

Some coaches seem to think that the emotional highs of coaching come from getting awards and praise from the fans and the media. Not Tony Dungy. The retired NFL coach says, "The joy I receive from coaching in this game comes from the preparation and the winning, not getting the credit or the attention."[4]

Former UCLA basketball star Bill Walton agrees. As a guest on my radio show, he once told me, "I love the pressure and anticipation of the game. I love the preparation and practice. Coach Wooden taught us to love the preparation of getting ready for a game. He said that you create a routine and good habits by the way you prepare yourself ahead of time.

"You prepare yourself mentally for anything that could happen in the game. You visualize the game a thousand times in your mind before it happens. And in practice, you get into a flow with your teammates. You memorize all of their moves, so that you begin to move in sync with them. Through intensive practice, your body and your mind memorize all the moves—and in the game, it becomes automatic, like pushing a button."

Pete Blackman, who played basketball at UCLA from 1958 to 1962, can testify to the intense preparation of Coach John Wooden. "He was fantastically prepared," Blackman said. "Literally every practice was planned down to the minute. You don't lose track of lessons like that. When you are preparing for a major business presentation, fifteen years later, you look around and you're probably the best prepared person there. Well, why is that true? Because people like Coach Wooden proved to you, at an early stage of development, that the time spent in preparation will pay off."[5]

Preparation opens doors of opportunity. You never know when a golden opportunity will present itself to you, whether on the field of competition or in everyday life. Preparation is the key to being ready to seize an opportunity when it comes your way. Leadership guru John Maxwell put it this way:

> There's an old saying: "You can claim to be surprised once; after that, you're unprepared." If you want to take advantage of opportunities to use your talent, then you *must* be prepared when the opportunities arise. Once the opportunity presents itself, it's too late to get ready.
>
> If you study the lives of dynamic men and women, you will find that preparation for opportunity is a common theme. President Abraham Lincoln said, "I will prepare and some day my chance will come." Prime Minister Benjamin Disraeli of England remarked, "The secret of success in life is for a man to be ready for his time when it comes." Oprah Winfrey asserted, "Luck is a matter of preparation meeting opportunity."[6]

In athletic competition, there is no time to think, "What is my next move?" Actions must be immediate, instinctive, and natural. NCAA basketball coach Jerry Tarkanian has a career coaching record of 990-228 (81.3%) across all college divisions, and has led three different schools to 20-win seasons during his first year as head coach. "The more your players have to think on the basketball court," he once said, "the slower their feet get."[7]

Don Shula put it this way: "I want our players to be so familiar with assignments that when the game starts, they don't have to worry about what they're supposed to be doing. They can simply turn themselves loose physically to do whatever it takes to win the game. … They should be so familiar with their assignments that when the game starts they're operating on auto-pilot."[8]

And music legend Jimi Hendrix put it this way: "Learn everything, forget everything, and play."

A Culture of Winning

John Wooden had an expression he repeated every day in practice: "Be quick—but don't hurry!" In other words, basketball must be played at a quick pace—but you should never be stampeded into playing out of control. "If you hurry," he'd say, "you're more likely to make mistakes. But if you're not quick, you won't get things done." The key to being quick but unhurried is *preparation*.

Coach Wooden learned the importance of quickness in preparation when he was a young basketball coach at South Bend High School in Indiana. Legendary Notre Dame football coach Frank Leahy took a shine to young John Wooden and invited him to attend Notre Dame football practices. Wooden never imagined he would learn so much about basketball while watching a football practice.

As Wooden watched the Notre Dame players going through their paces, he noticed how quickly the players shifted from drill to drill as Leahy blew his whistle. The Notre Dame players responded like a precision machine. They were so well prepared that their responses were fine-tuned and automatic. They were quick—but unhurried. Wooden realized that he could apply the same principles to his basketball practices—and he did. The lessons Coach Wooden learned from Frank Leahy became the foundation of the system he employed for the rest of his career.

In the early 1960s, Coach Wooden introduced the full-court press to college basketball. His Bruins weren't the tallest or most talented players in the NCAA, but they were the best-prepared—and the quickest. As a result, Coach Wooden won his first NCAA championship in 1964.

Predictably, other coaches began copying John Wooden's Bruins, including the full-court press. But few coaches understood what Wooden was doing. They mistakenly thought that the purpose of the Bruin press was to force a turnover. In reality, Coach Wooden used the press to force the opposing team to play at a faster tempo than they were used to. A team which hurries is more likely to make mistakes.[9]

Bill Walton recalls that Coach Wooden's practice sessions at UCLA were "nonstop, electric, supercharged, intense, demanding … with Coach pacing the sidelines like a caged tiger, barking instructions, positive reinforcements and maxims: 'Be quick—but don't hurry.'" The brilliant reasoning behind this fast-paced preparation became apparent on game day when, according to Walton, everything seemed to take place in a "slower gear" than in practice, because "everything we did in games happened faster at practice."[10]

Bobby Bowden, longtime football coach of the Florida State Seminoles, once told me he had calculated that he and his coaching assistants spent at least one hour of planning and preparation for each minute his players were on the football field, which works out to a 60-to-1 ratio of preparation time to playing time.

In his bio on the Florida State University website, Bobby talks about his love of the planning and preparation that are a huge part of a coach's job. "I just love to coach," he says. "I have always gotten my greatest pleasure out of breaking down film, learning about opponents and yourself, then implementing a game plan to take advantage of your strengths and their weaknesses. I love to take a group of young men in the late summer and mold them into a team."

His love of strategic preparation goes back to 1943, when a sports-obsessed 13-year-old Bobby Bowden was hospitalized with rheumatic fever, and forced to spend more than a year in confinement and recuperation at home (including six months of bed rest). In those pre-television days, Bobby had only a radio for entertainment, and even the entertainment shows were frequently interrupted with news from the European and Pacific theaters of the war.

"I basically listened to a play-by-play of World War II for a year," he later told an interviewer. "I would imagine what every place looked like, what the terrain of the battlefield was like, what the army units looked like, and how the sounds and smells of the war must have been."

At some point in his life, Bowden realized that there were similarities between leading troops in battle and coaching a sports team. "You face similar tasks of motivation, preparation, teamwork, discipline," he said. "I'm sure my interest in coaching, in real X's and O's coaching, probably stems a lot from listening to those accounts of the war and trying to imagine the movements of the battles. I still believe that winning is the greatest feeling there is in coaching, but I probably get the most satisfaction out of putting in the strategies and watching them play out."[11]

In short, Bobby Bowden finds the greatest reward of coaching in the process of *preparation*, which produces winning results. And his career record at Florida State (208-51-4) is all the proof you need that *preparation pays*.

Aron Bassoff, head women's soccer coach at the University of the Cumberlands, agrees that preparation is a key function of coaching at any level, in any sport. Bassoff says that his women's soccer program continually stresses preparation in order to "establish a culture of winning. Understanding preparation is the key to us getting to the level [where] we want to be."[12]

Six Keys to Preparing Your Team

Let me suggest to you six keys to effective preparation. I didn't invent these six insights. Rather, I learned them from the top coaching minds in many sports, at all levels of competition. They are:

First, *preparation must be relentless*. Rex Kern quarterbacked for the Ohio State Buckeyes from 1968 to 1970, including an undefeated season and a national championship in 1968. His coach was the legendary Woody Hayes (1913-1987), who won five national titles and 13 Big Ten championships during his 28-year tenure at Ohio State.

In 2002, WOSU-radio in Columbus produced a special documentary program on the life and times of Woody Hayes. Rex Kern was interviewed for that show and shared this insight about Hayes' approach to preparation:

> [Woody Hayes] believed in repetition. He believed that, in the heat of battle, you react, you respond to what you have been taught. And so, good gosh, we would run plays over and over and over again, until we got it right.
>
> And I will never forget, early on when I was a varsity player, Woody said to us, "Guys, we will run this play until we get it right. And you know what? We've got lights on this football field, and those lights will burn out before I'll lose a football game because I failed to prepare you well enough on this practice field."[13]

That is relentless preparation. That is a commitment to doing the same drill over and over and over again until your players know it in every fiber of their being and can run those plays in their sleep. Preparation must be relentless.

Second, *preparation must be meticulous*. Grant Teaff took over a dying football program at Baylor University in 1972, and he quickly turned the Baylor Bears into a winning team. Over a 20-year career, he compiled a winning record, and his teams won the Peach Bowl, the Liberty Bowl, the Bluebonnet Bowl, and the Sun Bowl.

I once heard Grant Teaff describe his philosophy of preparation as a coach and a leader. He explained, "I always say, 'You've got to plan like you're robbing a bank.' People always find that statement a little shocking, but it's actually a good way to approach the challenge of preparation. If you want to be successful, you have to plan out every detail, anticipate every possible problem, and leave nothing to chance.

"You have to ask yourself, 'If A happens, what's my Plan B?' In football, that's called an 'adjustment.' When your opponent throws something at you that you didn't expect, you have to adjust your plan. You have to have a fall-back plan, a Plan B. And you have to have it figured out in advance. That's what preparation is all about."

My friend Ernie Accorsi, former general manager of the New York Giants, has worked with some of the greatest coaches in football, including Joe Paterno, Don Shula, and Marty Schottenheimer. He once told me that all of these great coaches have two qualities in common. "First," he said, "these coaches simply refuse to accept defeat. They hate it. Losing any game sticks in their craw and eats them up inside. And this first quality produces the second quality: These coaches are absolute fanatics about preparation. They are thorough and meticulous in their planning and daily preparation. They try to account for every contingency, and they attempt to have a solution ready for any problems that might arise."

Third, *preparation must be as realistic as possible.* In your practice sessions, try to create real-world conditions that prepare your players for the actual conditions and opposition they will face.

LPGA golf instructor Cindy MacNider doesn't discount the value of the driving range, but she insists that the only way to become proficient at golf is to practice the game on a real course—bunkers, hazards, and all. "You will not have perfect, flat lies on the golf course," she explains, "so create real situations. Put yourself into competitive situations, buried lies in a bunker for instance."

And Stanford women's golf coach Caroline O'Connor agrees. "In practice," she says, "try to simulate on-course pressure." She suggests exercises, such as sinking 100 consecutive putts—one miss and you start all over. "If you are trying to make 100 putts in a row," she says, "at 90 your palms perspire." Now, that's pressure. If you are able to overcome that kind of real-world pressure in a practice session, then you will be better able to handle the pressure in actual competition.[14]

Fourth, *preparation must help players stay focused on the essentials.* On February 3, 2008, in Super Bowl XLII, Eli Manning and the New York Giants upset the heavily favored New England Patriots, becoming the first NFC wild-card team ever to win a Super Bowl. The Giants head coach was Tom Coughlin.

Five months later, as the team was heading to training camp for the new season, Coach Coughlin held a press conference and told reporters, "Successful teams out-think, out-prepare, out-practice, and out-play the opponents. It lies in our preparation. And if the hearts and minds are in the right spot, we can overcome any obstacle, and that is where we will start right out again. No one ever gave us anything and we don't expect it. We are not asking for anything. We expect that the only road to the quality football team that we want to be is through this hard work that occurs right now."[15]

Unfortunately, one of Coughlin's key players, Plaxico Burress, got involved in off-the-field problems that proved costly to himself and his team. The Giants had to play out the season without their star wide receiver. Though the Giants didn't make it back to the Super Bowl the following year, they managed to win the NFC East with a 12-4 record.

Bottom line, Coach Tom Coughlin knew how to prepare his Super Bowl champions for the season ahead. He had to help his players screen out distractions, fan expectations, and their own overconfidence. He had to get his players focused on the essentials of preparation. And your challenge is no different.

Fifth, *preparation must be all-consuming—for the coach as well as the players.* Football coach George Allen took over two losing teams—first, the Los Angeles Rams, then, the Washington Redskins—and he turned them into winners. In fact, he never had a losing season as a pro football head coach, and he closed out his NFL career with a record of 116-47-5 and a .705 winning percentage.

In his *Handbook of Winning Football*, Allen wrote, "Winning is the science of being totally prepared. Preparing a team to win is what football coaching is all about. My definition of preparation can be stated in only three words: leave nothing undone. That is what 17-hour workdays and 110 percent effort are all about. You have to want to win so badly that everyone else around you will work just as hard to win."

Preparation must be all-consuming—nothing left to chance, nothing left undone. Coach Allen went on to say, "The head coach himself has to put in the time. As I tell my players, a 100 percent effort is not enough. The world belongs to those who aim for 110 percent. You cannot win if you are not willing to pay the price." When the coach himself puts out a 110 percent effort, his players are inspired and motivated to work just as hard.

Former Rams defensive end Deacon Jones once told *Investor's Business Daily,* "George got his team ready. We never went into battle when we weren't ready."[16]

Sixth, *you must approach preparation with a positive attitude*. Both coaches and players should look forward to preparation with anticipation. Former UCLA women's softball coach Sue Enquist put it this way:

> I'm going to ask you from this day forward to really love the preparation of your game. I'm going to ask you to love the struggles of hard practices. I'm going to ask you to love the anticipation of game day because the preparation is the longest part of your life as an athlete. So if we enjoy the anticipation, which takes the longest amount of time, win or lose, we can all look back and say, "Oh, man, I had a good time." I want you to love the anticipation, but you can't love the anticipation of your training if you're not authentic in it. If you're authentic in your training, you're going to reach your potential in the competitive arena.[17]

Bear Bryant, college football's winningest coach, summed it up this way: "It's not the will to win that matters—everyone has that. It's the will to *prepare* to win that matters."[18]

Championships Are Won Behind Closed Doors

March 28, 1992: If you saw that basketball game, you'll never forget it. It was the NCAA East Regional Final. Number one Duke hoped to become the first team to successfully defend their championship, since John Wooden's Bruins ended a seven-year run in 1973. Kentucky hoped to reclaim its prestige following an embarrassing three year NCAA probation. It was Duke's Mike Krzyzewski versus Kentucky's Rick Pitino, a battle of the titans, played out in the Spectrum in Philadelphia before 17,848 fans.

In the second half, Kentucky battled back from a 12-point deficit to tie the game at 93 with 33.6 seconds to play. At the buzzer, Duke point guard Bobby Hurley missed— and the game went into overtime.

In the closing 31.5 seconds of the overtime period, the lead changed hands five times. With the score knotted at 98, Duke center Christian Laettner got the ball in the post, made a spin move, and launched a line drive as the shot clock expired. The ball banked off the backboard and dropped through the net.

On Kentucky's next possession, forward Jamal Mashburn was fouled while making a lay-up. After he sank the free throw, Kentucky had the lead, 101-100. Kentucky fans nearly blew the roof off the arena.

On Duke's possession, the ball went back to Laettner, who had not missed a field goal attempt all night. As Laettner pounded his way inside, Mashburn fouled him—and fouled out. Laettner made both free throws—and the crowd went quiet. Duke led 102-101. In 7.8 seconds, one of these two teams was going to the Final Four.

Rick Pitino called time-out and drew up an offensive play for his Wildcats. Meanwhile, Mike Krzyzewski huddled with his Blue Devils. As Duke came out of the huddle, point guard Bobby Hurley shouted to his teammates, "Call time-out if Kentucky scores!" (Krzyzewski later admitted, "I couldn't believe it. I forgot to remind the guys of that!")

Kentucky's Sean Woods, who had already scored 19 points, took the inbounds pass and launched a one-handed floater from 10 feet out. The shot cleared the fingertips of Christian Laettner by millimeters, kissed the backboard, and fell through the hoop. Kentucky led, 103-102, with only 2.1 ticks left on the clock.

The Blue Devils looked to their coach. Mike Krzyzewski knew what they were thinking: *Can we win—or is it over?* What he said to his players at that moment would be absolutely crucial to what happened next. He had to make them believe that winning was not only possible but inevitable. He had to put his players in a mindset where they would rely on their preparation.

"We're gonna win," he said —and instantly, a change came over his team. He could see it in their eyes. They *believed*.

Coach K reminded his players that the clock wouldn't start until the inbounded ball was touched, which meant that the inbounds pass could travel most of the length of the court while the clock remained frozen.

Grant Hill took the ball to the baseline while Laettner positioned himself far upcourt. The crowd was on its feet as the opponents lined up. Hill fired a long pass, Laettner dashed to the free-throw line, and the ball sailed past the outstretched hands of defender John Pelphrey and into the hands of Laettner.

Christian Laettner whirled, dribbled once, faked right to create separation from a Kentucky defender, spun left, leaped, and fired the 17-foot fadeaway. For everyone in that building, time slowed down. The final buzzer sounded as gravity pulled the ball back to earth. The ball never even grazed the hoop, but fell through the net with a swish of victory.

Duke won, 104-103. Kentucky fans were dumbfounded. Coach K and his Blue Devils celebrated wildly. They were going to the Final Four![19]

When an entire season hinges on what happens during 2.1 pressure-filled seconds, everything comes down to preparation. Championships are not won under the glare of the lights, while the crowd chants. They are won on the practice field and in the locker room. As Christian Laettner himself once said, "We won championships at Duke because of what happened behind closed doors."[20]

7

Maintain Balance in Your Life

©Randy Pench/ZUMA Press

As a coach, you can't perform well if your mind and body are not at their best. You can't focus on your leadership role when you are distracted by insomnia, exhaustion, heart palpitations, headaches, backaches, and indigestion. So, you must maintain your balance in all the dimensions of your life—spiritual, mental, physical, and relational.

Dayton Moore is the general manager of the Kansas City Royals. He has also worked for the Atlanta Braves organization as a scout and in other player-development roles. Moore believes that coaches and managers owe it to their players to help them achieve balance in their lives. "One thing I've learned," he said, "is that baseball players have been gifted to be athletes; but the only way they are able to use those gifts day in and day out and be successful is if they have the balance they need in their lives."[1]

As a leader, you also need to maintain balance in your own personal and professional life. Leadership expert Gregory K. Morris, Ph.D., put it this way: "Balance in life and leadership is difficult to come by and even harder to maintain. If you desire to lead with effectiveness over the long haul, balance will be a hallmark of your leadership. But the currents of change and temptation are so subtle that we usually do not recognize the shifts until we're significantly off course."[2]

Leadership coach Monica L. Wofford agrees. In her *Lessons in Leadership* newsletter, she writes, "One deceptively small concept that can produce big results is balance. It is a simple word and a fairly simple concept when dealing with weights and a scale, yet much more difficult when the weights are people and the scale is life. Balance can best be described in one sentence … 'If you don't have a life, get one.'"[3]

A Balanced Approach to Coaching—And to Life

Greg Morris, a former pastor in Florida, is a good friend. He studies leadership issues constantly and recently shared with me this important concept. Greg explains:

"For even the most veteran leader, life can seem overwhelming when things seem out of balance. The demands for your time, energy, and emotions come from all corners. As we attempt to juggle the demands of mental, physical, spiritual, social, and emotional needs, it seems as if the only time things are in balance is when the pendulum of life is passing from one extreme to another. If you are to maintain the cutting edge of your leadership effectiveness over an extended time, balance is needed. If you do not strike a balance, your leadership will lose its impact, your family life will suffer, and your perspective becomes distorted."

Brian Dyson, former vice chairman and COO of the Coca-Cola Company, delivered the commencement address at Georgia Tech in 1996. In it, he made this observation about balance in life:

"Imagine life as a game in which you are juggling some five balls in the air. You name them…work, family, health, fiends, and spirit, and you are keeping all of these in the air. You will soon understand that work is a rubber ball. If you drop it, it will bounce back, but the other four balls—family, health, friends, and spirit—are made of glass. If you drop one of these, they will be irrevocably scuffed, marked, nicked, damaged, or even shattered. They will never be the same. You must understand that and strive for balance in your life."

The Georgia Tech class of 1996 was fortunate to hear those insights. I hope they were listening attentively and have applied Mr. Dyson's wisdom.

Retired NFL coach Tony Dungy says he learned the importance of balanced living during his two years as a player and eight years as an assistant coach under Chuck Noll of the Pittsburgh Steelers. Coach Noll, he said, "had a strong belief that you had to be well-rounded. Family life was part of that. He was a great family man. He also enjoyed flying planes, boating, cooking, theater—a lot of things. He showed me as a 22-year-old player and a 25-year-old coach that you can do this job very well and do a number of other things along the way. That was important for me to grow up in this league with his type of leadership, to see that it could be done the right way and the winning way at the same time."

When Dungy was hired as head coach of the Tampa Bay Buccaneers in 1996, his team finished with a 6-10 record. Many fans and reporters blamed Dungy, claiming he wasn't up to the job. He was tempted to yield to public pressure, put in hundreds of extra hours at work, and ignore his family and his own needs.

But the words of Coach Noll, his mentor, reminded him to maintain balance in his life: "When you're not successful, when you're struggling, do *less*, don't do *more*." In other words, instead of working overtime to stuff a few more plays into the playbook, pull back and take an unhurried, unpressured look at the situation. Go back to the basics. Focus on the fundamentals that lead to success.

Tony Dungy received a lot of criticism for his approach to life. Some fans felt he didn't work hard enough at coaching, and that he spent too much time with his family or doing service to the community. Dungy silenced his critics on February 4, 2007, when he coached the Indianapolis Colts to victory in Super Bowl XLI.

"When you do win it all," he later said, "it validates your approach in many people's eyes. It's now much easier for me to talk about being balanced between work and family and still be able to win, as opposed to just saying, 'In theory, you can win this way.'"[4]

Keeping Winning and Losing in Perspective

What is the most important attribute a coach—and a team—should have? The answer, says John Wooden, is *balance*. He writes:

> Although a good argument could be made for the attributes "experience," "concentration," "skill," and the like, it is possible that the simple personal characteristic of "balance" is the most important for a leader and team.
>
> From a mental point of view, balance means keeping all things in perspective, maintaining self-control, and avoiding excessive highs or lows that occur because of luck or misfortune. Balance means not permitting the things over which you have no control to adversely affect the things over which you do have control, and it means retaining your poise during times of turmoil *and* triumph.
>
> These areas of balance are invaluable in leadership because they enable you to keep winning and losing, ups and downs, in perspective.[5]

One player who was profoundly affected by Coach Wooden's focus on balance is Gail Goodrich, who won two national championships (1963-1964 and 1964-1965) as a member of John Wooden's UCLA Bruins. Goodrich was on the team at the same time Coach Wooden was introducing the full-court press as a defensive strategy. Unfortunately, Goodrich was having a hard time getting into the right mind-set for Wooden's new system. He was the kind of player who always wanted to have the ball in his hands—and Coach Wooden was having a hard time getting Goodrich to understand that he still had a role to play when he *didn't* have the ball.

Finally, Coach Wooden sat Goodrich down and said, "Gail, the game is 40 minutes long. The opponent has the ball approximately half the time. That leaves us 20 minutes with the basketball. We have five players. In my system, balance is important, so each player should handle the ball about the same amount of time. That means you'll have the basketball for approximately four minutes per game. Gail, what are you going to do for the team during those *other* 35 minutes when you do not have the ball?"

For the first time, Goodrich understood what Coach Wooden had been trying to teach him. Coach Wooden was trying to get Goodrich—and everyone else on the team—to stop thinking like an individual and start acting as part of a balanced and cohesive team. He wanted every player to see himself as playing a role within a carefully balanced system. Goodrich recalled:

> He always talked about balance: body balance, scoring balance, team balance, and most of all, mental and emotional balance. Your feet have

to be in balance. Your body has to be in balance over your feet. Your head needs to be in balance with your body and your arms. He said if you're not in balance, you'll eventually fall over, and he meant it in more ways than one.

I came to see balance as one of the keys to success, not only in basketball, but in life. When things get out of balance, it's generally not good. Everything needs balance. That one word he kept drilling at us—balance—has stuck with me.[6]

Balance may be one of the most underrated and underrecognized weapons in a coach's arsenal. It's not an attribute we hear discussed very often in coaches' clinics or in books and articles for coaches. But the great John Wooden believed that balance was the most important single characteristic any coach or leader should have.

Balance Is Poise

Walt Frazier is one of the best point guards in the history of basketball. During his long career with the New York Knicks (1967 to 1977) and Cleveland Cavaliers (1977 to 1980), he averaged almost 19 points and more than six assists per game. But the statistic he takes the most pride in is "zero." Over his entire 13-year career in the NBA, Frazier was never charged with a technical foul.

Is this because Walt Frazier was born with a calm, easygoing demeanor? Hardly. "I used to be a hothead," he once said. "But when I was in the eighth grade, my coach called me over and said, 'Son, don't lose your head. Your brain is in it.' I never forgot that."[7]

Walt Frazier's eighth-grade coach taught him a crucial life lesson in the importance of maintaining emotional balance. Another word for emotional balance is *poise*. The dictionary defines *poise* as "a state of balance or equilibrium, as from an equal distribution of weight; a dignified, composed manner; steadiness; stability."

A person of poise maintains balance in all situations—in the highs and the lows, amid both praise and criticism, amid both advancement and adversity. Coaches and teams need to learn to maintain their poise in all situations. One coach who learned balance and poise the hard way was Dr. Jack Ramsay. In his book *Dr. Jack's Leadership Lessons Learned from a Lifetime in Basketball*, he recalled:

With few exceptions, I got along well with officials. When I started coaching in the NBA, there was a widely held belief that the coach who got the first technical called on him got the breaks from the referees, and his team usually won the game. ... So, for a few years, I became a sideline tyrant, frequently badgering officials, becoming one of the league "leaders" in technical fouls received. It wasn't really who I was, but I thought it was necessary for my team to win.

When I went to Portland to coach the Trail Blazers, I started with the same approach until one particular game when I went out to half-court to berate an official instead of going to the bench to talk to my team at a timeout. Bill Walton intercepted me before I got within shouting range of the official and said, "Coach, don't you know that we don't play well when you do that?" That stopped me dead in my tracks and changed my bench behavior for as long as I coached after that.[8]

Coach Mike Krzyzewski also wrote about the importance of poise as a leadership tool—and as a weapon for intimidating your opposition. In his book *Beyond Basketball: Coach K's Keywords for Success*, he observes:

Poise: keeping your composure in spite of circumstances.

Poise requires maturity. It's about remaining mentally and emotionally balanced all the time, no matter what is taking place around you.

In competition, the element of poise can make you appear much stronger in the eyes of your opponent than can your talent alone. I tell my players that you never want to show your opponent a weakness through your words, facial expressions, or body language. No matter what they're saying to you, no matter what the crowd is chanting, if you can show poise, you demonstrate to your opponent that they cannot rattle you. Just keep your mind on what you're doing and maintain that inner balance. Act like you have been there before and that you expect to do well.[9]

So if you want to keep your balance—and make your opponents lose theirs—keep your poise. Whether you're up or down, whether you are winning or losing, maintain your composure. Never show weakness. Let the opposition know that you are still in the game, you are still in control, and you intend to win.

Balance Means Taking the Middle Path

One of the most brilliant strategists ever to coach in the NBA is Phil Jackson, who has won 10 NBA titles as a coach, six with the Chicago Bulls and four with the L.A. Lakers. Phil gives much of the credit for his success to his coach and mentor, William "Red" Holzman (1920-1998). Holzman was head coach of the New York Knicks from 1967 to 1982, and he won NBA championships in 1970 and 1973. Phil played for Holzman and the Knicks from 1967 to 1978.

"The pivotal moment in my life was when I was injured, a career-ending type of injury with a spinal fusion, necessary for recovery," Phil recalled. "I missed the championship season in 1969-1970. ... During that period of time, Red took me under his wing. He didn't have an assistant coach, so he made me his assistant coach and taught the game to me."

Red Holzman also taught Phil Jackson the importance of balance in the game of basketball. "He talked philosophy with me," Phil said, "and he talked about the importance of staying not too high, not too low, and not letting victories or defeats send you tumbling one way or the other. He believed in what was called the middle path."

One way Holzman exemplified "the middle path" was by treating all of his players fairly and equally. "That ability to handle people," Jackson said, "probably was the trademark that I learned more than anything else. He treated the superstars and role players very much in the same manner."[10]

The elusive "middle path" all coaches need to find is that path of balance between a professional coaching career and a personal life. All coaches need to balance the demands of an intense work ethic with the need for rest and relaxation and family time. Coaching can destroy families quicker than anything—I've seen it happen many times. Don't let it happen to you.

Coaches are driven by a fear of failure. After all, as a coach, your failures are all out there in the open for the whole world to see. It's easy to become consumed by the games, the wins and losses, the criticism in the media. It's easy to lose your equilibrium and fall off the middle path. If you don't discipline yourself to maintain a balanced life, you can easily destroy your health, destroy your marriage, and lose your children. If you don't discipline yourself to eat properly and get adequate sleep, your body will break down. When your body falls apart, your coaching ability goes with it.

So, find that balance in life, and guard it with your life. Take time to nurture the most important relationships in your life. Your spouse and your kids need you—and you need them to keep you anchored in the things that matter most. Take time for your devotional life, for prayer and meditation, for worship and rest. Take time to recharge your spiritual batteries.

Keep your feet on that middle path, Coach. Maintain your balance in every dimension of your life. Keep your poise in every situation. Don't let victory send you too high, nor let defeat drag you too low. Maintain balance in all things—and if you don't have a life, *get one*!

8

Be Bold and Confident

©Elsa/Getty Images Sport

Bart Starr was a "poet." That's what they called students at Sidney Lanier High School in Montgomery, Alabama, since the school was named after a famous Southern poet of the 19th century.

Bart's football coach at Lanier was Bill Moseley, who had studied the game under then-Kentucky coach Bear Bryant. Bart Starr did not impress his coach as having any special talent for football. "He was one of those silent boys out for the team," Moseley once told an interviewer, "but that first year of high school he was kind of small for the team and there was nothing about him that made me pay him any special attention."

Young Bart was a bit undersized, and he lacked the kind of flashy, assertive personality that would make him stand out in a crowd. But he had talent and heart and a fierce work ethic. Bart Starr could withstand a coach's yelling and punishing workouts. The one thing he couldn't stand was being ignored—because then he had no opportunity to prove himself.

Frustrated at being overlooked by the coach, Bart decided to quit the team during his first year. Had he stuck to that decision, the world might never have heard of Bart Starr.

When Bart went home and announced he was quitting, his father applied psychology. "All right," the elder Starr said, "it's your decision. I'm glad you'll be home in the afternoons. I need you to weed the garden." He knew how much Bart hated gardening. The next day, Bart was the first to dress out for football practice.

So, Bart Starr remained on the team, even though his coach ignored him throughout his freshman and sophomore years. It wasn't until the third game of his junior season that he got a chance to prove himself.

It was September 1950, and Lanier High faced Tuscaloosa High, an intimidating opponent seeking to extend a 17-game winning streak. A crowd of more than 12,000 fans filled Lanier's Crampton Field, cheering for Lanier's quarterback Don Shannon. Meanwhile, future Super Bowl legend Bart Starr sat on the bench.

Early in the game, Don Shannon was gang-tackled. When the dust cleared, Shannon couldn't get up. His leg was broken and his season was finished. A murmur of dismay passed through the crowd.

Coach Moseley turned to his bench—and there was Bart Starr, the back-up quarterback he had ignored for the past two years. Moseley saw Starr as nothing more than a "150-pound scrub." But what choice did he have? He sent Starr into the game.

Starr knew that, as quarterback, he had to be a leader. He had never led this team before. His teammates didn't know if he had the right stuff to lead, and they didn't see him as a leader—not yet. If he was going to take charge of this offense, he'd have to prove he had the confidence to lead.

The team's lack of respect for his leadership was apparent the moment he stepped into the huddle. Several players started talking at once, all suggesting different plays. "You guys stop jabbering," Starr said. "I call the plays. You guys just do your job. Is that clear?"

Starr called the play, they broke huddle, and he proceeded to lead a drive that rolled up some respectable yardage, but ended in a punt. Even though he did not score, it was clear to all that Bart Starr was a leader.

The game was scoreless at the half, but in the third quarter, Starr broke the tie with a keeper into the end zone on an end-around. In the fourth quarter, he threw a 38-yard touchdown pass to clinch the win—a 13-0 stunning upset. Bart Starr established himself as a hero, a leader, and a quarterback of destiny.

And it began in the huddle, when a quiet, unassuming benchwarmer made the decision to assert himself as a bold, confident leader. It began with the words, "I call the plays."[1]

Choose the Bolder Course

Leaders must be bold. They must make decisions with confidence, never showing weakness or timidity. Field Marshal William Joseph Slim, the World War II British general who turned back Japan's invasion of India and Burma, warned that an overabundance of caution can lose the battle. "When you cannot make up your mind which of two evenly balanced courses of action you should take," he said, "always choose the bolder."

I vividly remember 1967, the year I met Bart Starr. I was running the Phillies farm club in Spartanburg, South Carolina, and as one of our promotions that summer, we brought Bart in for a personal appearance at the ballpark. We paid him $500, which was top dollar in those days. Bart spent the whole day with our fans. He spoke at a luncheon, signed autographs, played golf with some of our boosters, tossed a ball around before the game, and threw out the first pitch. Bart could not have been more kind and gracious—a true gentleman. That was the beginning of a friendship with Bart Starr that has lasted well over 40 years.

The experience of getting to meet Bart Starr during the summer of 1967 made it all the more meaningful, later that year, when I turned on the TV and watched him battle his way through the most notorious game in football history—the "Ice Bowl," which is the nickname given to the 1967 NFL Championship game at Green Bay's Lambeau Field on December 31, 1967. The Ice Bowl has acquired the status of legend because it had everything: hostile sub-zero weather, high stakes (the winner would play in Super Bowl II), intense rivalry (Vince Lombardi's Packers versus Tom Landry's Dallas Cowboys), and a heart-pounding conclusion. In fact, the game came down to a single bold decision on a final play as time expired.

Bart Starr and the Packers faced Don Meredith and the Cowboys. Frostbite conditions turned the football into a rock, making deep passes impossible. The game was played out in short-yardage passes and slippery sprints across an ice-slick field. Dallas halfback (now retired NFL coach) Dan Reeves later recalled, "I remember getting my lip busted, and no blood came out. My throat burned from breathing in that cold air."

It was a slugfest, and the Packers led 14-10 at the half. The third quarter was scoreless. In the fourth quarter, the Cowboys scored a touchdown and led 17-14.

With 4:50 remaining, Bart Starr directed the Packers' final drive from his own 32. Managing the clock with precision, he steadily advanced the ball with a series of short slants and handoffs. Finally, with 16 seconds remaining in the fourth quarter, the Packers were at third and goal inside the Cowboys' one-yard line. At that point, Bart Starr burned his final time-out and went to the sidelines to talk it over with Coach Lombardi.

The Packers had two fairly safe and conservative options: First, they could kick the chip-shot field goal and send the game into overtime. Second, they could try a pass. An incompletion would stop the clock and leave a few seconds for a fourth-and-goal attempt.

But Bart Starr saw a third option—a bold option. At the sidelines, he told Coach Lombardi that his linemen, Jerry Kramer and Ken Bowman, were sure they could open a hole in the middle for a quarterback sneak. Coach Lombardi liked the audacity of Bart Starr's plan. "Run it," Lombardi said, "and let's get outta here."

Starr went back to the field and called one of the most famous plays in NFL history. Bowman snapped the ball. Jerry Kramer charged into Cowboys defensive tackle Jethro Pugh, standing him up. Bowman plowed into Pugh, forcing him off the line. Starr tucked the ball and lunged through the hole, into the end zone.

And the Packers had it all: Touchdown. Win. League championship. Trip to Super Bowl II. And they owed it all to Bart Starr's bold plan and Vince Lombardi's bold decision: "Run it, and let's get outta here."[2]

Boldness to Confront

In 1999, my wife, Ruth, and I had dinner with Larry Catuzzi, who coached college football for many years, including four years as an assistant to Woody Hayes at Ohio State. Larry and I go way back. He was a quarterback at the University of Delaware when

I was in high school in Wilmington, and we were teammates for one summer on a semi-pro baseball team, Wilmington Sporting Goods. (Larry later became co-chairman of the Flight 93 Memorial Task Force after his daughter, Lauren Catuzzi-Grandcolas, died on 9/11 aboard United Flight 93, which crashed in Pennsylvania.)

As we shared an evening together over dinner, Larry and I talked about leadership. He offered insight after insight, and as he talked, I wrote down many of his thoughts for later reference.

One nugget of Larry's leadership wisdom I preserved that night was this: "The one character trait all the great leaders have is toughness—mental and physical toughness to deal with hard situations and difficult people. A real leader takes bold stands. You can't intimidate him, and he doesn't hesitate to wade into tough situations and confront people when necessary."

One coach who truly exemplifies these qualities of bold leadership is Amanda Butler, head women's basketball coach for the University of Florida Gators. A Florida alum herself, she was a Lady Gator from 1990 to 1994, playing guard and lettering all four years.

Known for her toughness and strong leadership abilities, Butler took part in 73 victories during her tenure—the best four-year total in Florida history. She never missed a game in four years, and started 99 out of 114 games. She averaged 29 minutes per game, played a full 40 minutes in three games, and a full 45 minutes in one overtime game.

The 5'8" Butler was known for her strong, confident, aggressive approach to the game. No matter how big the opponent, she always took charge. In one game during her senior year, she sustained a severe cut over her right eye; 12 minutes and seven stitches later, she was back in the game.

"Amanda is by far the toughest and hardest-working person I know," says former teammate Crystal Parker. "We were in practice one day when she was mixing it up in the paint and Takilya Davis came out with the ball, but Amanda just laid there for a second. I remember thinking something was wrong because Amanda always gets up quickly. Everyone else was continuing to play and ran down to the other end of the court, but she was standing there holding her face and blood was everywhere. I ran over to her and she kept saying, 'I'm all right, I'm all right.' I stood there scared, looking at her with tears in my eyes and she was telling me that she was all right. She had broken her nose and had to be taken to the hospital. Amanda was back at practice the next day."

In fact, it took 10 injections of painkiller in her face to reset her broken nose, but a short time after the injury, she played 20 minutes against Florida State, helping the

University of Florida Gators win an 81-78 victory. She was also the first female athlete in history to wear a Bill Laimbeer-style plastic facemask to protect the cast on her nose. That's toughness.

Her former coach, Carol Ross, remembers Amanda Butler as "the toughest player I have ever coached. She's not just physically tough, but mentally strong and competitive. Everything that Amanda has done since I first met her as an 18-year-old has prepared her and led her down the path to become the Gator head coach."[3]

Her players agree. One of Coach Butler's stars, guard Kim Critton, says, "Since getting to know Coach Butler, the word that best describes her: she has *swagger*."[4]

Great leaders have toughness—both mental toughness and physical toughness. They can't be intimidated. They won't back down. They won't yield to pain or injury. They boldly, confidently confront the people and situations that must be confronted.

Share Your Confidence With the Team

Leaders have a duty to build boldness and confidence in their players. One of the great coaches to inspire boldness in his troops was North Carolina's Dean Smith, who retired in 1997 with 879 wins to his credit. Smith's assistant (now head coach of the Tar Heels), Roy Williams, recalls:

> Against Georgetown in 1982, when Coach Smith called time with 32 seconds left, I didn't like the looks on our [players'] faces. For the first time I thought we could actually lose the game. But he told the team, "We're in great shape. I'd rather be in our shoes than theirs." He said it so confidently that I had to sneak a peek at the scoreboard to make sure it said Georgetown 62, North Carolina 61. Then he said, "We are going to determine who wins this game." And he grabbed Michael [Jordan] and said, "Knock it down."
>
> When our guys broke the huddle, the looks on their faces had changed 180 degrees. The way he talked to them had more to do with us winning the national championship than anything else that happened that season.[5]

Coach Smith faced an even tougher situation against archrival Duke on March 2, 1974. With only 17 seconds remaining, North Carolina trailed by eight. In those days, there was no three-point shot, so Smith's team needed four scores to tie. Center Mitch Kupchak recalls, "His calm throughout was amazing. The way he walked us through those 17 seconds, it was as if he said, 'Don't think about this. Just do as I say and we'll win.'"

Dean Smith inspired his players by breaking those 17 seconds down into steps. First, he told forward Bobby Jones to make his two free throws, and then the team would go on defense, steal the inbounds pass, score, and instantly call time-out. Says Kupchak, "Bobby made both free throws. We stole the pass. We scored. We called time-out. It all happened so fast."

Smith proceeded to the next step, forcing another turnover. North Carolina executed and scored. Next, Duke's best free-throw shooter, Pete Kramer, missed two free throws. North Carolina rebounded the ball and called a final time-out.

Kupchak remembers, "We had the ball under their basket and had to go the length of the floor. Coach calmly told us to run the 5-3-5. The five man, me, took the ball out and threw it to the three man on a five pattern, which is a square-out at midcourt. ... The plan was to get Walter the ball, have him take one dribble and shoot." Walter Davis unleashed a 35-foot bank shot as time expired—and he scored. Tie game.

All of that happened within 17 seconds. The game went into overtime—and North Carolina won it, 96-92. Widely regarded as one of the best games in college basketball history, that contest proved that a coach who inspires confidence in his players can make miracles happen with 17 brief ticks of the clock.[6]

Bold, confident coaches build bold, confident teams by infusing their own confidence into their players. As Coach Mike Krzyzewski said, "Confidence shared is better than confidence only in yourself."[7]

Be Boldly Decisive

One of the most basic tasks of leadership—and especially of coaching—is decision-making. For some, decisiveness comes easy. Others seem to postpone the moment of decision until the last possible moment, as if waiting for some piece of information to fall from heaven and decide the matter for them.

Delaying a decision is usually more dangerous than simply deciding, firmly and finally, even before all the facts are in. When you have a decision to make, make it. Decide quickly—and decide boldly. Odds are, you'll make a good decision. As Theodore Roosevelt once observed during the Spanish American War, "In any moment of decision, the best thing you can do is the right thing. The next best thing is the wrong thing. And the worst thing you can do is nothing."

Homer Rice served as head football coach at Rice University and at Cincinnati. He also served as athletic director at North Carolina, Rice, and Georgia Tech. One of Homer Rice's seven "Principles of Motivation" is decision-making. He observed, "We must be able to make a decision. Lack of decisiveness is the major cause of failure. Successful people reach decisions promptly and change them slowly, if there is ever a need for change."[8]

In his autobiography *Undefeated*, Bob Griese, quarterback of the undefeated 1972 Miami Dolphins, reflects on the bold decisiveness of his coach, Don Shula: "Why is Don Shula such a great leader? No mystery: The man takes charge. Wherever he is, whatever situation he is in, he just takes charge. He takes charge in the meeting room. He takes charge on the practice field. He takes charge on the sidelines. He even takes charge on the golf course."

Griese goes on to describe a golf outing with Don Shula, retired Cowboys quarterback Eddie LeBaron, and former Cowboys general manager Tex Schramm. Normally, you choose partners by throwing the players' balls in the air, and the two that land closest together are partners. But Shula didn't leave anything to chance. Even on the golf course, he was boldly decisive. "All right, Eddie," Shula said, "you and I will take on those two. We'll tee off first."

"Same old Coach," Griese concludes, "in complete charge wherever he goes. ... I always liked that in Don Shula. Having a take-charge coach got our team places we couldn't have gone without him. Thanks to Shoes, I got to be a part of NFL history. He knew exactly what he wanted to do with that team, and he did it."[9]

Coach Mike Krzyzewski warns against making too many rigid rules as a means of avoiding the tough decisions. "Too many rules get in the way of leadership," he says. "The truth is that many people set rules to keep from making decisions. Not me. I don't want to be a manager or a dictator. I want to be a leader—and leadership is ongoing, adjustable, flexible, and dynamic. As such, leaders have to maintain a certain amount of discretion."[10]

Trust Your Gut—And Live With the Consequences

Phil Jackson draws upon his early coaching experience to illustrate the importance of sticking to your decisions. In his book *Sacred Hoops: Spiritual Lessons of a Hardwood Warrior*, he describes an incident that took place in 1985, when he was coach of the Albany Patroons of the Continental Basketball Association (CBA). Phil's nemesis on the Patroons was a talented but headstrong player named Frankie J. Sanders. Phil had instituted an equal-pay plan for all the players—but after the Patroons had won the CBA championship, Sanders demanded a big raise.

Over Phil Jackson's objections, Patroons president Jim Coyne gave in to Sanders' demands. In addition to operating the team, Coyne was also an Albany County elected official. "Coyne had no appreciation for the subtleties of the player-coach relationship,"

Jackson lamented. "All he cared about was winning reelection—and keeping the Patroons on top was part of his campaign strategy."

Once Sanders went over Phil's head and got his raise, he became uncoachable. He demanded more playing time and expected that everything revolve around him. As the Patroons headed into the playoffs against the Toronto Tornadoes, Phil knew he had to do something to rein Sanders in. In the second game of the playoffs, played in Albany, Phil benched Sanders.

Soon after the benching, Phil was looking down the bench and saw Frankie relaxing with his shoes off. "What are you doing?" Phil shouted. "Put your shoes back on!"

"No," Sanders replied, smirking. "I'm going down to the locker room. My foot hurts." And he walked off the court.

Afterwards, Phil punished Sanders with a two-game suspension. The team headed to Toronto for game three—but Sanders stayed behind. After losing the first two games on their home court, the Patroons lost again in Toronto, 117-105. If Phil's team lost game four of the best-of-seven series, it was over. Even so, Phil had no regrets about suspending Sanders.

Jackson stood by his decision—until Jim Coyne called from Albany. "Phil," Coyne said, "we need Sanders. We can't live without him. I want him reinstated."

When Jackson explained that Frankie Sanders had become uncoachable and a detriment to the team, Coyne replied that Sanders had experienced a change of heart, and he would fly in formation from then on. He had even agreed to apologize to the team. Reluctantly, Jackson agreed to lift Frankie's suspension and let him play in game four.

Coyne and Sanders flew to Toronto, and Sanders stood up in front of the team and, as Phil recalls it, "mumbled a few meaningless words." So much for the promised apology.

Then Frankie J. Sanders and the Patroons went out on the court and demolished the Toronto Tornadoes, 123-111. Frankie made 35 points that night. "After that," Phil recalls, "he was impossible to control." Phil sums up the lesson of that experience:

> The unspoken laws of basketball are strange and mysterious. When you violate them, as Sanders did in the Toronto series, you pay a price, but never in a predictable way. I felt as if I had invited disaster by caving in and letting Sanders return. ... It taught me something important— above all, trust your gut. This is the first law of leadership. Once you've made your move, you have to stand by your decision and live with the consequences because your number one loyalty has to be to the team.

In the case of Sanders, I compromised my principles to placate my boss, and the players picked up on my ambivalence immediately. The solidarity that had taken so long to build suddenly evaporated. Not only did we lose the series, we were lost as a team.[11]

Making decisions and standing by them is tough. But that's what leadership is all about.

Audacity, From Head to Foot

Jack McKeon (aka "Trader Jack") is a former manager in Major League Baseball. He has worked for the Kansas City Royals, the Oakland A's, the San Diego Padres, the Cincinnati Reds, and the Florida Marlins. His 1984 Padres won the National League pennant, and he was honored as National League Manager of the Year in 1999 and 2003. In his book *I'm Just Getting Started*, Trader Jack reflects:

> You can't be afraid to make the tough decision. … The most important thing is to go with your heart, don't worry about what other people think about your decision. Make your decision based on what you think is best. …
>
> Sometimes you have to make the hard decisions and trade the popular guy for a chance to win. I traded the Hall of Fame shortstop Ozzie Smith in San Diego when I was GM after the 1981 season. There was no more popular guy in a city than the Ozzie Smith. … What I got in return was an All-Star shortstop in Garry Templeton. I got right fielder Sixto Lezcano and relief pitcher Luis DeLeon, both of whom made our club better. We made it to the World Series two years later. It wasn't a popular decision at the time, but nobody was complaining when we went to the World Series. …
>
> Don't go sideways or backwards, go forward. Don't be afraid to make the bold move. Be creative.[12]

What if you make a mistake? What if you make a really bad decision? Well, if it's clearly and obviously a bad decision, then you may need to reverse yourself. But don't be too quick to do a 180. Remember, your players are watching you. If you appear to be dithering and indecisive, you could undermine yourself as a leader. Think long and hard before taking action that could make you look weak and vacillating.

Before you reverse yourself, ask, "Is there a way to make this bad decision work? As a bold and confident coach, can I turn this bad decision into a good one?" More often than not, you can.

"The Old Perfessor" himself, baseball manager Casey Stengel, once told his protégé Whitey Herzog, "There are three ways to do anything: the right way, the wrong way, and my way. If my way turns out to be the wrong way, nobody's ever gonna know, because my way is the only way we're ever gonna do it anyway."[13]

And an even older "Perfessor" by the name of Will Shakespeare put it this way in Act I, Scene vi, of his play *Cymbeline*:

> Boldness be my friend!
> Arm me, audacity, from head to foot!

Don't hesitate to decide boldly, act boldly, and speak boldly and confidently. Don't be afraid that someone's going to think you're arrogant and conceited. One of the boldest leaders in the game of football, Johnny Unitas, put it this way: "There is a difference between conceit and confidence. Conceit is bragging about yourself. Confidence means you believe you can get the job done."[14]

Lou Holtz tells a story from his early coaching career. In 1972, he had just accepted the position as head football coach at North Carolina State. At the time, the Wolfpack's record was (to put it charitably) mediocre, and its football program was decidedly substandard. Holtz—a young, untested coach—had a hard time convincing prospective players that he was going to turn things around at NC State. His recruiting tour in the region was an abject failure. Deeply discouraged, he headed north to Chicago for the National Football Coaching Clinic.

At the clinic, he ran into an old friend, Wayne Harden, head football coach at Temple University. They sat down for a talk, and during their conversation, Harden asked Holtz, "Lou, are you the best football coach in the country?"

It was a startling question. Holtz thought about some of the other college football coaches around the country, such as Bear Bryant and Woody Hayes. Did he have the audacity to brag that he belonged in that august company? Certainly not!

"No," Lou Holtz replied sincerely, "but I want to be."

"In that case," Harden replied, "you're stealing North Carolina State's money—and you should resign. They hired you because they think you *are* the best coach in the country for that job. For you to say anything less is a disservice to your employer."

Those words shook Lou Holtz to the core of his being. Years later, he recalled:

> Few conversations ever cost me any sleep; that one did. After a night's reflection, I concluded that Wayne was right. If the university thought I

was the best man to coach its team, then my performance had to match those expectations. This should be your attitude whenever you accept a job. Someone hired you because they believe you have more talent than anyone else who applied for your position. Reward the confidence they have placed in you. Think as highly of yourself as your employer does.[15]

In other words, be bold and confident. Assert your ideas boldly. Communicate your vision with passion and self-assurance. Act decisively and stand by your decisions. Believe in yourself, and others will believe in you—the players, the fans, the media, and management. Fortune favors the bold.

9

Be a Teacher and a Learner

©Albert Dickson/Sporting News/ZUMA Press

Jim Calhoun was 15 years old, talented at basketball, football, and baseball, while growing up in Braintree, Massachusetts. One day, while Jim was playing in a Babe Ruth League All-Star game, one of the adults at the game took him aside and matter-of-factly said, "Hey Jim, you'd better go home. Your dad just died of a heart attack."

Young Jim Calhoun ran all the way home. At the doorstep, he saw that it was true. He went to his grief-stricken mother and promised that he would take care of her and his five siblings.

Jim kept his word. He already had a couple of part-time jobs, pumping gas and working at a junkyard. After his father's death, he landed a job cutting granite headstones for the cemetery. The job required him to get up every morning at 4:30. As he grew older, he put off going to college, so he could continue providing for his family.

From an early age, Jim Calhoun learned what life is all about: responsibility, loyalty to family, and hard work. He also learned some tough lessons about loss, suffering, and sacrifice.

Today, Jim Calhoun is the head men's basketball coach at the University of Connecticut. He has coached his UConn Huskies to two NCAA titles (1999 and 2004) and the 1988 NIT championship. He is also a teacher who is eager to share what he has learned about life.

In his book *A Passion to Lead: Seven Leadership Secrets for Success in Business, Sports, and Life*, Jim shares his inspirational formula for success in life: "Talent determines what you can do in life. Motivation determines what you decide to do. And attitude determines how well you do it."[1]

Jim sees coaching as a form of teaching. He told an interviewer for *Investors Business Daily*, "The most important thing to having a successful practice is to design the practices to teach. Every practice, I do two things: teach the mechanics of the game and have a theme for the practice."

Calhoun's players see him as a teacher and mentor who imparts lessons in basketball and lessons in life. Donny Marshall played under Coach Calhoun for four seasons before going on to play in the NBA. He recalls, "Coach was instilling in me one big idea: That you always have to believe in yourself, and you always have to fight, because there's something better out there for you, if you're willing to go get it. As a coach, he never gave you anything. You earned it."[2]

Coaching is teaching. Leadership is teaching. If you aren't teaching, you aren't leading. And if you aren't learning something new every day, what do you have to teach anyone else?

"I Am a Teacher"

In an interview for *UCLA Magazine*, Coach John Wooden described his philosophy of coaching this way: "I've always considered myself a teacher. Whether I was in an English classroom, where I taught for 11 years, or whether I was on the tennis court, the baseball diamond or the basketball court, I am a teacher."[3]

ESPN sportswriter Rick Reilly notes that Coach Wooden "never made more than $35,000 a year, including 1975, the year he won his 10th national championship, and never asked for a raise."[4] In fact, in the late 1960s, when Coach Wooden's Bruins were at the height of their success, L.A. Lakers owner Jack Kent Cooke offered to hire him as head coach of the Lakers. Wooden said he wasn't interested. Cooke offered Coach Wooden a salary 10 times what he made at UCLA.

"Nobody's worth that kind of money," Coach Wooden replied. "It's not about money."

Cooke was incredulous. He'd never met anyone who said that it's not about money. Coach Wooden explained that there were several reasons he didn't want the job. First and foremost, he *liked* being a coach on the college level, because it meant that he was a teacher. Coach Wooden refused to give up teaching, no matter how much money he was offered.[5]

Bill Walton—Coach Wooden's star center from 1971 to 1974—said this about his old coach:

> John Wooden … taught life at UCLA for 27 years before officially retiring in 1975, establishing records for success that will never be touched. All of the approximately 168 UCLA basketball lettermen John Wooden coached know that when he stopped actively running Bruin basketball, it did not signify an end to his life-long commitment to teaching. … John Wooden teaches by example. He never asks or expects anyone to do anything that he hasn't already done himself. He teaches by creating an environment that people want to be a part of, where we want what he has to give. While we haven't always known this—and some of us are certainly very slow learners—learn we eventually did. That is what John Wooden teaches, the ability to learn how to learn.[6]

Believe it or not, Coach Wooden even taught his players how to put on their shoes and socks. "I want to see you do it," he'd say. "Pull up the socks, make sure there are no wrinkles. Now, put your shoes on, start from the bottom and tighten them from the bottom up."[7]

In one of his books, Coach Wooden explained why he took the time to teach such seemingly basic and trivial matters to his players:

> Wrinkles, folds and creases can cause blisters. Blisters interfere with performance during practice and games. Since there was a way to reduce blisters, something the player and I could control, it was our responsibility to do it. Otherwise, we would not be doing everything possible to prepare in the best way. …
>
> Next I'd instruct the player on how to lace and tie his shoes precisely: Lace snugly, putting some pressure on each eyelet, and then double-tie each shoe so it won't come undone during a practice or a game. … It was something under our control that we could prevent, and so we did.[8]

One of Coach Wooden's greatest admirers is another UCLA coach known as Miss Val—Valorie Kondos Field. Under her leadership, UCLA gymnastics teams have won five NCAA titles. And one of Miss Val's biggest fans is Coach John Wooden. Though Valorie Field was all of 15 when Coach Wooden retired from coaching in 1975, she considers herself a Wooden disciple. And John Wooden is a fan of Miss Val. He has a regular spot (second row, floor level) at Pauley Pavilion for all Bruins gymnastics home meets. Though they were born a couple of generations apart, Coach Wooden and Coach Field share a common commitment to coaching—and teaching. In her column for the UCLA Bruins website, Valorie Kondos Field explained her philosophy of coaching this way:

> Gymnastics is an amazing venue through which to learn life lessons such as discipline, focus, and commitment to a goal. … One thing that we talk about a lot with our team … is the discussion of "learning" [and] "acquiring knowledge." … Going to class and studying isn't about making the grade but enriching your knowledge to help make living your life more colorful. It's about having an enthusiasm for learning about all sorts of different things in life. These always turn into interesting discussions with our team.
>
> From a coaching perspective, along with teaching our athletes how to compete well and teaching them better form, my personal gift and goal is to help our athletes understand the importance of the quality of movement. Regardless of what event they are on, or whether they are focusing on dance or gymnastics skills, the quality of their movement is what makes their movements come to life. This holds true in moving through daily life as well.[9]

John Wooden left a legacy as a basketball coach that Miss Val carries on with the Bruins gymnastics team. It's a legacy of coaching as teaching—of instructing young athletes not only in the skills and principles of competition, but in what it means to be an effective human being.

"I Loved the Meetings"

Roy Williams, head coach of the men's basketball team at the University of North Carolina, is proud of the many former Tar Heels players who have gone on to important leadership positions. He believes that's because his program doesn't just teach basketball. It teaches discipline, hard work, and strong character—the very qualities people need to have a successful life in the real world. "Think of the self-sacrifice involved in playing basketball at Carolina," he says. "Think of the discipline. Think of the work—the willingness these players had, to spend extra time at something to try and push themselves past the place where they thought they could go. All of that correlates to life after basketball."[10]

Duke University's men's basketball coach Mike Krzyzewski said, "I am a teacher and a coach. I surround myself with other good teachers on my staff. And our whole approach to coaching revolves around teaching. Teaching is at the heart of my coaching style. If I teach them well, winning games will be the natural result."[11]

Hall of Fame basketball star Magic Johnson observes that Lakers head coach Phil Jackson is, above all, a teacher. "The great thing about Phil is the way he has handled players," Johnson said. "He has a different style, too, that old Zen thing. I love him because he never gets too high and never gets too low and always wants to help the guys grow as men. He teaches them basketball and also teaches them outside the sport."[12]

Great leaders are almost always great teachers—and most of them have had great teachers during the formative years of their own lives. Celtics legend Bill Russell remembers Ross Guidice, his freshman coach at the University of San Francisco, as a committed teacher:

> Guidice always supported a player's love of the game, and he did so with a generosity and good spirit that I've never seen since. If a player wanted to spend three hours being drilled after practice, Guidice would stay. All the player had to do was ask.
>
> I took him up on the offer. On many occasions, we worked for hours at a stretch, just the two of us alone in the gym on Saturdays, holidays, at night. As many hours as I put in, he'd put in. … He was excited over every bit of progress I made. …
>
> He simply loved to help people who wanted to be helped. For many years after Guidice left basketball and went into business, I used

to think that if a kid were to walk into his office and ask for coaching help, Guidice would go right down to the gym. I'd have bet that he'd walk right out on the customers in his store, in his street shoes, just to teach basketball. He was that unselfish.[13]

Notre Dame football coach Knute Rockne was committed to teaching as an integral dimension of coaching. He once said, "The average professor goes into a classroom, gives his lecture, and leaves. His attitude is distinctly 'take it or leave it.' He may flunk half the class and everyone is awe-stricken. The coach, however, has to be a super-teacher. He must see to it that the class learns what he has to teach. If he flunks half the class, he flunks with them. It is not what a coach knows. It is what he can teach his boys, what he can make them do."[14]

One of the most flamboyant coaches in NFL history is O. A. "Bum" Phillips (Houston Oilers, New Orleans Saints). Phillips, the father of Dallas Cowboys head coach Wade Phillips, was mentored by Bear Bryant. Bum described his philosophy of coaching this way: "I teach them to get along with their fellow man—the other players. If you don't teach that in coaching, then you're not coaching."[15]

Of course, one of the greatest teachers in NFL history was Vince Lombardi. Executive coach John Baldoni describes Lombardi as a role model for the coaching and teaching profession:

> Vince Lombardi, who began his career in coaching as a high school teacher of math and sciences, was first and foremost a teacher. With a piece of chalk and a blackboard, he could talk for hours to players or to fellow coaches at clinics about the X's and O's of football. Dressed in a sweatshirt and a baseball cap and with a whistle around his neck, Lombardi was the archetypal image of a football coach of his era. …
>
> Coaches must be active listeners, attentive to communication clues. Blank stares or bored looks indicate that the lesson has no meaning. Conversely, head nods and questions mean that the lesson may be getting through. The coach must work to find methods to engage the employee's interests and hold it so that learning does occur.
>
> It is no coincidence that many coaches are good storytellers. Stories offer the opportunity to impart important life lessons in a manner that is accessible and even enjoyable rather than condescending and preachy. For this reason, coaches keep a personal inventory of stories intended to evoke the appropriate emotion for the situation—admiration, inspiration, tears, or laughter.[16]

Lombardi began his football career as an offensive lineman, one of the legendary "seven blocks of granite" at Fordham University in the mid-1930s. Following graduation, he considered entering the priesthood. After a great deal of soul-searching, Lombardi decided to go into teaching. He accepted a position at St. Cecilia High School in Englewood, New Jersey, where he taught physics, chemistry, and Latin. He also coached St. Cecilia's basketball team, and served as assistant football coach (later head coach).

After eight years at St. Cecilia's, he became an assistant at Fordham, and later at the military academy at West Point, where he was mentored by the legendary Army football coach Earl Henry "Red" Blaik. From there, he moved to an assistant position with the New York Giants. Five years later, he took the job as head coach of the Packers. When he arrived in Green Bay, the Packers were the laughingstock of the NFL. In a single season, he transformed the Packers into a winning organization.

"Lombardi was first and foremost a great teacher," writes John Baldoni. He describes Lombardi as a master psychologist who knew how to prepare his players to learn. His practices were short and precisely orchestrated—no longer than 90 minutes twice a day. His team lectures were fiery and unforgettable. He told his players that his expectations were simple: They were to keep themselves in physical shape to play football. He would do the rest. He would teach them. He would motivate them. He would draw up the tactics and strategies. Lombardi deliberately wanted to take the pressure of winning off his players and onto himself.

Some players didn't appreciate the intensity of Lombardi's loud, impassioned lectures. But one of Lombardi's Packers couldn't get enough of them. "I loved the meetings," Bart Starr recalls. "I never, ever was bored or tired at any meeting we were in with Lombardi. I appreciated what he was trying to teach."[17]

Baldoni observes that Lombardi's "greatest football lesson" was the Green Bay Sweep—a play which shifted the action to the strong side of the field, right into the face of the opposition. The sweep was designed to keep the opponent off-balance. From that formation, Lombardi's Packers could run a number of running and passing options. He drilled his team intensively in the sweep. His goal was to have one play that the team could consistently run with good results—a "go-to" play. Not only could the Packers count on the sweep to gain yardage, but he knew that it was one play that would always "instill confidence and rally the team."

Teaching With All Your Being

Chuck Noll was head coach of the Pittsburgh Steelers from 1969 to 1991. As coach, he earned four Super Bowl rings, more than any other head coach in NFL history. A profile of Coach Noll in *Investor's Business Daily* gives us a fascinating insight into what it means to be a teaching coach:

Chuck Noll was a head football coach for 23 seasons. But he considered himself a teacher first.

Noll put a premium on educating players. He worked with them, mostly on basic techniques, whenever possible. He considered post-practice one-on-one drills the best time to teach them fundamentals. He was devoted to bringing out the best in players.

He didn't care who the player was. Someone could be on the verge of being cut. But if he asked the coach to help him learn the game, Noll welcomed the chance.

Noll expected the same education-first mentality from his staff. When hiring assistants, he preferred people with no pro coaching experience. The reason: He thought college assistants were more likely to be excellent teachers, and he didn't want to deviate from his pet philosophy.

"I'm a teacher," Noll said. "Players win, coaches teach them. I teach."

Upton Bell, a front-office executive with the old Baltimore Colts when Noll was an assistant there, said: "Chuck is unique in that he doesn't fit that winning-is-the-only-thing coaching philosophy. With him, teaching is the only thing, developing a man to fulfill his potential. If he does a good teaching job, winning is a natural by-product."[18]

What do you do with a player who is uncoachable—and unteachable? Mike D'Antoni, head coach of the Phoenix Suns and 2005 NBA Coach of the Year, believes in giving players a *chance* to learn—and cutting them if they *refuse* to learn. "I don't yell and scream," he says. "I try to teach the guy exactly what I want. If the player doesn't give [maximum effort] to me, that's when I say to [general manager] Donnie Walsh, 'He's got to go.' … If the player is unteachable, if he's a selfish person, then you get rid of him and move to the next guy."[19]

The former North Carolina State women's basketball coach, the late Kay Yow, shared her views on coaching and teaching with *Coach and Athletic Director*. Asked if she thought it was important to teach ethics and moral principles as well as basketball, she replied that coaches must be, first and foremost, teachers and role models of strong ethical character. She added:

I know that if I were approached by someone who asked me to cut some corners in recruiting or do something less than straightforward, I would know exactly how to respond—right now. Anytime you know the answer to a situation, you're not going to have to sit around wondering what to say. Preparation is the key.

And what I'm going to do must be based on my belief that you can't ever compromise ethics. People say, "Don't worry, no one will ever know about it." Well, someone will know about it.

I recently read a story about a man who was taking his two young sons to a movie, and the guy in the box office told him the movie was three dollars for adults and free for any kids under six years old. So the man hands over six dollars, as one of his sons is three and the other is seven.

The clerk tells him he could have gotten in for free, because no one could have known his son was seven. The father answered: "My son would have known."

That is what I mean by "setting an example."[20]

Kay Yow lived and died teaching her players about ethics and character, about basketball, and about life. Blogger Bud Bilanich of the *Fast Company* online community summed up Kay Yow's example this way:

She battled breast cancer for 22 years. She was first diagnosed the year before she coached the U.S. team to the gold medal at the Seoul Olympics. She had a mastectomy, underwent chemo and kept coaching.

Kay Yow's cancer returned with a vengeance in 2006. She took a 16 game leave to focus on her treatments during the 2006-07 season. She returned to coaching and her team won 12 of its final 15 games. … Her players wore pink shoelaces in honor of their coach. That team got into the NCAA tournament and made it to the Sweet 16. She was so weak during those games that she spent most of her time sitting on the bench. Her assistant coaches stood to shout instructions to players, and helped her to her feet during time outs.[21]

That is what it means to teach your players with every dimension of your life, with every fiber of your being. Kay Yow was not only a role model to her players, but to coaches and leaders everywhere.

A Teacher Is a Continual Learner

Great teachers are lifelong learners. They read, study, ask questions, and learn all they can about every field of knowledge. "I have a very inquisitive nature," said former Dolphins coach Don Shula. "When I was a player, I didn't only know what I was supposed to do but also what the people around me would be doing. I was always thinking how the offense would attack the defense, how they would try to beat the things we were trying to do. Very rarely was anything put on the blackboard that I didn't ask, 'Why do we do this?' or 'What do we do if they do this?' … Being inquisitive like that broadened my scope and gave me a well-rounded football background."[22]

John Wooden, too, affirms the importance of being a lifelong learner. He once observed:

> Early on, I came to believe that you should learn as if you were going to live forever, and live as if you were going to die tomorrow. What does this mean? In the simplest way, I would explain it like this.
>
> Always be learning, acquiring knowledge, and seeking wisdom with a sense that you are immortal and that you will need much knowledge and wisdom for that long journey ahead. Know that when you are through learning, you are through.
>
> But I want to live [my] life as if I were going to die tomorrow: with relish, immediacy, and the right priorities.[23]

One of my personal heroes as both a baseball player and manager is Lawrence Peter "Yogi" Berra. Yogi may well have been the greatest catcher in the history of the game. He was named American League MVP three times and is one of the few managers in major league history to lead teams to the World Series from both the American and National Leagues. Though he quit school in the eighth grade, Yogi Berra is an inquisitive soul and a student of life who preaches the importance of lifelong learning. He said:

> Even when you get older, you should never be a know-it-all. You can always learn from someone else's experience. When I became a manager, I always listened to my coaches. I figured what's the use of having coaches if you can't use their opinions and experience? I'd always make the final decision, but I wanted their input. For years and years, Frank Crosetti was a great Yankee coach, a manager's coach. Serious as heck, but smart. He played when Ruth and Gehrig played. How can you not use all those smarts? I know some managers who barely talk to their coaches—maybe it's an ego thing. They act like they invented the game. That's not good. … Experience is a great thing—everyone can learn from it.[24]

Vince Dooley was the head football coach (1964-1988) and athletic director (1979-2004) at the University of Georgia. As head coach, he amassed an enviable record of 201-77-10, and won an NCAA national title (and Coach of the Year honors) for the 1980 season. In his book *Dooley: My Forty Years at Georgia*, he writes:

> I've always said that the great thing about being a teacher or a coach is that you continue to enjoy it for the rest of your life through your players and students. All the memories of competition don't become less important, but what becomes increasingly more important are the players who come back and say two simple words: "Thanks, Coach."
>
> Some thank me for teaching them the simple lessons of discipline. Or they're grateful because I taught them to win—and to lose—with dignity and class. Or I taught them the work ethic that they would take with them and use for the rest of their lives. Or I taught them how to work through adversity in order to achieve their goals.
>
> That's because the teachers you always remember are the ones who are the most demanding. … When someone like Billy Payne, who has accomplished so much since his days at Georgia, expresses his appreciation, that is something I just can't put a value on.[25]

If you impart more than athletic skills and game instruction, if you truly teach your players how to win at the game of life, they'll be back. And they'll thank you.

10

Care for Your Players as People

Trivia time: Name the only player ever to be ejected from a Major League Baseball game without ever appearing in one. I'll give you a hint: This player was twice enshrined in the Hall of Fame—but *not* the Baseball Hall of Fame. No, he made it into the *Basketball* Hall of Fame—as a player in 1976 and as a coach in 2004.

Time's up. The player's name: Bill Sharman. From 1950 to 1955, Bill was an outfielder in the Brooklyn Dodgers farm system. He was briefly called up to the majors and was sitting on the bench during a September 27, 1951, game against the Boston Braves. When Braves runner Bob Addis was called safe at home, the Dodgers' objection was loud and strenuous, prompting umpire Frank Dascoli to clear the entire Dodger bench—including Bill Sharman, who had yet to step onto the field as a major leaguer. And he never did.

But Bill Sharman went on to earn fame during 11 seasons with Red Auerbach's Boston Celtics. He played in eight NBA All-Star games (winning All-Star Game MVP honors in 1955). He later coached the L.A. Lakers to an NBA record 33-game win streak (in the Wilt Chamberlain–Jerry West era), and coached the 1967 Philadelphia 76ers to an NBA championship (again, with Wilt Chamberlain).

When Bill Sharman played in Boston in the late 1950s, he became concerned that the Celtics' opponents had decoded the Celts' playbook. He went to Coach Auerbach and expressed his worries. Auerbach listened to Sharman's concerns, and then replied, "Okay, here's what we're going to do. We're changing all the numbers. From now on, number one play is number two. Number two is number three." And so on. They practiced the new system, and it seemed to work.

Before the next game, Auerbach reminded his players of the new play numbers. Sharman and his teammates all said, "We've got it." So the game began, and point guard Bob Cousy called "Two!" Unfortunately, amid the pressure of the game, half the players forgot the new system. Three guys were running one play, two guys another. It was a disaster. "We looked like Keystone Cops out there," Auerbach said.

Coach Auerbach allowed chaos to reign until his Celtics were down by 10, then he called a time-out and told his team, "Forget the new system! From now on, a one is a one, a two is a two—and if those guys can figure it out and stop us, good for them!"

Now, here's the point: Red Auerbach knew at the outset that the new system wouldn't work. He also knew there was no need to disguise the plays. Auerbach was sure that, even if the other side knew which play they were running, they still couldn't stop it. He listened to Sharman's concerns and changed the playbook for one simple reason: He wanted Bill Sharman to feel valued and listened to. He wanted his players to know that he respected them and cared about them as people. Auerbach summed up his philosophy:

Players are people, not horses. You don't handle them. You work with them, you coach them, you teach them, and, maybe most important, you listen to them. The best players are smart people and a good coach will learn from them. Sometimes when guys came to me with ideas, I knew they couldn't possibly work. But I didn't just say no, because they would see that as a sign that I didn't respect them.[1]

One of Auerbach's players, center Wayne Embry, affirms his coach's way of dealing with his players. "Red was the ultimate team builder," Embry said after Auerbach's death. "He was a great motivator because he made an attempt to know and understand people. He knew the needs of his players emotionally and mentally. He respected you and your family and made us all welcome to the Celtics family. He had great compassion and created a family environment."[2]

Winning is important—but you win with people. This means that people are every bit as important as winning. One of the greatest coaches in NBA history put an unworkable idea into practice so that one player would feel valued. What are you doing to let your players know you care about them as people?

Coaching Is a People Business

My friend Jay Strack has conducted many chapels in professional sports. Years ago, when Tony Dungy was coaching the Tampa Bay Buccaneers, Jay was invited to conduct a pre-game chapel for the Bucs. Jay arrived early and found the room where the chapel would be held. The only person in the room was a man who was setting up chairs for the chapel.

Jay walked in and said, "Hi, I'm Jay Strack."

The man who was setting up chairs looked up and said, "Hi, I'm Tony."

Then Jay recognized the man. "Coach Dungy?"

"Yes, I'm Tony Dungy."

"I'm here to conduct the chapel. Let me help you set up these chairs."

"Oh, no thanks," Coach Dungy said. "I like to set up each chair myself. I know where each man sits. I know his needs, what's on his mind, and where he's hurting. So I pray over each man's chair as I set it up."

Now, that's a coach who cares about his players. Tony Dungy understands that coaching is not just about X's and O's and winning championships. Coaching is a people business.

The late Yankees outfielder-turned-broadcaster Bobby Murcer once said: "A good manager is someone you can talk to about anything, not only about baseball, but also about your own personal life, your family life, whatever. You might not think that players need anyone like that, but they do. They need to have somebody they feel they can trust, and they need to know that a private conversation stays just that: private."[3]

If you want your players to perform well and make you look good as a coach, you've got to care about them and help them believe in themselves. Coaches have to say some very tough things to their players. If you want them to hear you, trust you, and believe what you say, it helps if they know you care.

Several years ago, while researching my book *The Ultimate Coaches' Clinic*, I had an interesting conversation with Seth Greenberg, head men's basketball coach at Virginia Tech. I asked Seth what it takes to get players to play hard every night. Seth told me, "If your players know you care about them as human beings, they *will* play hard for you."

Edward W. "Moose" Krause was nicknamed "Mr. Notre Dame." He competed in just about every sport offered at Notre Dame, and was known primarily for his accomplishments in basketball. But Moose also played football for Knute Rockne's Fighting Irish. He graduated cum laude in 1934 and later coached basketball at Notre Dame.

Moose Krause recalled being one of 300 freshmen who came out for Notre Dame's freshman football team in 1930. Yet, though he was only one frosh face out of 300, Coach Rockne knew his name and all the others. After Moose and his brother Phil had only been on campus for half a semester, their dad came to visit. The three of them had lunch at the cafeteria, and Mr. Krause mentioned that he'd heard a lot about Knute Rockne and would like to meet him.

"Well, maybe," Moose said, trying to duck the subject, "but you know, the coach is really busy … "

But as they were walking out of the cafeteria, who should they see walking toward them but Knute Rockne himself! In fact, Rockne walked right up to the three of them and said, "Moose! Phil! How are you fellows doing in your studies?"

Moose and his brother were amazed that the famous coach knew them by name. Recovering from his surprise, Moose introduced his father, and they chatted for a few moments.

Years later, Moose Krause reflected that Coach Rockne "knew the players by their names; he had a fabulous memory for names. And … he was always concerned with the academic progress of every student he had under his wing as a coach. And this was the greatest thing that I remember about him."[4] Indeed, that's about the greatest thing anyone could ever say about a coach.

"The Man Made Me Feel Important"

Dr. Ed Gubman, in his book *The Engaging Leader*, describes NBA coach Phil Jackson as a master psychologist who made a point of understanding each of his players as an individual—and relating to each one on an individual basis. His was no cookie-cutter, one-size-fits-all approach. Gubman writes:

> Jackson discovered that Shaquille O'Neal wanted a close, father-son type relationship because of O'Neal's family background. So that's what Jackson worked on, even before he started coaching him. He also joined with O'Neal's family to encourage him to finish his degree. O'Neal, with the Lakers' blessing, left the team for a few days during the 2000-2001 season to attend graduation ceremonies at LSU. To Jackson, it was a matter of supporting O'Neal and his family and getting priorities right.[5]

"Deep down," said Michigan football coach Bo Schembechler, "your players must know you care about them. This is the most important thing. I could never get away with what I do if the players feel I didn't care for them. They know, in the long run, I'm in their corner."[6] Or as former Jets general manager Terry Bradway put it, "This is a people business, and the way you win in this business is dealing with people."[7]

Willie Davis was a dominant defensive end for the Green Bay Packers during the Lombardi era. A few years ago, he told me the story of his last conversation with Vince Lombardi. It took place in 1970, the first year of Willie's retirement from football.

He was at San Diego Stadium for an exhibition game, the New York Giants versus the Chargers. There, he encountered Giants owner Duke Mara, who told him that Vince Lombardi was in a D.C. hospital and fading fast. The coach was not expected to last the week.

Willie immediately left the stadium, drove to L.A., and flew all night to Washington. He took a cab to Georgetown University Hospital and was met there by Mrs. Lombardi. She led him into the hospital room to see the coach.

"That was the only time," Willie told me, "I ever saw Coach Lombardi not in control. You should have seen the smile when he saw me. He didn't have much voice, but he whispered, 'Willie, you were a great player. That was the best deal I ever made.' He started to cry, and I did too. I was only in the room about two minutes. Then Mrs. Lombardi led me out and said, 'He gets very emotional when the old Packers come to visit.'"

Willie walked out of the hospital to get a cab to take him back to the airport. He had flown cross-country for just two minutes with his old coach, and he felt it had been well worth it.

As he reached the curb to flag a cab, a group of reporters recognized him. They crowded close as he got into the cab, and one of them asked, "Willie, why did you fly all the way across the country to see Coach Lombardi?"

"Because the man made me feel important," Willie Davis replied. "I love the man." Then he closed the door and the cab pulled away.

That's what great coaches do. They make their players feel important.

And remember, your team doesn't consist only of your players. Every person in your organization is a member of your team, and you need to care for them as individuals. Raymond Berry was head coach of the New England Patriots from 1984 to 1989. At the beginning of one season, Berry had the entire team and the ball boys line up for a photo. Then, at a team meeting, he passed copies of the photo out to each player. The boys' names were printed by their pictures.

"Those boys know who you are," Berry told his players. "Now I want you to know them and call them by name. Everybody's important on this team. Everybody."[8]

It's true. There are no minor roles, and no insignificant people on your team or in your organization. Everyone deserves to be cared for as an individual.

Teams Are Made of Individuals

There's a lot more to coaching than mapping strategy, teaching skills, giving speeches, and holding practice sessions. Coaching is *persuasion*. You have to get your players to buy into your vision, your values, and your passion. You have to find a way to transplant *your* will to win into *their* hearts. Vince Lombardi put it this way: "How does one achieve success in battle? I believe it is essential to understand that battles are won primarily in the hearts of men. Men respond to leadership in a most remarkable way. Once you have won their hearts, they will follow you anywhere."[9]

How did Vince Lombardi win the hearts of his players? His son, Vince Lombardi, Jr., said that Coach Lombardi made it a point to find each players "hot button," that individual aspect of a player that motivates him and enables him to respond to coaching. Sometimes, finding that "hot button" wasn't easy. Coach Lombardi was not a warm-fuzzy guy, and there were times when his intensity worked against him. One incident during Lombardi's first season with the Packers involved guard Jerry Kramer.

During practice, Lombardi put the team through goal line scrimmages—and Kramer was struggling. He missed assignments, jumped offside, and generally had a bad practice. Lombardi got right in his grill and yelled, "Mister, the attention span for a grade school kid is 30 seconds, for a high school kid a minute, for a college kid three minutes! Mister, where does that leave you?" Then he proceeded to level a number of insults, including "fat cow" and some less-printable terms.

Do that to some players, and they will kick up their performance to prove you wrong. But insults were not Jerry Kramer's "hot button." In fact, Lombardi's tirade served only to make him feel defeated, frustrated, and angry. After practice, he went to the locker room and sat on the bench, pondering whether he should quit the team. (My friend Ernie Accorsi, who knows Jerry Kramer well, told me that Jerry was actually thinking, "Today's the day I punch him in the mouth!")

Coach Lombardi walked into the locker room, took one look at Jerry Kramer, and realized he had gone too far. He walked over to Kramer, put a hand on him and tousled Kramer's hair. "Son," he said, "someday you are going to be one of the greatest guards in football."

He had found exactly the right words. He had pushed Jerry Kramer's "hot button." Kramer often told that story, and pointed to that moment as the turning point in his career. From then on, Kramer envisioned himself as "one of the greatest guards in football" and did everything possible to fulfill Coach Lombardi's prophecy.

Vince Lombardi, Jr. concludes, "Not everyone responds the same way. The leader must find each person's 'hot button.'"[10]

Football coach Dick Vermeil, who has won Coach of the Year at four different levels—high school, Junior College, NCAA, and NFL—agrees that you can't coach X's and O's. You must coach people as individuals. "We don't coach football players," he once said. "We coach people who play football for a living. We approach it that way. We do everything we can both on and off the field to help them be what they have the ability to be. If we are successful, then they help us all get better."[11]

Walter Alston managed the Brooklyn and Los Angeles Dodgers to World Series championships in 1955, 1959, 1963, and 1965. He once explained his management approach this way:

> My philosophy of managing is rather simple. I believe in keeping everything simple, allowing a great deal of room for the individual to think on his own and respond within general confines we have set down for the whole Dodger organization. The most important thing in my opinion is to know your players. Know them as players in terms of their assets and liabilities, but more important know them as persons. That's where you determine how you can get the best from them.[12]

Never forget that you are in the people business, and that people are unique individuals. Like snowflakes, no two are alike. To get the best results on the playing field, get to know your players as more than a set of skills, as more than a sheet of statistics. Get to know them as people.

The 33 Percent Rule

They call Sue Enquist "the John Wooden of women's softball." She started her UCLA career as a student and center fielder on the Bruins softball team. She played from 1975 to 1978 and completed her career with a batting average of .401. She came back to UCLA in 1980 as an assistant coach, helping coach the Bruins to four NCAA championships over nine years. She served as head coach from 1989 to 2006, winning an additional four NCAA championships. As player and coach, she has helped win a total of 11 NCAA softball titles. She retired in 2006 with an 887-175-1 career coaching record, and her .835 winning percentage places her among the top five NCAA coaches, regardless of sport or gender. She was twice named Pac-10 Coach of the Year.

Sue Enquist is a 5'5" ball of fire who now divides her time between delivering rousing motivational speeches across the country and indulging her passion for surfing. During her career, she not only coached softball, she coached *life*. "It's kind of corny," she says "and the kids think it's funny, but if people can carry out those two things—a positive attitude and 100 percent effort—their lives end up being more enjoyable."

During her Bruin coaching days, she not only waved runners around third, but coached 22 to All-America honors and nine to Olympic gold. Those who know Enquist say she maintained that delicate balance all coaches need: She asserted her authority, she was tough and demanding, yet she was supportive and compassionate. Her players knew she cared about them as people.

Catcher Stacey Nuveman, a two-time Olympic gold medalist and NCAA Division I home run record-holder, played for Enquist from 1997 to 2002. "Sue was about life as much as she was about softball," Nuveman says. "What she taught superseded any fielding, hitting, or softball lessons. She made sure every player walked away with a degree and life lessons."

Infielder Clair Sua played for Enquist from 2001 to 2004, and now coaches at Cal Poly. Enquist, she says, "was one of the biggest influences in my life. ... She always focused on our careers outside of softball."

Under Sue Enquist's leadership, the Bruins softball team had a "family" feel. Her parents, Bill and Jane Enquist, attended most of her games as both a player and coach—and they came to be affectionately known as "Slap" and "Mamma E." They not only supported their daughter, but joined in celebrating team victories and players' birthdays.[13]

Sue Enquist always approached coaching with a "process-oriented philosophy." In other words, her coaching was focused on producing a winning attitude, a game-winning level of effort, regardless of the numbers on the scoreboard. After every game, the team met in the clubhouse and Enquist evaluated the team effort. A win on the scoreboard didn't shield players from a tough, fair critique. And a tough loss on the field could yield praise in the meeting if players expended every ounce of effort.

Sue Enquist became infamous for her sayings, known as "Sueisms." Some examples:

- "I don't coach to the scoreboard and they don't play to the scoreboard."
- "There are only two things you can control—your effort and your attitude."
- "Don't look left and don't look right. Keep your eye on the goal."
- "Leap into the unknown. If you fall, the team will pick you up."

The most famous "Sueism" of all is her "33 Percent Rule." Enquist says you can divide people into three categories—the top, middle, and bottom thirds. She says The 33 Percent Rule applies "in school, on your team, and when you graduate. You can use it in life."

She explains that the bottom third are people who "suck the life out of you." Bottom third people may even be on your team—the people for whom nothing is ever good enough. They whine and complain and take energy and motivation *out* of an organization instead of contributing to the team effort. You find bottom third people wherever you go.

Next, Enquist describes the middle third—the ones whose attitude is determined by circumstances. They are happy and positive when things are going well. They are down in the dumps in times of adversity. Middle third people are on an emotional roller coaster, continually tossed about by people, obstacles, and problems. They get too high in the good times, and too low in the tough times.

Finally, there is the top third. Enquist encourages her players to join the top third. The top third of people maintain a positive attitude even in tough times. They are leaders, influencers, and game-changers. "We do more as the top third," she says. "We get it done in the classroom. We compete hard. We serve our community. We stand up to that high standard."

Top third people live in a "bubble" of high standards. When players practice teamwork and strive for excellence, they are inside that bubble. In fact, they may not always realize how special that "inside-the-bubble" experience is. "The day you graduate and go out and get that job," she says, "watch how you're surrounded by the mediocre. You will be the standard others will emulate, which is an awesome compliment. ... You're going to learn how special it was to be in the bubble."[14]

So live in the bubble of coaching excellence, and urge your players to become top third people. They'll win games for you, then go on to be winners in the game of life.

Players Need Tender Loving Care

The late football coach Eddie Robinson began his tenure at Grambling State University in 1941 and retired in 1997. He holds the record (408) for the most victories of any head coach in Division I-AA football (now called the Football Championship Subdivision). He said in 1959, "The most important thing in football is the guy who plays the game. … You can't coach a person unless you love him. I loved these guys and looked at them as though they were the ones I wanted to marry my daughter."[15] Do you love the players you coach? (And would you want one of them to marry your daughter?)

Retired Dodger manager Tommy Lasorda truly loved his players. He showed it by *hugging* them. In the book *I Live For This*, sportswriter Bill Plaschke wrote about Tommy's "hugginess":

> He would scream at a player in the dugout, then hug him in his office after the game. Break them down and build them up. Show them how much he cared about winning, then show them how much he cared about them. Some of his players played hard because they wanted to avoid the scoldings. Others played hard because they couldn't wait for the hugs. Either way, they played. …

> From his first days as a minor league manager … Lasorda embraced his young players, turning them into the sort of loyal major leaguers who would win him a World Series. He literally embraced them, becoming one of baseball's first managers at any level to hug players after home runs, a tradition he continued throughout his career. …

> The secret to his managing success was simple. He knew his people. He knew who would react to a swift kick and who needed a long hug.[16]

Have you hugged your players today? And do they know that if they ever need anything, you are there for them? Do they know how to reach you if they have a problem? Dean Smith, former head basketball coach at the University of North Carolina, used to tell his players, "If you ever need me, call." And he gave them a number where he could always be reached.[17]

Another way to show your players you care about them is to lift them up from failure. One of the great role models of a coach who uplifts his team is Lenny Wilkins. Twice inducted into the Basketball Hall of Fame (both as player and coach), Lenny has coached the Seattle Sonics, the Portland Trail Blazers, the Cleveland Cavaliers, the Atlanta Hawks, the Toronto Raptors, the New York Knicks, and the 1996 Olympic champion USA men's basketball team. After a 35-year coaching career, he retired in 2005.

San Francisco sportswriter Ron Thomas, in his book *They Cleared the Lane*, tells how Lenny Wilkins lifted up his team after a heartbreaking playoff loss. It happened in 1989, when Wilkins was head coach of the Cleveland Cavaliers. In four years, Wilkins had turned the Cavs into a winning team and coached them into the playoffs. Unfortunately for Lenny, this was the beginning of the Michael Jordan era—and this was the night Jordan fired what sports history remembers as "The Shot."

It was May 7, 1989, the fifth and final game of the first-round of the NBA playoffs. The Bulls and Cavaliers had each won two games in the best-of-five series, and the deciding game was played on Cleveland's home floor. Cavaliers guard Craig Ehlo had just scored on a driving lay-up, giving his team a 100-99 lead with four seconds remaining.

After a Bulls time-out, Chicago forward Brad Sellers prepared to inbound the ball. Michael Jordan broke free of a double-team by Craig Ehlo and Larry Nance, caught the inbounds pass on the right sideline, dribbled twice, streaked to the foul line, leaped and hovered in midair, while Ehlo stretched himself out to block the shot. Jordan fired—and as the buzzer sounded, the ball rattled home.

While Jordan celebrated, Craig Ehlo fell to the floor in dejection. Later, Ehlo and his teammates went to the locker room knowing their entire season had been wiped away by a single shot—by "The Shot."

In the locker room, Lenny Wilkins stood before his team and said, "You guys gave everything. You played your hearts out. This guy [Jordan] is the best player in the league, maybe the best player ever, and it took him and three seconds and that shot to beat you. The greatest player maybe of all time beat you on a great shot. You did the best you could. Let it go."

Craig Ehlo later recalled, "I heard that and all the pain escaped me. Lenny just had this presence about him. He didn't come stomping in and throw a chair or cuss everyone out. He built something positive out of the whole situation, something positive that could carry us through a long, hard summer."[18]

It Don't Cost Nuthin' to Be Nice

Bear Bryant, the late head football coach of the Crimson Tide, told a story that took place in 1958, his first year at Alabama. He took off in his old car down the back roads of South Alabama to recruit a prospect for the team. After crisscrossing those dusty roads for a while, he couldn't find the school.

Finally, Bryant saw a cinderblock building with a hand-painted sign that read "Restaurant." He stopped and went inside—and all eyes turned in his direction. Bryant realized that he was the only white person in that eating establishment. Segregation was in full force in those days, and white people simply did not patronize black restaurants in rural Alabama.

Bryant walked up to the counter and took a seat. He asked the man at the counter what was on the menu.

The man replied, "You probably won't like it. It's chitlins, collared greens, and black eyed peas with cornbread. You know what chitlins are?"

(Chitterlings, in case you didn't know, are pig intestines.)

"I'm from Arkansas," Bryant replied. "I've probably eaten a mile of chitlins. Sounds like I've come to the right place."

A few minutes later, the man served up a big plate of food, then stayed to chat while Bryant ate his lunch. "You ain't from around here, then?"

"No, I'm the new football coach at the University up in Tuscaloosa. I'm down here to recruit a player." He named the player and the school.

"Yeah," the man said, "I've heard of him. He's pretty good." And he proceeded to give Coach Bryant directions to the school.

After lunch, Bryant thanked the man and reached for his wallet—but the man at the counter wouldn't take his money. "If you have a photograph or something I can hang up behind the counter," he said, "that's all I want."

So Coach Bryant took down the man's name and address on a napkin, and promised to send an autographed photo. He left and followed the man's directions to the school. He talked to the coach and player, but he wasn't impressed. He chalked it up as a wasted day. When he got back to Tuscaloosa, he found an 8 x 10 photo of himself, and he wrote on it, "Thanks for the best lunch I've ever had, Paul Bear Bryant." He mailed it the following day.

Years passed. Bear Bryant went on to win a string of championships and became known nationwide. One day, having heard good things about a black offensive lineman in the southern part of the state, Bryant got in his car and drove to the school to recruit him. But when Coach Bryant met with the player, the young man said his friends were going to Auburn, so he was going to Auburn, too.

Coach Bryant left empty-handed and returned to Tuscaloosa. Two days later, he got a phone call from the player who turned him down. "Coach," the young man said, "would you still have an opening for me?"

"Son," Bryant said, "I sure do."

"Well, I'd like to come."

"What changed your mind?"

"My grandpa. When I told him I passed up a chance to play for you, he pitched a fit and told me I wasn't going nowhere but Alabama, and I wasn't playing for nobody but Coach Bryant."

"Who's your grandpa?"

"You probably don't remember him, but you ate in his restaurant that first year you were at Alabama. You sent him a picture, and that picture has hung behind his counter ever since. To this day, he tells everybody about the time Bear Bryant came in and had chitlins at his counter. My grandpa said that when you left that day, he didn't expect you to remember him or send that picture, but you kept your word. That means everything to Grandpa. He said you would teach me more than just football, and I need to be coached by a man like you. So I guess I'm going to."

Bear Bryant choked up a bit when he heard that. He later said, "I learned that the lessons my mama taught me were always right. It don't cost nuthin' to be nice. It don't cost nuthin' to do the right thing most of the time. In fact, it would've cost me a lot if I had broken my word that day."

Bryant later went back to that restaurant, posed for more pictures with the restaurant owner, and gave him a signed football. Then he sat down and had a big plate of ribs.[19]

Coach Bryant often told that story to make a point: It doesn't cost anything to care for your players, for fellow coaches, and for people in the community. And you never know what dividends it might pay.

11

Maintain Passion, Enthusiasm, and Fun

©Elsa/Getty Images Sport

Jim Valvano coached the Wolfpack, the men's basketball team at North Carolina State University, in the 1980s. Jimmy V enjoyed a 19-year coaching career, followed by a successful tenure as a network broadcaster and motivational speaker. He died of cancer in 1993.

Jimmy's younger brother, Bob Valvano, remembers him for his sense of *fun*. Jimmy grew up in the Corona neighborhood of Queens, New York, surrounded by uncles, aunts, and cousins. Jimmy wandered the neighborhood with his older brother Nick, and there was always something fun to do. One of Jimmy's favorite relatives in the neighborhood was his Aunt Marion.

Bob recalls, "She let him try to re-create the latest experiments from the Mr. Wizard TV show in her apartment. [Jimmy] loved to retell the story of boiling eggs in vinegar, making them as hard as rubber balls, and then bouncing them off the walls. Great fun, but more so for him, no doubt, than for my aunt, who was left with an apartment reeking of boiling vinegar!" Jimmy's Aunt Marion would offer him the meal of his choice—and Jimmy would order a bottle of Nedick's orange soda, nothing else. She would serve it to him. "I think he may have been more excited about that than he was about winning the national championship," said Bob.

The theme of Jim Valvano's life, says older brother Nick, was *fun*. "Jim had to—just had to—have fun in whatever he did," Nick recalled. "He had a tremendous desire to make other people laugh, and to make himself laugh, and that was rooted in his childhood. The nuns at St. Leo's school used to take him from classroom to classroom when he was in first grade, and he'd do Jimmy Durante impersonations …'Good night Mrs. Calabash, wherever you are!' When he came into my class, I'd sink down in my chair, humiliated. My friends would say, 'Hey, isn't that your little brother?' and I'd claim I didn't know him."[1]

From a very early age, Jimmy Valvano understood the need for fun, both on the basketball court and in life. Great teams thrive on fun. When players enjoy their work, they don't see it as work. They see it as *fun*. As Robert D. Ramsey writes, "Fun is good for people. It strengthens the immune system, stimulates endorphin production, and increases energy. … Fun promotes creativity, builds teams, and relieves tension."[2]

When people experience that "endorphin rush" of fun, they want to experience it again and again. That's why fun is addictive. When work is fun, *work* is addictive. As people work together, become comfortable with each other, and bond together, they unleash each other's peak performance. That's how fun builds teams and produces championships.

It's All About Fun

Dean Smith, former head basketball coach at the University of North Carolina, taught his players to "play hard, play smart, play together"—that was the North Carolina basketball philosophy. He added:

> *Hard* meant with effort, determination, and courage; *smart* meant with good execution and poise, treating each possession as if it were the only one in the game; *together* meant playing unselfishly, trusting your teammates and doing everything possible not to let them down.

> That was our philosophy: We believed that if we kept our focus on those tenets, success would follow. … When we put these elements together, the players had fun, which was one of my goals as their coach. I wanted our players to enjoy the experience of playing basketball for North Carolina. Each player on our team knew he was important. They all did a terrific job of sharing the ball, which also made the game enjoyable for more players.[3]

One of Dean Smith's goals for his players was *fun*—and he knew how to make basketball *fun* for his players. For him, fun was serious business. Fun is the product of playing the game as it was meant to be played—playing hard, playing smart, and playing together. If his players would play the game according to his philosophy, they would enjoy the game. They would have fun. And they would experience success and winning—and winning is *always* fun!

Sports marketing expert Jon Spoelstra (father of Miami Heat coach Erik Spoelstra) says we should never forget that the whole purpose of sports is *fun*. It's supposed to be fun for the players, fun for the fans, and yes, fun for coaches and managers. Spoelstra writes:

> What I like about being in pro sports is that it means *nothing*. In sports, you don't pollute the rivers, the fields, or the skies like some companies do. You don't manufacture anything tangible. You just pay young men an illogical amount of money to play games in front of people. …

> Pro sports provide a relief for individuals from the problems of the world. … A movie or a concert lasts for a couple of hours and there is no ongoing emotional attachment. With pro sports, the emotional attachment is year-long. The season lasts about seven months, and there is the off-season. A fan can be mentally entrenched with

his/her team for 12 months out of the year, year after year, decade after decade. … For most fans, the teams provide a mental ballpark to which they can escape for a short time each day.[4]

Spoelstra is writing about the pro sports world, but much the same can be said for sports at *any* level, professional or amateur. It's all about fun. A baseball game or a basketball game won't solve the problems of the world, but it will help you forget your problems for a while. And you'll have *fun*.

So, amid all of the serious business of preparation, discipline, laying strategy, and motivating, let's not forget what it's all about. Let's not forget to have fun. The more fun players have, the more fun the fans will have.

Coaching Is Fun (If Not, Why Do It?)

Whether you are coaching a bunch of little tee-ball players, or a high school or college team, or coaching at the highest level of the pros, you should have fun coaching. Marv Levy coached the Buffalo Bills to four consecutive AFC championships and was inducted into the Pro Football Hall of Fame in 2001. He says that he is often approached by high school and college football coaches wanting to know how they can get into coaching in the NFL. That question, he says, "really frosts me." Why? Because the people who ask that question are not living in the present—and they don't know how to truly enjoy coaching at their present level. He adds:

> Goals are great, but if you live in constant anticipation of something else, of getting somewhere, you're never fully involved in what you're doing now. And I think that means you're probably not doing a great job.
>
> I entered coaching because I loved it. … Wherever I was, that was my dream job. I even loved coaching high school. My philosophy is that, whatever your job, do it as though you're going to be doing it for the rest of your life. Because once you start to see it as a stepping stone to something else, you're not doing your best; you're not fully involved.[5]

Mike Martz won a Super Bowl ring as offensive coordinator for the St. Louis Rams at the end of the 1999 season (Super Bowl XXXIV, January 30, 2000). He began coaching at the college level in 1980, and moved to the NFL in 1992.

But it wasn't until 1998, when he was the offensive coordinator with the Washington Redskins, that he stumbled upon a realization that changed the way he coached—and the way he looked at life. The Redskins starting quarterback, Gus Frerotte, struggled on the field and was eventually replaced by backup quarterback Trent Green. The 'Skins were winless in their first seven regular-season games. It was a humiliating start, and some in the media blamed Martz for the Redskins' offensive woes.

That's when Martz experienced his epiphany. "The revelation came in Washington," he told sports writer Larry Weisman. "I was coaching what I thought was as hard as I could and as good as I could, and we were 0-7. It was frustrating because you're working as hard as you possibly can, and you're miserable and you're 0-7."

What was Martz's revelation? It wasn't a vision. It wasn't a religious experience. It was a simple-yet-profound insight: "I just had this realization that I should just enjoy what I do," he said. "I changed my attitude completely, to enjoy [coaching] and have a little bit more fun."

Martz realized that if he, as the coach, was having fun coaching, then his players would be positively affected. "The players," he said, "get a take on what your attitude is without you saying a word. The body language is pretty loud, actually. I just decided we can do it a different way."

The life of the coach is filled with hard work and serious responsibility. The hours are long, the pressures are great, and the criticism can be vicious, whether deserved or not. If you, as a coach, are not having fun at your work, then all of the stress and tension will eat you alive. It will rob you of your reason for living. In 1998, Mike Martz realized that he needed to get his life back into perspective.

"My whole life I was so goal-oriented," he said. "Gotta do this, gotta go, gotta go, gotta go. And I turned around and looked back, and the years had flown by so quickly, the kids were grown, and I said to myself, 'Whoa, let's put the brakes on and enjoy this thing as we go.'"[6]

Mike Martz learned in time. He came to the realization that, even in times of adversity, coaching should be fun. And the more fun you have coaching, the more success you're likely to have as well. Soon after this revelation, Martz moved from the Redskins to the Rams. He eventually succeeded Dick Vermeil as Rams head coach and led the team to the playoffs four out of six years, including a trip to Super Bowl XXXVI (where the Rams were narrowly beaten by the Patriots, 20-17).

If you're coaching, you'd better have fun. If it's not fun, why do it? Fun makes better coaches and better teams. Just ask Mike Martz.

The Secret Is Passion

What is the secret to fun? Simply this: Do everything with passion! Jim Calhoun, head coach of the UConn Huskies men's basketball team, put it this way in his book *A Passion to Lead*:

> *Passion* is another word for enthusiasm, which translates into energy, which in turn produces action. The more passion and energy you have,

the more things you're likely to get done in the course of the day or a week or a year—and the better off you and your organization will be. It's called being productive—and it means that you are working harder than your competitors, whether you're flipping pancakes in a New Mexico diner or trading bonds in Manhattan.

I ask our players all the time: "How did you feel at six this morning?"

My players *don't* get up at six in the morning. How many teenagers do you know who do? The question is rhetorical—my way of letting the student athletes know that *every* day is full of great possibilities, if you have an optimistic attitude. What I'm really suggesting is that they take an aggressive, can-do approach to life.[7]

All the great coaches and sports stars of every game, of every age, have been people of great passion for what they do. Christy Mathewson (1880-1925) was one of the most renowned pitchers of the "dead-ball era" of early Major League Baseball, playing for the New York Giants and Cincinnati Reds. He was one of the first five players inducted into the Baseball Hall of Fame in its inaugural year (1936).

"A person must enjoy playing baseball," Mathewson once said. "He must not go at it as he would seat himself in an office desk at nine in the morning and then keep his eye on the clock until five in the evening. He must like it, must love it, must put his whole soul in it."[8]

Passion was the key to playing the game in Christy Mathewson's day, and it is still the key today. It was a passionate sense of fun that motivated Orioles third baseman Cal Ripken, Jr. to show up at the ballpark every day for 17 seasons, breaking Lou Gehrig's supposedly "unbreakable" record for consecutive games played. Ripken sometimes had to shake off injury or illness in order to maintain "The Streak," an unbroken string of 2,632 games played from May 30, 1982 to September 20, 1998.

In 1999, Cal wrote the foreword to his dad's book, *The Ripken Way*, and gave a word of tribute to his first coach, Cal Ripken, Sr. (who spent 36 years in the Orioles organization as a player, coach, and manager). "The Streak," Cal Jr. wrote, "was born because my father taught me to come to the ballpark with a desire and a passion to play."[9]

Passion and fun are equally important in football. Wide receiver Vince Papale played three seasons with the Philadelphia Eagles, and was the inspiration for the movie *Invincible*. He once said of Eagles coach Dick Vermeil, "He always had a hop in his gait, as if he couldn't wait to get where he was going. And he had a big smile on his face. Every practice, you felt like there was no place in the world he would rather be."[10]

When you think of a passion for football, you think of John Madden. As head coach of the Oakland Raiders (1969-1978), he became the youngest coach in NFL history to reach 100 career wins. He did so at age 42 after only 10 full seasons. His 1976 Raiders went 13-1 in the regular season and beat the Vikings 32-14 in Super Bowl XI, January 9, 1977. He later brought his passion for football to his career as a sports broadcaster. These words of John Madden typified his approach to the game: "I'm not a journalist, I'm not an actor. I'm a football coach doing television. It's fun. It's my life, my passion. I'll do it as long as I can."[11]

I once went fishing with Curt Gowdy, the NBC sports announcer and longtime voice of the Boston Red Sox. Curt had come to Florida for an event at the Ted Williams Museum and Hitters Hall of Fame. While we were fishing, I enjoyed the chance to discuss sports history with a man who had seen a lot of it firsthand.

Curt told me that when he was a boy, growing up in Wyoming, he worshiped Coach Knute Rockne of Notre Dame. "I never met Rockne," Gowdy told me, "but I once had a chance to talk to the great sportswriter Grantland Rice at a reception. Rice had known Rockne very well, so I asked him to tell me what, in his opinion, made Knute Rockne so inspirational and successful as a coach. Rice said, 'That's easy. The man had a passion and enthusiasm that lent force to his personality. If Churchill, Stalin, FDR, and Knute Rockne were all in a room together, Rockne would dominate the room.'"

A great leader in another realm, the South African statesman Nelson Mandela, once said this about the importance of approaching everything in life with a great passion and enthusiasm: "There is no passion to be found playing small, in settling for a life that is less than the one you are capable of living."[12] Those are true words. So play large. Play with passion.

This Coaching Bug Has Bitten Me

Where do teams learn to play big, to play with enthusiasm and fun and passion? They learn it from the example of enthusiastic coaches, who exemplify a grand sense of fun, who live their lives with intensity and joy.

Jon Gruden—NFL coach (Raiders and Buccaneers) and TV color commentator (*ESPN Monday Night Football*)—became the youngest coach at that time to win a Super Bowl when his Bucs beat the Raiders 48-21 in Super Bowl XXXVII (January 26, 2003). Passion and fun define this guy. He talked about his approach to the game in a book entitled *Do You Love Football?!: Winning with Heart, Passion, and Not Much Sleep*:

> Football really is all I know. … I'm not a scratch golfer. I don't know how to bowl. I can't read the stock market. … But I can call, "Flip Right Double X Jet 36 Counter Naked Waggle at Seven X Quarter" in my sleep.

I love the competition of the game. I love the players who play it. I love the strategy, the variables. I love the smell of the grass, the sound of the stadium. I love the thrill of victory. I like to see how we respond to the adversity that a loss brings and to the sudden changes that we have to deal with, whether it's a fumble, an interception, a 15-yard penalty, or something worse. ... The game day experience is what really gets me juiced.[13]

Gruden's passion for the game also comes through in an interview he gave to sportswriter Mike Freeman. He said, "I know there are some people, even coaches, who might think the way I do things is over-the-top. I feel like I have to work harder to be the best. Part of it is I have a sickness. This coaching bug has bitten me. I love what I do. I always will, and I don't know if I'll ever be able to change."[14]

Great coaches all have the "sickness" Gruden talks about. To be a winning coach, the "coaching bug" must bite you and infect you with a passion and enthusiasm for the game. You must be bitten and smitten with a sense of *fun*—an I-can't-wait eagerness to start the team meeting, to get on the practice field, or to take the field of competition on game day. When you love coaching and competing with that kind of intensity, then every day is the best day of your life.

In Chapter 1, I talked about Maggie Dixon, sister of Pittsburgh men's basketball coach Jamie Dixon. Maggie was an assistant coach at DePaul for several years before landing the job as head women's basketball coach at the United States Military Academy at West Point. Her career record as a head coach was .645. Tragically, her entire head coaching career was only one season long—a 20-11 record at Army.

On April 5, 2006, just weeks after leading her team to the NCAA tournament, she died at Westchester Medical Center in Valhalla, New York, after collapsing in the home of a friend. A couple of years before her death, she told an interviewer that she got into coaching because she loved basketball and she loved working with kids.

"I always thought that I'd become a teacher or teach at some level," she said. "When I got into high school, I worked a couple camps with Jamie. ... I always liked working with the younger kids and it just kind of developed into that. It was just something that I always enjoyed. I loved basketball and I liked being a role model to kids and helping out."

Those who knew Maggie always seemed impressed by the sense of passion and fun that radiated from her life. Her mentor, DePaul Blue Demons head coach Doug Bruno, said, "I liked her enthusiasm. ... I felt a good energy from her."

Her brother Jamie shares Coach Bruno's view. Before Maggie's death, before she even landed a job at West Point, he said, "She really has a passion for [coaching]. That's the most important thing. She really enjoys doing what she's doing. … She has always been a pretty happy person and seems to have fun wherever she's at."[15]

From the beginning of her all-too-brief tenure at West Point, Maggie Dixon was preaching fun to her players. As Ira Berkow of the *New York Times* observed, "Dixon told her assembled players on the first day of practice: 'There will be no excuses. We're going to play to win, and we're going to have fun doing it.'"[16]

After Maggie Dixon's death, her players and fellow coaches memorialized her as a person who taught the value of fun. Stefanie Stone played her senior year under Maggie's coaching, and she credits Coach Dixon for sharpening her abilities and reviving her career. Said Stone, "She taught us about perseverance, about [the need to] keep going and never give up and to have fun while you're playing. … I will never forget anything she taught me."

Maggie's assistant, Dave Magarity, succeeded her as head coach at Army. He, too, learned from Maggie how to coach with a sense of fun. "What I've tried to do is just keep that attitude that she brought every day," he said. "She always wanted the kids to have fun—she thought that was an important thing. That is something that I learned from her."

In fact, he says that having Maggie as a role model has enabled him to keep *fun* as a principal element in his game plan. He recalls that on one occasion, while coaching a women's team, it occurred to him that his players were not having fun. They were not enjoying basketball. "So I backed off a little bit," he said, "and we worked things out. That's what Maggie taught me. With these kids, I want to make sure they enjoy coming to practice and enjoy being together."[17]

Maggie Dixon is gone, but the players and coaches she inspired and the lessons she taught live on. She left a legacy of winning—and she left a legacy of fun.

12

Take Care of the Little Things

©Stephen Dunn/Getty Images Sport

Ted Williams (1918-2002) tops the list of my sports heroes. His 19 seasons with the Boston Red Sox are the stuff of legend. He retired with 521 home runs and a career batting average of .344. In 1941, he batted a thundering .406.

After I moved to Orlando, I began attending induction ceremonies every February at the Hitters Hall of Fame and Ted Williams Museum in Hernando County, north of Orlando. The event included a ceremony and dinner, and even though Ted was in poor health following a stroke, he always attended in his wheelchair. When he was wheeled into the room, all conversations stopped. There was a sense of reverence in the room for Ted and all he had accomplished.

At one of these events, a fan came up to Ted and held out a baseball bat for him to examine. "They tell me," the fan said, "that this is one of the bats you used in 1941, the season you hit .406."

Ted took the bat in his hands and worked his hands around the grip. He closed his eyes, remembering. Then he said, "Yep, this is one of my bats. In 1941, I used to cut a little groove in the handle for my right index finger to nestle in. I can feel that groove. Yep, this is one of my bats all right."

I was amazed. After 60 years, Ted Williams was still able to focus on the little things that contributed to his greatness.

According to the Hillerich & Bradsby Co. of Kentucky, makers of the Louisville Slugger bat, Ted Williams used to come out to the manufacturing plant to personally meet with the craftsmen who made his bats. He would climb ladders and hand-pick the timber he wanted, and he'd remind the lathe-operators, woodworkers, and finishers to maintain his meticulous standards for each bat. The workers at Hillerich & Bradsby recalled an incident which illustrated just how particular Ted was about his Louisville Slugger bats:

> Ted Williams … once complained about the way the handle tapered on his favorite bat. He sent them back, saying their grips didn't feel right.
>
> They weren't. H&B staff members measured the grip with calibrators against the models he had been using. They discovered that Williams' new bats were 5/1000ths of an inch off.
>
> Williams also could tell differences in the weight of his bats. J.A. Hillerich, Jr., a late president of the company, once tested Williams. He gave him six bats, five weighing exactly the same, the sixth weighing one-half ounce more. Williams picked out the one with the minute difference.[1]

Boston Celtics coaching legend Red Auerbach described an encounter he once had with Ted Williams in the 1950s. As the two men discussed their respective games, basketball and baseball, Ted Williams asked the Celtics coach, "What do your guys eat on the day of a game?"

Auerbach said, "What do you want to know for? You seem to be doing all right with what you're doing."

"I'm always looking for new ways to improve what I do."

So Auerbach told him, "On the road, the way it's set up, they get so much per diem and they eat on their own. When we play in Boston, they eat at home. But the smart ones, for a 7:30 game, will eat around 3:30. You don't want them to be full going into a game."

Then the coach asked Williams what his pre-game meals were like. Williams replied that he ate after the game, not before. His post-game meals usually consisted of a couple of lamb chops, a piece of toast, and hot tea.

Auerbach concluded, "He thought of the little things, what's important to being great. When you're great and you excel, some athletes would coast on that. ... Here's the best hitter in baseball, and he's trying to get another little percentage point."[2]

"Inches Make the Champion"

When Doc Rivers was head coach of the Orlando Magic, the coaching staff wore T-shirts that had these words printed on the back: "It's all the little things." Doc wanted his coaches and his players to always remember that the little things matter.

Ever since I got into professional sports management, I have been intrigued by the little things—all the details that make a sports organization work. I like to wander around the facility and talk to the players, the coaches, the staffers, the interns, the secretaries, the concessionaires, and the janitorial staff. I like to schmooze with everyone about all the little details that make the organization function well. The little things fascinate me, and I feel I have a better handle on "the big picture" because I take time to pay attention to the individual "brush strokes."

The little details are not merely fascinating; they are vitally important. The late *Chicago Daily News* columnist Sidney J. Harris once observed that, in Major League Baseball batting averages, it's the little things that make all the difference. "One batter hits .275 for the season," he wrote. "The other hits .300. The one who hits .300 may easily have a contract awarding him twice as much money as the one hitting .275. Yet the difference between the two over the season is only one extra hit in forty times at bat."[3]

Former Major League Baseball outfielder, coach, and manager Whitey Herzog offers this perspective on the little things:

> Baseball, when it's played right, is made up of a lot of smaller plays, and each one gives you an edge if you work at it. It's also a game of large samples: Over 154 or 162 games, the little things accumulate and pile up and turn into big ones. That's the game's most essential fact. It's a game of percentages, and any way you can tilt the wheel your way a little, you do. … Writers and fans hardly ever notice these little things, and you hardly ever hear anybody mention 'em, but they decide championships.
>
> Take baserunning … [Longtime MLB manager Casey Stengel] taught it better than anybody I ever saw. Thinking ahead was part of it. … The leftfielder, for example. Does he throw left-handed? If he does, you've got an edge. If you hit it right down the line, you know he has to turn his back to the diamond to pick it up. To throw to second, he has to turn back around and come across his body with the ball. That gives you a little extra time, and it means if you hustle a little bit, you can turn a single into a double. … It added up to runs, and runs added up to leads, and leads added up to … wins.[4]

Or as Cal Ripken, Sr., observed so succinctly, "Do two million little things right, and the big things take care of themselves."[5]

In the same way, the little things can make or break a football game, a season, a team, or a coach. Vince Lombardi said, "Football is a game of inches, and inches make the champion."[6] And former Notre Dame coach Lou Holtz, who has coached teams from four different schools to top 20 rankings, made this observation about the little things:

> If two seminars were held at the same time, one conducted by successful teams and one by losing teams, the similarities between the two would be amazing. The offensive and defensive theories both employed would be virtually identical. The amount of time they spent practicing wouldn't vary by more than a few minutes and their practice format would be the same. The main difference would be attention to detail. In the successful organization, no detail is too small to receive attention. No job is minor, and everyone takes great pride in realizing that they are important and their responsibilities are critical to the unit's success.[7]

Business expert Harvey Mackay, in *Swim With the Sharks Without Being Eaten Alive*, offered an instructive example of how Lou Holtz pays close attention to the little things—and teaches his players how to follow his example. MacKay writes:

The [Notre Dame] team has a road game at Purdue. They've been instructed to wear coats and ties to the stadium because they'll be closely observed as representatives of the University of Notre Dame. They're waiting to board the bus to go to the stadium for the game. And waiting. Coach Holtz shows up. Doesn't say a word. Just goes down the line and looks them over. And over. Finally he goes up to one of the players, smiles, reaches up and straightens the player's tie, and then nods to the driver of the bus. Not until then is the door to the bus opened and the team permitted to load up. …

If you're going to be a winner, guys, look like a winner. Little things mean everything. … You can preach about little things and discipline until your tongue hangs out, but it won't work unless *you* yourself find a way to dramatize it and make it seem important enough so the message gets through.[8]

The same principles hold true in basketball. Jim Calhoun, head men's basketball coach at the University of Connecticut, put it this way:

What is a basketball game? It's really a long series of little battles played out over forty minutes, hundreds of momentary skirmishes—battles for loose balls and rebounds, one-on-one matchups between a guy who, with the shot clock running down, is going to shoot the ball and a defender who must keep him from putting it in the basket. Win enough of those little fights and you win the game. You've got a few more points on the scoreboard than your opponent when the final horn sounds. By doing lots of little things well, you've accomplished a very big goal.[9]

A Matter of Patience

To the uninitiated, baseball is all about big hits and big plays. To those who know the game, baseball is a game of finesse, percentages, and fine increments. The better your team gets, the stiffer the competition you'll face—and as the competition gets tougher, the little things become increasingly more important. Former Houston Astros manager Phil Garner (2004-2007) explained it this way: "The more you win, the more important the little things matter. You have to be able to cut off guys, you have to be able to execute bunt plays. It all boils down to if you can execute when the game's on the line. When the pressure is at its highest, can you execute the little things? That's going to be the difference between winning and losing. That's why we have to go back to the very simple basics."[10]

Dodgers manager Joe Torre also stresses the importance of mastering the details and playing with finesse instead of pressing too hard to make the big plays. "To me," he said, "detail is very important. ... The only thing we try to express to [new players], starting in spring training, is that we deal with small things here. You want to think small, and then big things will happen. ... Don't go up there and try to hit home runs. That thinking may work rarely, but never on a regular basis. When you face those real good teams, being in the habit of having quality at-bats probably helps you win more games than anything else."[11]

Former NFL quarterback Phil Simms (currently a sportscaster for the CBS television network) had an outstanding football career at Morehead State University in Kentucky. He was drafted in the first round (seventh selection overall) by the New York Giants and played his entire pro career for that organization. Simms was named MVP of Super Bowl XXI (January 25, 1987) for leading the Giants to a 39-20 victory over John Elway and the Denver Broncos.

I once had Phil Simms as a phone-in guest on my Orlando sports talk show—and the whole time he was talking, I was writing down his stories and insights in a notebook next to my microphone. I asked him if he had any advice for coaches. "Yes, I do," he said. "You know what brings coaches down? You know why some coaches lose their edge in this game? It's because, sooner or later, they get tired of doing the little things. When you get tired of doing the little things, it shows up in the team's performance. It shows up on the scoreboard. Coaches get tired, the same as players. Over time, it just gets harder and harder to sustain an intense focus on the little things."

What are some of the "little things" Simms refers to? He described them in his book *Sunday Morning Quarterback*. Reflecting on the 1986 season, when the Giants won the Super Bowl, Simms recalled that it was a long, intense, demanding process—and it didn't happen in just one season. "It took three seasons of a lot of yelling and a lot of work," he said. "It took coaches stressing the little things, over and over, such as showing a linebacker the proper technique to stop a tight end from blocking him."[12] Mastering the little things requires patience and perseverance from both coaches and players.

In his book, Simms also talked about how a coach—Giants quarterbacks coach Jim Fassel—helped him extend his playing career by teaching him the little things that make a quarterback more effective. Fassel (who would later serve as Giants head coach) joined the organization in 1991, Simms' thirteenth season, and began instructing Simms in the fundamentals of the West Coast Offense.

One day, Simms was out on the practice field, throwing short passes to his receivers. Fassel stood on the sidelines. He had been on the job for a month, teaching Simms a variety of "little things," techniques to improve his step, his body position, his throwing, and even his grip on the ball. After a few throws, Simms turned to Fassel and said, "This is messed up."

Jim Fassel nervously asked what Simms meant, fearing that the quarterback was rebelling against his coaching.

Simms replied, "I should have known this stuff thirteen years ago. I'd have been setting records in the NFL if I'd known this thirteen years ago." Simms concluded:

> It was that big of a difference. It was unbelievable. In my last year, my fifteenth season, I was beat up, but I went to the Pro bowl because I had learned with Jim for two years and I was starting to piece those lessons together well—how to hold the ball, how to relax, the proper steps to take, all the little things. Of course, I couldn't throw the ball anywhere near as hard as I could earlier in my career because I had had arm injuries and my feet hurt. However, in my fifteenth year, I could control the ball much better than I ever had in my career because of the techniques I have finally learned.[13]

Simms continued to have success in the waning years of his career because a coach took the time to help him master the little things. It's the little things that make or break a player—and a coach.

One Little Step at a Time

Alan Hobson understands the importance of the little things—and he's living proof of the power of taking thousands of little, incremental steps in order to reach big goals. He spent nearly two decades preparing to climb Mount Everest. In 1997, he achieved that childhood dream at age 39 on his third attempt.

In his 1999 book *From Everest to Enlightenment*, Hobson described his intense training regimen for his assault on Everest:

> To develop the exact muscles used in climbing, I spent as much time as possible hiking up mountains in the Canadian Rockies to achieve as much vertical gain as possible, usually 3,000 to 5,500 vertical feet. … I often did this with up to a 50-pound pack so as to make the important transition from "aerobic fitness" to "pack fitness." …
>
> Because of my heavy speaking schedule … the bulk of my day-to-day physical training usually took place in the fitness centers of hotels. Usually, this involved loading up a backpack with 50 pounds of weight, … strapping five pounds of weight on each ankle, cranking the incline on the treadmill up to its maximum … for two hours at a time. …

I did not climb Everest in a single step on a single day at a single moment. I climbed it during those endless hours on treadmills scattered in hotels and health clubs from Los Angeles to New York and from London to Paris. … I suited up and I showed up. I invested in my dream, my future, and in my very survival.[14]

Hobson compared his training for Everest to the kind of symbolic "treadmills" we all walk in our daily lives. We all struggle against the "gravity" of obstacles and opposition we encounter in our careers, in our relationships, and in the daily and hourly problems we must deal with.

"Our everyday Everests," he said, "are not climbed in a single day or even in a single step. They are climbed by taking an apparently endless series of small steps that, over years and decades, may amount to something."[15]

Three years after his successful conquest of Everest, Alan Hobson was diagnosed with leukemia—cancer of the blood—and told that he had less than a year to live. Suddenly, he faced a very different kind of mountain. Refusing to surrender to the diagnosis, he elected to undergo a risky high-dose chemotherapy treatment regimen. He bet his life that the chemo would kill the cancer before it killed him—and the bet paid off. In his book *Climb Back from Cancer*, Hobson describes how the same step-by-step approach to climbing Everest became his approach to conquering cancer:

> While preparing for Everest, I have developed my own training mantra. For every step I took on the treadmill, I said to myself, "CAN … WILL. I CAN climb Everest, I WILL climb Everest" … over and over again.
>
> On my medical mountain, I had another mantra. For every step I took on the ward while receiving chemotherapy I said to myself, "I CAN get better. I WILL get better." …
>
> The first infusion was to last about a week, roughly the same amount of time it takes to climb from the base of Mount Everest to the summit once a person is acclimatized. The closer we got to the end of the chemo cycle, the worse I was likely to feel, just like getting closer to the summit of Everest. Headaches were common. So was acute fatigue, nausea, vomiting and insomnia—precisely the same side effects chemo produced.

As he progressed through his treatment, Hobson imagined that each round of chemotherapy was a camp on the way to the summit of Everest. He used notes taped up around his hospital room to remind him of where he was along his medical "climb." The notes read, "August 12. Day 1. Base Camp," then, "August 13. Day 2. Camp 1," then, "August 14. Day 3. Camp 2," and so on.[16]

Whatever challenge you face in your coaching and leadership career, take a lesson from Alan Hobson. Take your first step, then another and another, and start climbing your Everest. It may not seem like you're getting anywhere. You may have to take a lot of steps on the treadmill before you ever set foot on the slopes.

But small, patient steps lead to great accomplishments. Little things add up to great things. Millions of little water droplets make an ocean. Take care of the little things and the big things will take care of themselves.

13

Surround Yourself With Loyal People

©Mitch Stringer/Cal Sport Media/ZUMA Press

Buddy Ryan was one of the toughest, loudest, cussin'est, hard-nosed coaches in the NFL. And he inspired intense loyalty from his players.

He won his first Super Bowl ring as the defensive coordinator for the New York Jets. In Super Bowl III, Jets quarterback Joe Namath powered the offense and Buddy Ryan coached a Jets defensive squad, which held the Baltimore Colts to a single touchdown. Though the Colts were heavily favored, the Jets won the NFL championship game 16-7.

From the Jets, Buddy moved to Minnesota, where he coached the Vikings defensive unit known as the Purple People Eaters. There, he gained notoriety for paying a "bounty" to his players for making big hits.

In 1978, he became defensive coordinator for the Chicago Bears. While in Chicago, he shook up the entire NFL with his 46 Defense, a blitzing scheme in which four linemen, three linebackers, and three defensive backs crowded the line of scrimmage, leaving the free safety in the backfield. The 46 Defense not only changed the defensive game, but led directly to the development (by Bill Walsh and the 49ers) of the West Coast Offense. So, it would be fair to say that Buddy Ryan radically changed the way football is played—on *both* sides of the ball.

As defensive coordinator of the Bears under head coach Mike Ditka, Buddy Ryan collected his second Super Bowl ring in Super Bowl XX, January 26, 1986, with a resounding victory over the New England Patriots, 46-10. After that victory, the Bears carried Coach Ditka on their shoulders—but in a tradition-breaking demonstration of love and loyalty toward their defensive coordinator, the Bears defensive players also carried Buddy Ryan.

After Super Bowl XX, the Philadelphia Eagles hired Buddy Ryan as their head coach. He quickly turned a losing Philadelphia team into an organization that consistently won 10 games or more per season. In the process, Buddy earned the respect and loyalty of all his players—and especially a defensive lineman named Reggie White.

My writing partner, Jim Denney, who assisted Reggie White on his autobiography, told me that Reggie had a lot to say about Buddy Ryan. Reggie described him as "a coach who relentlessly pushed you to be the best, but was also a good friend, someone you'd go to battle for."

The first time Reggie met Coach Ryan, he was impressed that his new coach took an interest in the welfare of his family. Reggie's wife, Sara, was expecting their first child at the time. Coach Ryan told Reggie, "Make sure you spend plenty of time with your wife. Family is your most important priority. Football is a great game, but family's number one."

Reggie soon learned that Buddy Ryan had a tough side, too. The Eagles training camp was held in August at the stadium of West Chester University, about 35 miles west of Philadelphia. It was humid, temperatures were in the 90s, and Reggie recalled, "We were all stewing in our juices." As Coach Ryan put the players through their drills, Reggie thought he was seeing a whole different Buddy Ryan.

"It was like he was mad at us," Reggie recalled. "He was screaming at us and pushing us in that heat, making us run sprints, then making us run laps. Guys were dropping from dehydration, but he'd yell at us to get up and do it all over again. I thought he was going to kill us!

"I had just about reached my limit. I was sitting on a bench, taking a break, and wondering why Buddy hated us so much. Just then, Buddy came over to me and said something that shocked me. He said, 'Reggie, I just want to tell you that you are the best defensive lineman I've ever seen. You do things I've never seen guys do before.' I didn't know what to say. He'd never seen me in a game, only in practice. And I knew he had coached some of the best defensive linemen in the game—Richard Dent, Alan Page, Carl Eller, Jim Marshall, guys like that.

"To this day, I don't know if Buddy really meant that or if he was just trying to motivate me. But those words challenged me. I wanted to be worthy of the praise he'd given me, so I worked harder for Buddy Ryan than for any other coach I had played for. That was my second year in the NFL, and I got 18 sacks that season.

"That was a tough training camp. I think Buddy deliberately designed it to be that tough in order to weed out anyone who wasn't a thousand percent committed to the team and committed to winning. I saw a lot of guys up and quit because Buddy was so tough on us. I saw guys throw down their helmets and walk away. I remember one guy saying, 'Shucks, my dad's rich. Who needs this? I'm going home!' And he did.

"Some of the guys who left the team were talented players. For a long time, I couldn't understand why Buddy chased them off that way. Later on, I figured out what he was doing. He was cutting the team down to a hard core of committed guys who'd be loyal to him. And it worked.

"I respect tough coaches, and Buddy was one of the toughest I ever played for. But he was fair. I only had one request of my coaches: I asked them not to cuss at me. I told my coaches, 'I can take anything—yelling, hollering, even working me till I drop. I just can't take someone cursing at me.' I didn't care if they cussed around me. I just didn't want them cursing me personally.

"One night during training camp, Sara came to visit. She was staying in a hotel near the campus, and I wanted to spend the night with my wife. So I went to Buddy's office to ask if he'd let me stay at the hotel with Sara. When I got to the office, some of the other coaches were hanging around, and they said, 'Hey, Buddy! Reggie White's here! He wants to talk to you!'

"I heard Buddy griping from a-way down the hall. He said, 'Reggie White! He wants me to stop cussing—and I've been coaching and cussing for twenty-odd years! I've been cussing ever since I was in the National Football League!' Then he came stamping into his office with his face all red, and he said, 'Reggie White, I've cussed every day of my life and I can't stop cussing now!'

"I said, 'I ain't coming to ask you to stop cussing. I just want to ask if it's okay for me to stay overnight in a hotel with my wife.'

"He looked surprised and said, 'Oh, okay, go ahead.'

"And that's why I loved Buddy Ryan. He was tough but fair. We all loved him and wanted to work hard for him."

When a coach inspires that kind of loyalty in his team, he knows he's got players who will run through walls for him. You can't *demand* that kind of loyalty. But you can *inspire* it.

Circle the Wagons

What does every team, business, and organization need? "Loyalty," says retired MLB manager Yogi Berra. "For me, loyalty to teammates trumped everything. … I couldn't achieve what I wanted to without the trust and help of my teammates. And vice versa. We just had a loyalty to each other. I know loyalty is more fragile in business. It's fragile in professional sports. People are more transient than ever. But being a trusted coworker or a good teammate should never go out of style."[1]

Loyalty may be defined as the quality of being faithful and devoted to a person or a cause. Loyalty is not based on feelings; it's based on commitment. You can be loyal to a friend even if you are angry with him. You don't even have to like someone in order to be loyal to him. For example, you can be loyal to a coach with the disagreeable personality. And you can be loyal to a player who has disappointed you on the field. Why? Because you have made a commitment of your loyalty to that team, to that coach, and to those players. You have committed yourself to a cause, to a goal, and as a person of character you will keep that commitment regardless of your feelings.

The best way to teach loyalty is through acts of loyalty. As a coach, you can be hard-nosed, demanding, and as loud as a foghorn—but if your players know you care about them, you want them to succeed, and you are shaping them into winners, they will accept your ranting and screaming.

Loyalty begets loyalty. Always defend your staff and your players against attack. If anyone in your organization is accused of wrongdoing, always withhold judgment until the facts are in. When your players and staff know you are loyal to them, they will pay back your loyalty many times over.

As a coach, you demonstrate loyalty by speaking the truth. Tell your coaches and players that you expect the truth from them. Tell them you want to know about any problems on the team, including personal problems that would affect team unity and performance. Tell your coaches and players that you expect them, out of loyalty, to embrace the changes you implement, such as changes in strategy, changes in personnel, changes in preparation, and so forth.

Even though loyalty must be earned, you should still demand it—loyalty toward you, and loyalty toward teammates. Make sure your players know that you expect loyal behavior from them, and that any disloyalty will be met with consequences. Make sure they know that a loyal player does not belittle or attack his teammates. A loyal player does not spread rumors or speak ill of his coach. Loyal people treat their teammates with unconditional respect. They build each other up; they don't tear each other down.

Every team faces adversity, and adversity can divide a team, pitting one player against another. Don't allow adversity to weaken team unity. If your players or assistants are criticized by the media or the administration or the fans, circle the wagons and demonstrate loyalty to your people. As a coach, always remember that you, your coaches, and your players succeed or fail as a team. Don't let adversity divide and conquer you.

A Paragon of Loyalty

When I was growing up in Wilmington, Delaware, my best friend, from kindergarten all the way through high school, was a young man named Robert Ruliph Morgan Carpenter III—though I knew him as Ruly. I didn't realize it at the time, but one of the biggest breaks of my life was having Ruly Carpenter as my best friend.

In 1943, when Ruly was three years old, his grandfather purchased the Philadelphia Phillies baseball team for $400,000. Ruly's grandfather owned it, and his father, Bob Carpenter, ran it. In socioeconomic terms, Ruly's family and mine had nothing in common. Ruly's parents were heirs to the DuPont fortune, while my dad was a $4,000-a-year school teacher at Tower Hill School, the prep school Ruly attended. (The only reason I attended a swank private school was because my dad taught there.)

Even though we came from different social strata (his family even had a chauffeur named Alfred!), Ruly Carpenter and I were best friends. We did everything together—fishing, swimming, shooting BB guns, skating, basketball, and a fair share of mischief. We also spent countless hours playing baseball, either on the sandlot or on Ruly's own field. That's right, Ruly had a baseball field right on his property. I'll never forget the time, back in 1957, when Phillies first baseman Ed Bouchee worked out with us on Ruly's baseball diamond (he was rehabbing after missing spring training).

Hanging out with Ruly, I got a lot of free trips to Shibe Park and I got to meet a lot of major leaguers. After the games, Ruly would take me to the locker room and we'd rub shoulders with all my heroes—Del Ennis, Richie Ashburn, Robin Roberts, all the "Whiz Kids" of the early 1950s.

Every spring when we were in high school, Ruly would get a bunch of guys together and we'd take the night train to Clearwater, Florida, and watch the Phillies in spring training. Ruly was an outstanding athlete and won a dozen varsity letters in high school. On the high school baseball team, Ruly was the pitcher and I was the catcher, so he was throwing to me. On the football team, I played quarterback and he was an end, so I threw to Ruly (in fact, I threw him 10 touchdown passes our senior year). Our football team was undefeated throughout our last two years in high school, and we only lost two games the whole four years.

After high school, I went on to Wake Forest and Ruly went to Yale. After graduating in 1962, he joined his dad in the Phillies front office. By 1972, Ruly had become the president of the Phillies organization. His tenure was extremely successful. Under his leadership, the Phillies began making postseason appearances almost every year. He presided over the Phillies' first-ever World Series championship season in 1980.

In 1981, Ruly sold the team. The financial strain of operating an MLB franchise in the era of free agency was more than Ruly wanted to deal with. He sold the team for $32.5 million, which, even allowing for inflation, is a pretty hefty return on his grandfather's $400,000 investment in 1943.

Sports historian William C. Kashatus chronicled the Phillies' magical season in his book *Almost a Dynasty: The Rise and Fall of the 1980 Phillies*. In that book, he captured a dimension of Ruly Carpenter's personality that I appreciated throughout the years that Ruly and I grew up together—Ruly's deep sense of loyalty. Kashatus described "Ruly Carpenter's vision of the 'Phillies family,' an organization based on unconditional loyalty to all its members regardless of their place in the club hierarchy."[2] Kashatus went on to cite this example of Ruly's sense of loyalty:

> "It didn't matter if you were in the front office, on the playing field, or the grounds crew, everyone mattered," said Mark Carfagno, who worked on

the team's grounds crew from 1971 to 2002. "That was Ruly's goal and he set the example for everyone else. This was a rich guy with a degree from Yale, but it didn't stop him from sitting down with us and watching games from the tunnel in back of home plate. We were the 'little guys' in the organization, but he would sit and joke with us like he was one of the gang.[3]

Ruly Carpenter was a paragon of loyalty and one of the most exemplary and gentlemanly executives in the history of professional sports. He set a great example for leaders to follow. I'm proud that I have been able to call him my friend.

When Loyalty Says "No"

Pat Summitt, head basketball coach of the Lady Volunteers at the University of Tennessee, is one of the most successful coaches in collegiate sports history. In July 2009, *The Sporting News* ranked the 50 greatest coaches of all time, in all sports, both collegiate and professional—and not only was Pat Summitt the only woman on the list, but she was ranked number 11, right after Knute Rockne.[4]

In her 1999 book *Reach For the Summit*, Coach Summitt talks about the importance of loyalty in any organization—and she makes it clear what loyalty is and what it isn't. She writes:

> The single most common reason organizations self-destruct is disloyalty. … I seriously doubt whether [loyalty] is something that can be "taught." But it can be developed, and earned. To build a sound organization you must surround yourself with people who share the same basic values, people who are constant and who will be true to your organization. …
>
> When I say surround yourself with loyal people, I don't mean yes people. I want to make that clear. In fact, it is a crucial distinction. … People who say yes to you all the time are, in my opinion, insulting you. They assume you are either too immature or unstable or egotistical to handle the truth.
>
> The absolute heart of loyalty is to value those people who tell you the truth, not just those people who tell you what you want to hear. In fact, you should value them the most. Because they have paid you the compliment of leveling with you and assuming you can handle it.[5]

This is a principle of leadership that transcends the world of coaching and sports. Whether you are a business leader, a political leader, or a military leader, you need to surround yourself with people who will be loyal enough to level with you and tell you the truth. General Colin Powell, former chairman of the Joint Chiefs of Staff and former secretary of state, put it this way: "When we are debating an issue, loyalty means giving me your honest opinion, whether you think I'll like it or not. Disagreement, at this stage, stimulates me. But once a decision has been made, the debate ends. From that point on, loyalty means executing the decision as if it were your own."[6]

So, it's important to remember that loyalty sometimes says "no." The most loyal members of your staff or your team are those who will tell you the truth. The way you respond when they tell you the truth may well be a test of *your* loyalty toward *them*.

Loyalty Given, Loyalty Returned

The late George Allen took over two floundering NFL teams, the Los Angeles Rams and the Washington Redskins, and he engineered miraculous turnarounds with both teams. In fact, George Allen never had a losing season in his career.

Question: How did he do it? Answer: He demanded—and received—a 110 percent effort from his players. He once said, "As I tell my players, a 100 percent effort is not enough. The world belongs to those who aim for 110 percent. You cannot win if you are not willing to pay the price."[7]

Great coaches inspire intense effort—and intense loyalty. In fact, the depth of loyalty of your players and staff may well be the most reliable test of your effectiveness as a leader. After all, a coach's job is to inspire his players to run through walls for him. You can't expect a team to give 110 percent to a coach who doesn't inspire an incredible depth of loyalty.

Hall of Fame NFL coach Marv Levy was an assistant coach under George Allen with both the Rams and Redskins. He recalled that George Allen "was loyal to people who worked for him and he inspired us to be loyal to him. You had to work tremendously long hours, he was somewhat demanding, yet he cared deeply about the people who worked for him and played for him. Despite the hard work, he made the game fun."[8]

My old friend and mentor, baseball magnate Bill Veeck, once said, "For my dough, loyalty is the greatest virtue in the world."[9] And former LSU football coach Paul Dietzel put it this way: "The greatest word in the English language is loyalty. ... You are loyal to the people you're working for and to your players as well. You expect loyalty back from them. Loyalty is how you act when no one is looking. You have to go to bat for your associates, even if you don't like them or you disagree with them. Loyalty is being honest."[10]

Before his retirement in 1997, basketball coach Dean Smith coached the University of North Carolina Tar Heels to 897 wins, the most ever by an NCAA coach. His career statistics as a coach include two NCAA championships, 11 Final Four appearances, and 33 consecutive top-three finishes in the Atlantic Coast Conference. And in the process, he earned a reputation as one of the most caring and beloved human beings in college sports. He was never in too big a hurry to take time for his fans. Unlike many sports figures who seem annoyed and rushed when asked for an autograph, Dean Smith is known for personalizing each autograph he signs with the fan's name and an inspirational message.

Famed for his generosity, Coach Smith always shared his annual Nike endorsement contract, worth $300,000, with his assistant coaches and office staff. His players knew him as a mentor and counselor. Michael Jordan called him a "father figure," adding that Coach Smith "had an impact on so many players' lives. … He's left a legacy that we all can reminisce about."

Former North Carolina point guard Phil Ford remembers Coach Smith as the man who saved his life. Ford played four years at UNC, won gold with the U.S. Olympic team in 1976, and finished his college career as the only player in ACC history to score over 2,000 points and more than 600 assists. He was drafted second overall in 1978 by the Kansas City Kings, and played in the NBA—but his pro career was cut short by an eye injury. Soon afterward, Ford was battling depression and alcoholism.

Dean Smith, who always kept in touch with his former players, learned of Ford's problems and helped him get into a rehab center. Ford recalls, "He saved my life. It was like, 'Hey, I'm here for you. You and I are going to solve this problem together.'" After getting his life back together, Ford joined Dean Smith's coaching staff.

Is there one word that, more than any other, defines Coach Dean Smith? Paul Hardin, former chancellor at the University of North Carolina at Chapel Hill, knows the perfect word. "Loyalty is his defining grace," Hardin says. "Dean probably knows the whereabouts of every player who ever played for him whether he was an All-American or a bench warmer."

As writer Donald W. Patterson said in a profile of Dean Smith in the *Greensboro News & Record*, "He gives loyalty to his players, coaches and office staff and they give it to him in return."[11] What a great legacy for any coach to have—a legacy of loyalty given, and loyalty returned.

14

Empower Your Players

After a nine-year career quarterbacking the Cleveland Browns, Otto Graham retired. He had been the Browns' starting quarterback since the inception of the team in 1946. With Graham's retirement, head coach Paul Brown needed a new quarterback. There were two QBs he liked in the upcoming draft—Len Dawson and John Brodie. But with the sixth pick in the draft, Brown had little hope that either player would be available when his turn came.

Sure enough, when it was Cleveland's pick, both quarterbacks were gone. But Paul Brown could hardly believe his good fortune when he saw that running back Jim Brown of Syracuse University was available. An amazingly versatile athlete who excelled in football, basketball, track, and lacrosse, Brown had finished fifth in the Heisman voting and was a unanimous first-team All-American. Averaging 6.2 yards per carry in his senior year, he had finished the regular season by spearheading a 61-7 blowout of Colgate, in which he had rushed for 197 yards, scored six touchdowns, and kicked seven extra points. No question, Paul Brown wanted Jim Brown to play for the Cleveland Browns.

Football franchises were not as flush with cash in those days as they are today, so Paul Brown had to convince Jim Brown to sign with the team for a standard rookie contract, a $12,000 first-year salary plus a $3,000 signing bonus. Coach Brown told his new running back that he would join the team as a backup to fullback Ed Modzelewski.

Jim Brown agreed. In spite of his record-setting achievements at Syracuse, Brown didn't know how good he was, compared with other players in the NFL. As soon as he arrived at training camp, Coach Brown lined him up with the other running backs to time them on the 40-yard dash. Even though the rookie back was dead tired after driving all night to get to training camp, he easily beat the other backs.

In fact, after one day practicing with Jim Brown, Ed Modzelewski called his brother Dick, who was at that time a defensive tackle for the New York Giants. "Well," Ed told his brother, "I've just become a backup."

Cleveland's first exhibition game that season was against the Pittsburgh Steelers in the Akron Rubber Bowl. Coach Brown sent Jim Brown into the game to run a draw play. The rookie running back later recalled, "I broke free for a long run and a touchdown."

After the touchdown, he came back to the sidelines. As he sat on the bench, Coach Brown walked up and matter-of-factly said, "You're my fullback." Then he turned and walked away.

Jim Brown sat on the bench, stunned. His coach's words kept replaying over and over in his mind: "You're my fullback . . . You're my fullback."

That game was in August 1957. The years 1957 through 1970 became known as "The Jim Brown Era" of the Cleveland Browns. During those years, Jim Brown racked up

12,312 yards rushing, averaging 5.2 yards per carry, for 126 touchdowns. And throughout those years, and in the decades that followed, the words of coach Paul Brown continued to echo in his thoughts: "You're my fullback."

"Those words," Jim Brown told sportswriter Terry Pluto. "I'll never forget them. He told me that I was his fullback, and then never said another word about it."[1]

That's the power all coaches have to make a difference in the lives of the performance of their players. It's the power of empowerment.

Players Who Run Through Walls

NFL coach Jimmy Johnson (who won Super Bowls XXVII and XXVIII coaching the Dallas Cowboys) expressed his philosophy of empowerment this way: "Treat a person as he is, and he will remain as he is. Treat him as he *could* be, and he will become what he *should* be."[2]

In a 1992 profile of Jimmie Johnson in *Sports Illustrated*, sportswriter Ed Hinton recounted the story of how Jimmy Johnson empowered one of his rookie players the first day of a Cowboys minicamp:

> Rookie cornerback Clayton Holmes, a third-round draft choice out of little Carson-Newman College, was walking meekly off the Cowboy practice field, obviously awed by his surroundings. "Hey, Clayton, I saw you doing some really good things out there," said Johnson, out of the blue, from his seat on a bench near the locker-room entrance. Holmes looked up, surprised that Johnson even knew his name.
>
> "Got a lot to learn, Coach," said Holmes.
>
> "We think you can play here. We like you."
>
> Well, you should have seen Holmes's face.
>
> Now," Johnson [said later], "how was he going to know he really can make this team unless somebody told him?"[3]

Hinton interviewed Michael Irvin, then in his fifth year with the Cowboys and his fourth season under Jimmy Johnson. Irvin's impression of Johnson? "He'll sit there and listen—I mean, really listen," the Hall of Fame wide receiver said. "You know he's in your corner, no matter how the media caves in on you. It takes the load off. Then when you go on the field and the man says, 'I want you to run down there, catch that ball and run into that wall,' who are you to say no? You say, 'Okay, Coach, you were there for me, and now I'm going to give it up for you.' And you run into the wall."[4]

Another player who used to run through walls for his coach was Giants outside linebacker Lawrence Taylor. The coach in question: Bill Parcells. On a Monday night game in New York against the Saints, November 28, 1988, L.T. tore a pectoral muscle in his right shoulder—and kept right on playing. With every play, every hit, that muscle tore a little more and hurt a lot worse.

Taylor repeatedly went to the sidelines for treatment, and the network cameras frequently cut away to show him grimacing in pain as he was taped up and fitted with a harness to keep his shoulder in place. L.T. knew that the Giants defense desperately needed him. With quarterback Phil Simms sidelined, Parcells was forced to rely on two struggling backup quarterbacks to keep the offense going. If the defense collapsed, then this late-season game, with major playoff implications, would certainly be lost.

The Giants' entire season now rested on Lawrence Taylor's shoulders—and one of those shoulders was in excruciating pain while being literally torn apart. Yet even with only one good shoulder, Taylor was playing like a man possessed. In that game, he got three sacks, forced two fumbles, batted down a pass, and collected seven tackles.

Sportswriter Dave Anderson of the *New York Times* marveled that Lawrence Taylor played brilliantly and effectively "with an injury that would prevent some people from combing their hair."[5] Taylor and the Giants hung on, preventing the Saints from reaching the red zone even once that night. When time expired, the Giants had won 13-12.

After the game, as Lawrence Taylor headed for the trainer's room, Coach Parcells stopped him and put his forehead against L.T.'s forehead. Standing apart from the other players, coaches, and sportswriters, where no one else could hear, Parcells spoke a few private words to his wounded linebacker. L.T. smiled, nodded, murmured a brief reply, and then went on into the trainer's room.

Years later, Taylor described that brief conversation. The coach simply told Taylor, "You were great tonight."

And Taylor replied, "I don't know how I made it."

Reflecting on that exchange, Taylor once said, "That was probably the only time that Bill Parcells actually came up to me after the game and told me that I was great. We've always had this thing where Bill doesn't have to tell me I'm playing well. ... That was a big moment for me."[6]

Empowered to Win

I never cease to be amazed at how a simple word of affirmation, praise, or thanks can mean so much to a player or an employee. This profound truth was brought home to me by Gene Conley.

Back in the 1950s and 1960s, Conley spent 11 seasons pitching for the Phillies, Braves, and Red Sox. In the off-season, the 6'9" Conley was a backup center for the Boston Celtics, behind Bill Russell. Gene now lives in Clermont, near Orlando, and is a big Magic fan. I once had lunch with him, and we discussed baseball, basketball, and life. During our talk, I said, "Gene, of all the managers and coaches you played for, who do you remember best?"

"Eddie Sawyer," he said instantly. Sawyer managed the Phillies in 1948 to 1952 and 1958 to 1960; he passed away in 1997.

"What made Eddie Sawyer so memorable?" I asked.

"Kindness. Eddie was the kindest man I ever pitched for."

"Do you have an Eddie Sawyer story to share with me?"

"Oh, sure—but you'll have to excuse me, because I always get emotional when I tell it."

"I'd love to hear it, Gene."

"Well," he began, "back in 1959, the Phillies were playing a doubleheader with the Cardinals. It was bottom of the ninth, and I was in the bullpen. The Cardinals had two on and two out with Stan Musial coming up to bat. Eddie went out to the mound and removed the pitcher, and he waved to me. I was pitching."

I could hear the emotion in Gene's voice. "What happened?" I asked.

"Well, I struck out Stan Musial," Gene said. "We won. I was walking off the field and Eddie was standing in the dugout. He shook my hand and said, 'Thanks a lot, Gene. I appreciate that.'" He picked up the table napkin and dabbed at his eyes.

I waited for the rest of the story—but there was no more. That *was* the whole story. That was why Gene Conley got choked up: A handshake and a thank-you from Eddie Sawyer.

Then it came to me like a revelation—that was a *profound* story! Forty-five seconds after Eddie Sawyer spoke those words, he probably forgot all about it. But Gene Conley remembered those words *45 years later*—and he got teary-eyed and emotional over it.

It doesn't take much for a coach or a leader to have a huge impact on his players. A pat on the back, a handshake, a word of thanks—any gracious gesture can make an impression that lasts all season, and even for a lifetime. It takes so little to empower your players and build their confidence, and any act of affirmation can mean so much.

One of the most colorful and controversial coaches in college basketball history is Bobby Knight. He was head coach at West Point (1965-1971), Indiana (1971-2000), and Texas Tech (2001-2008). The quick-tempered Coach Knight is famed for his combative encounters with refs and reporters. What is less known is that Bobby Knight has always run a clean program, and over his 43-year career, he has never been sanctioned by the NCAA for recruiting violations. Bobby has always been intensely committed to the education of his players, and the percentage of Knight-coached players who graduate is significantly higher than the national average. He has also generously donated thousands of dollars to Texas Tech, especially the school's library fund.

In their book *Bob Knight: The Unauthorized Biography*, Steve Delsohn and Mark Heisler relate an incident that gives us a glimpse into a side of Bobby Knight that might surprise a few people. It's the story of Steve Alford, who played at Indiana. Delsohn and Heisler noted that people who knew Alford believed that the player "had suffered more at Knight's hands and was more angry about it than he cared to admit in public. Nevertheless, Alford also ached for Knight's approval." Steve Alford later wrote about playing basketball for Coach Knight, and Delsohn and Heisler recorded this incident in Alford's own words:

> During a lull, [wrote Alford] I looked around for Coach Knight. I finally spotted him sitting calmly in a folding chair with his sons, Patrick and Tim, beside him. I guess he could be calm; it was his third championship, our first.
>
> He waved me over and sat me down on his right. He put his arm around me and leaned toward my ear. "I want you to know, Steve, that I really appreciate all that you've done since you've been here. You've gotten everything you could out of your ability."
>
> I had tears in my eyes and I think he had tears in his. We both knew what the moment signified; the end of our relationship as player and coach. ...

He gave me a little squeeze. "Steve," he said, "I've never been prouder of a player than I am of you."

I had waited for years to hear that. It was worth the wait.[7]

That's the power of empowering words. It doesn't take much to make a player feel valued and confident: "Thank you." "I'm proud of you." "I appreciate your effort." You don't have to gush or overdo it. But if one of your player's has earned a pat on the back, make sure he gets one.

Nobody does this better than Rich DeVos, who (along with his family) owns the Orlando Magic. Rich and his partner Jay Van Andel started the Amway Corporation in 1959 with approximately $49 in operating capital they had pooled between them. Today, Amway is a worldwide enterprise, a $7.5 billion company.

When asked what his duties are with the company, Rich replies, "I'm the head cheerleader." That's what he's done for half a century—touring the world, speaking to employees and distributors, and cheering them on: "I'm so proud of you! Couldn't do it without you!" He makes you feel like a million bucks, like you could take on the world. He sends out many handwritten notes of encouragement. I have two of them framed on my wall.

As a coach, you have the same job: You're the head cheerleader for your players. Your goal is to empower your players to perform at the peak of their collective and synergistic ability. A fully empowered team is comprised of players who are:

- Publicly and privately praised for their accomplishments
- Boldly confident and optimistic
- Trusted and expected to exercise initiative and leadership
- Willing to take calculated risks for big returns
- Well-trained and well-prepared
- Adequately equipped with the resources to be successful
- Intensely committed to the team and to winning

If your players are empowered in these seven ways, then your team is ready to take on the world.

Empower Your Coaching Staff

Former Buccaneers head coach Jon Gruden recalls when he was a graduate assistant coach at the University of Tennessee under head coach Johnny Majors. During a home game against Auburn, Gruden noticed that Auburn's free safety was playing shallow against UT's play-action passes on crossing routes. He was sure that Tennessee's speediest receiver, Terence Cleveland, could beat Auburn's free safety to the post. So, he passed a note to offensive coordinator Walt Harris which read: "DP8 Go? Check the post" (shorthand for "Draw-Pass 8 Go and look for the post route"). Harris took Gruden's suggestion and called the play. Sure enough, Terence Cleveland outran the safety and made the catch for a huge gain.

Gruden recalls what happened the following day when the coaches gathered to watch game film:

> The moment the big pass to Terence appeared on the screen, my heart started beating fast with anticipation. "That's a good call, Walt," Coach Majors said. "That's a good job." I would have been satisfied if it ended right there, but then Coach Harris said, "Jon called that." Coach Majors walked over to where I was sitting, gave me a pat on the back and said, "Attaboy!" That was a highlight of my career. That was one of the greatest days of my life.
>
> I'll never forget Walt for giving me credit on that play. There are a lot of people in his position who wouldn't have done that.[8]

Jeff Turner was a 6'9" center at Vanderbilt University who went on to a 10-year career in the NBA with the New Jersey Nets and the Orlando Magic. After retiring from the game, Jeff went into broadcasting. After the death of our mutual friend Chuck Daly, I asked Jeff to share some remembrances of Chuck. Jeff told me this story:

"The Orlando Magic hired Chuck Daly in 1997. I had retired two seasons prior as a player, and had joined the Magic's radio broadcast team as the color analyst. My position put me at every practice, on the team plane, and courtside to watch one of the most fascinating men to ever work an NBA sideline. When I think of Chuck Daly, I think about the way he related to his staff and to those of us on the periphery of the team. There was never any doubt as to who was in charge, yet Chuck had a humorous and relaxed way of communicating with his staff and empowering us all to be our best.

"I remember one particular game in the middle of a long road trip. The Magic were not playing with energy or focus. Coach Daly used several timeouts to try to get the team revved up, to no avail. He prowled the sidelines in frustration. He made offensive adjustments, defensive adjustments, changed line-ups out on the floor, but nothing worked.

"During one possession, the clock expired before the Magic could get off a shot. In exasperation, Daly turned to his coaching staff and said, 'Okay, all you geniuses! Give me something! You all want to sit here in my seat, but it's hot up here!'

"Later that evening, I had dinner with some of the assistant coaches and we all shared a good laugh about the incident. Some of the coaches recalled other 'Chuckisms'—funny lines Coach Daly used that had a serious point to them.

"Several years later, I left broadcasting for a new challenge, accepting a position as an administrator in charge of leadership development and head boy's basketball coach at Lake Highland Preparatory School in Orlando. During my first game as head coach, Coach Daly's line came back to me: 'You all want to sit here in my seat, but it's hot up here!' Suddenly, I knew what it was like to sit in Coach Daly's hot seat—and that line wasn't funny anymore.

"I had a dozen young men looking up at me, expecting quick decisions, inspiring words to lift them up after a mistake, or that special play to boost their confidence and start them on a much-needed scoring run. That's when I realized I had never learned to think like a head coach before. I was like an assistant coach who focuses on individual players, or on defensive strategy or offensive strategy. But I was a head coach now, and my job required me to see the *big picture*—but I couldn't see it!

"That's when I understood what Chuck Daly had been trying to tell all of his 'geniuses.' None of us realized how hot it really was in the hot seat. Chuck understood that his assistants needed to start thinking like head coaches. That was his way of challenging them to think bigger, and to begin preparing themselves for the day when they would lead their own teams.

"Chuck Daly used to call me 'Left Hander.' He probably didn't realize how closely this player-turned-broadcaster was watching him, listening to him, and trying to learn from him. Even though it took a couple of years for the lesson to sink in, 'Left Hander' was listening—and learning. With practice, I got more comfortable in the hot seat, and I quickly began applying the many lessons I had learned while observing Chuck Daly. I count myself fortunate that I had the rare opportunity to watch and learn from such a great teacher.

"Thanks, Chuck. It's still hot in this coach's hot seat, but your teaching and your example have made the heat a little more bearable."

Those are instructive words from Jeff Turner. As a leader, as a coach, always keep in mind that you're not just coaching players. You're coaching your staff. You're coaching your other coaches. Your goal is to help them grow wiser, smarter, and stronger in their profession. Help them to see the big picture as well as their own little corner of the canvas. Empower them to fulfill their potential and their destiny as coaches in their own right.

Some Empowerment Tips

As a coach, always seek to create an environment where everyone in the organization becomes an empowerer of everyone else. It's crucial that empowerment not only flow from the head c oach down, but from coaches to coaches, staffers to staffers, and players to players. In a healthy, winning organization, everyone empowers everyone else. It's habitual. It's second nature. It's part of the organization's culture. An attitude of empowerment begins at the top, and should pervade every corner of the organization.

Denis Potvin is a retired hockey defenseman who served as team captain of the NHL's New York Islanders during the 1980s. He was a key factor in the Islanders' four Stanley Cup championships during his career. The first of those championships was the toughest—and the sweetest.

The Islanders had struggled for most of the 1979-1980 season, but they came down the stretch with a 12-game winning streak. They battled their way through the playoffs and earned the team's first Stanley Cup championship by defeating the Philadelphia Flyers in an overtime period of game six, May 24, 1980.

At the end of that game, Denis Potvin skated into the pile of his teammates, who were whooping and congratulating each other in the middle of the rink. In the midst of the wild celebration, Potvin turned and saw head coach Al Arbour skating up behind him. Potvin reached out and the two men embraced—then Coach Arbour spoke in his ear, so only he could hear, "Denis, make sure you let the other guys carry the cup."

"I was very impressed," Potvin later recalled. "He was still thinking about his players even though the Stanley Cup had just been won—his first time as a coach."[9]

That's a coach who understands the importance of empowerment. Moreover, he knows that empowerment doesn't just flow from the top down, but needs to flow outward in all directions, from one player to another. So, set an example of empowering others, and encourage your coaches, staffers, players, concessionaires, and janitors to follow your example.

Here are some additional tips for building a culture of empowerment in your organization:

Use praise sparingly. The great coaches don't lavish praise on every little thing a player does. When praise is dished out promiscuously, it quickly becomes meaningless. But when praise is used sparingly, then any little word of thanks or affirmation can have an enormous impact.

Lavishing too much praise on a player also tends to make that player lazy and complacent. If you praise a player when he is only giving 10 or 20 percent, what is left to say when you want to get 110 percent out of him? And if you give a player an easy assignment then praise him when he effortlessly accomplishes it, your praise will seem like an insult—as if you are treating him like a child (which, in fact, you are).

If a player gives you 110 percent, by all means, let him know it. Short of that, he's just doing his job.

Praise effort, not talent. Talent is unearned; it's a gift. Athletes can't help it if they are gifted. But they have total control over the effort they put out. A second-stringer who delivers maximum effort deserves far more praise than a star player who achieves the same results without breaking a sweat.

Praise performance and execution, not points on the scoreboard. If your team goes all-out, executes well, carries out assignments, makes few mental mistakes, and perseveres through adversity, then give them their due, even if they come up a few points short. No team should ever be complacent about losing, but no team should ever feel ashamed to lose if they did everything they could to win. Never berate a team that left every drop of sweat and blood on the field of competition. And never praise a team that fumbled and stumbled its way to a lucky win.

Praise players for being unselfish and for thinking "team first." The player who made the crowd-pleasing tomahawk jam already got his affirmation from the people in the stands. But what about the player whose unselfish assist made it all possible? He could probably use a high five or two from his teammates and a "good job" from his coach. See that he gets it.

Don't be too quick to take out a player when he's struggling. Instead, call a timeout, talk to him, help him settle down and rebuild his confidence, then let him work his way back into the game. Whatever you do, don't say anything to tear down his confidence or make him feel pressured and panicked. Players get "into the zone" when they are relaxed and confident. Pour on the pressure and condemnation, and all you've got is a rattled player.

Tell others how good your players are. Sometimes the best way to empower a player is to talk about him behind his back. Imagine how that player will feel when someone goes to him and says, "Do you know what your coach just told me?" When praise comes to a player by a roundabout means, it often carries more impact than if you praised that player directly.

If you plant the right words with the right people, you can bet it will get back to your players. And do you know what the result will be? That player will have to start working *twice* as hard to live up to your praise! A sincere but strategically targeted word of affirmation can be the best way to challenge your players to step up their effort and commitment.

Coach John Wooden made sure he planted words of affirmation where it would have the greatest impact: with the news media. He observed:

> Every single member of your team needs to feel wanted and appreciated. If they are on the team, they *deserve* to be valued and to feel valued. Do you want someone on the team who doesn't feel necessary and appreciated? How do they find out unless you let them know?
>
> Right after each UCLA basketball game, there would be a press conference with representatives from all the media. I could predict what questions they would ask and which players they wanted to interview.
>
> I always tried to use this opportunity to praise those individuals the media would overlook. I would say, "When I put so-and-so in just before the half and he made that steal, it quite possibly could have been the turning point in the game." I wanted to let other players know they were very important to the team. … I tried to let them know they were important, that they were valued. All members of the team are important.[10]

Coach John Wooden knew how to empower his players to win championships. Empowering *all* of his players at *every* level was a key element in his success. It just might be the key to your success as well.

Empower to Win

Empowerment is about winning. The goal of empowering your players is not merely to make them feel good about themselves. Your goal is to motivate them to deliver the maximum performance, effort, perseverance, and commitment of which they are capable.

Perhaps the greatest empowerer in the history of sports was Vince Lombardi, head coach of the Green Bay Packers. He took over a team that had a 1-10-1 record and quickly transformed them into champions. In 1960, just two years after that embarrassing season, Lombardi coached them to the NFL championship game. It was a battle of the titans, the Packers versus the Eagles, played the day after Christmas 1960 at the University of Pennsylvania's Franklin Field—and it was the Packers' first appearance in an NFL title game since 1944.

I was there that day, a 20-year-old junior in college, home for Christmas break. My dad had gotten tickets for the two of us, and we had driven from Wilmington to Philadelphia for the game. I remember it like it was yesterday. It was a cold day with snow on the ground, but the sky was clear—great football weather. The rabid Philly sports fans were screaming their lungs out.

In those days, nobody had a sense of who the Green Bay Packers were, nor how they were about to dominate the NFL for years to come. Nobody knew anything about Vince Lombardi or Bart Starr. The only truly famous Packer was Paul Hornung, who was a great running back for Notre Dame and was the number one pick overall in the 1957 NFL draft. But the Philly fans (myself included) saw the Packers as a perennial laughingstock team from the hinterlands of Wisconsin who had somehow lucked into the NFL championship game. We all figured the Eagles would blow them out and quickly send them packing back to Green Bay.

The game began, and the fans immediately saw that they had underestimated Vince Lombardi and his team. Over the course of the game, the Packers outgained the Eagles 401 yards to 296, and made 22 first downs versus 13 Eagles first downs. It all came down to the Packers' final drive in the waning seconds of the game. The Packers trailed 17-13. Quarterback Bart Starr completed a pass to fullback Jim Taylor from the Eagles 22 and seemed destined to score—and win.

My dad and I were high in the stands, and the action took place right in front of us. I had a good view of Taylor as he battered his way into the Eagles secondary, twisted out of the grasp of Eagles defensive back Bobby Jackson, and turned toward the end zone, just 10 yards away.

Just then, Eagles linebacker Chuck Bednarik blocked Taylor's path, wrapped his arms around Taylor's shoulders, wrestled him to the turf at the nine-yard line—then stayed atop Taylor while the clock wound down, denying the Packers time to run another play. Though Philadelphia fans celebrated, it was a bitter loss for the Packers.

Years later, I read about what took place in the Packers locker room after the game. Lombardi gathered his players. The air was heavy with gloom and frustration. The Packers had gone from the basement to the pinnacle of the league to compete for a championship—but had fallen just a few yards and a few seconds short.

Lombardi didn't intend to leave his players in that trough of despair. "Before this game," he said, "you may not have realized that you could have even won this game. Some of you doubted that a championship was even possible. But I don't think there's any doubt in your mind now. And that's why you will win it all next year. This will never happen again. You will never lose another championship."[11]

And the Packers never lost another championship game while Vince Lombardi was their coach. The following year, the Packers again played for a championship—and they made a resounding statement, defeating the New York Giants 37-0. It was the first of five NFL championships the Packers would win under his leadership.

Winning begins with empowerment. And empowerment begins with you, the coach of your team, the leader of your organization. You are the one who puts the *pow* in empowerment.

15

Unity of Purpose, Diversity of Skills

©John Pyle/Icon SMI/ZUMA Press

Following a stellar career with the Detroit Pistons, Isiah Thomas went on to become a part owner and general manager of the expansion Toronto Raptors, then he joined Bob Costas in the broadcast booth for NBC. In 1999, shortly before embarking on a new career as a head coach in the NBA, Isaiah Thomas talked to Mike Wise of the *New York Times* about what makes a championship team.

"Building and becoming a champion is an awful, awful lot of hard work," he said. "Going from 40 wins to 50 wins is a delicate balance. Trying to get from 50 wins to the championship, that's chemistry and balancing. It's not talent that takes you there, believe me. It's chemistry."

Asked to assess the talent and chemistry of the New York Knicks, a team that later hired him as president of basketball operations, Thomas explained his theory as to why the Knicks were about to miss the playoffs for the first time in a dozen years: "Though it may be a talented team, the chemistry is not working. ... The most important thing is chemistry on any team. To me, talent is not as important as chemistry. You've got to find a group of individuals committed and willing to work together. Then you can start identifying the proper talent."[1]

That is an insightful statement. One of the keys to winning, whether in sports, business, the military, or any other endeavor, is an elusive quality called "chemistry." And the key to good chemistry is a delicate and seemingly paradoxical balance of qualities I call "unity of purpose, diversity of skills."

On every great team, you will generally find paired opposites of personality types, skills, and areas of specialization. To have a well-balanced team, you need some leaders and some followers. You need some stellar slam-dunkers and some unselfish role-players. You need some players with size, some with speed, some with power, and some with finesse.

Yet all of these diverse skills, talents, abilities, attributes, and personalities must be focused on a single goal, a unified purpose: *Winning as a team*. All of your players have to be willing to set their own egos aside in order to serve the team. All of these high-flying talents must be taught to fly in formation. When you've got a well-rounded, well-balanced blend of personalities who relate well to each other, complement each other, and trust each other, you've got *chemistry*—and you've got a *team*.

Be Ready to Go to War

Every team must have diversity. But team unity is the glue that binds your diverse players together into a single force with a single purpose. A team that is diverse but lacks unity will probably rattle apart.

Sports is a realm that brings together not only people of diverse talent and ability, but people of diverse viewpoints, beliefs, and ethnicities. The world of sports, then, becomes a microcosm for what the world could and should be—a place where diversity is celebrated in the midst of an atmosphere of unity and singleness of purpose. As Bill Russell recalled from his days with the Celtics, "There were Jews, Catholics, Protestants, agnostics, white men, black men. The one thing we had in common was an Irish name. The Celtics."[2]

Every team should look like that—diverse yet unified. That's how America should look. That's how the world should look. Such a world would be a utopia.

John Wooden expressed his vision of unity of purpose, diversity of skills, in his book *Wooden: A Lifetime of Observations and Reflections On and Off the Court*:

> We all fit into different niches. Each of us must make the effort to contribute to the best of our ability according to our own individual talents. And then we put all the individual talents together for the highest good of the group.
>
> Thus, I valued a player who cared for others and could lose himself in the group for the good of the group. I believe that quality makes for an outstanding player. It is also why the best players don't always make the best team. I mean by this that a gifted player, or players, who are not *team* players will ultimately hurt the team, whether it revolves around basketball or business.
>
> Understanding that the good of the group comes first is fundamental to being a highly productive member of a *team*.[3]

Sometimes, the chemistry-killer on a team is that one individual who refuses to put team first, who refuses to play by the rules of teamwork. He won't respect his teammates—or his coaches. He ridicules ideas and resists coaching. He puts his teammates down in order to inflate his own ego. Sometimes, you can bring such individuals around by reminding them of the need for unity and cohesion and teamwork. But if you can't get his attention with a warning or two, it's time to cut him loose—regardless of how much talent he may have. Talent is useless if it serves a single ego instead of the entire team.

Brandon Marshall of the University of Central Florida was the 119th overall pick in the fourth round of the 2006 NFL draft. Selected by the Denver Broncos, Marshall was mentored by the great Broncos receiver Rod Smith (849 receptions, 11,389 receiving yards, 70 career touchdowns, two Super Bowl rings—XXXII and XXXIII).

"Marshall had his share of legal troubles in his early time with the Broncos, [so] it appeared Smith would be good for the kid," sportswriter Brian Howell wrote. "The Broncos hoped Smith would be a mentor to Marshall, and he was. … [Smith] became great by showing up to work every day for 14 years, not caring about his personal statistics and always putting the team ahead of himself."

In Marshall's first three seasons in the NFL, he gained a reputation as a formidable wide receiver who could regularly break tackles for extra yardage after the catch. Rod Smith, the top receiver in Broncos history, was a good role model and helped keep Marshall on the straight and narrow. After Rod Smith retired, however, Marshall seemed to come off the rails.

Brandon Marshall's troubles included assorted minor scrapes with the law and a three-game league suspension (later reduced to a single game). Marshall missed the Broncos 2009 exhibition opener against the 49ers because he had to stand trial for a misdemeanor battery charge regarding the alleged beating of his then-girlfriend (he was acquitted).

Openly resentful toward the Broncos new head coach Josh McDaniels (who replaced Mike Shanahan in 2009), Marshall began agitating for a trade or a new contract. He punctuated his demands with rebellious behavior during practice sessions. He refused to learn the new playbook. During one late-August practice, Marshall dogged it during warm-ups, walking instead of running with the rest of the team. He swatted down a pass that was thrown to him, and then punted the ball away instead of handing it to the ball boy. Video clips of Marshall's antics were broadcast on national TV.

The Broncos responded by suspending Brandon Marshall for the rest of the preseason. Howell wrote:

> It is a sad story about Marshall, whose desire to become the next Terrell Owens or Chad Ochocinco has gotten in the way of him becoming something greater—such as the next Rod Smith. … Marshall has elected to take the trail blazed by Owens and Ochocinco, the poster boys for malcontent, diva receivers.
>
> Oh, those two have put up big numbers. There's no denying their talent. Owens and Ochocinco also have got a grand total of zero championship rings and are better known for killing team chemistry and concocting creative touchdown celebrations than they are for being winners.[4]

When assembling your team, talent is important, but great talent combined with a chemistry-killing personality can destroy team unity—and it can cost you games and championships. Former baseball manager Whitey Herzog says it's crucially important to choose players who contribute to good team chemistry—and that's especially true of your role players, your second string, your backups. "You'd better pick your bench right," he observes. "You want good guys who are willing to sit, pinch-hit, and play roles, and who don't think they should be playing every day. ... They know they've got a job, but they ain't going to play unless somebody gets hurt. That son of a gun who thinks he should be out there when you know he can't—brother, that's when [you've got problems]."[5]

Your goal as coach is to assemble a cohesive group of people at all levels, from stars to role players, who represent a diversity of abilities and personalities, while sharing an absolute unity of vision and purpose. Once you have achieved that precarious balance, you've got chemistry. You've got a team of players, each a specialist in his own role, ready to go to war for each other—and for you.

How to Encourage Unity

In an article on his website, Joe Haefner, co-founder of Breakthrough Basketball, pointed out something about Duke head basketball coach Mike Krzyzewski that I never noticed before. Haefner writes:

> Have you ever watched a Duke game and noticed what happens if there is a Duke player on the ground after a dead ball?
>
> Every single Duke player on the floor runs to the player on the ground and helps him up. I'm certain that Coach K ingrains this into his players from day one and it's important that you do too.
>
> How does this help your team? It builds team unity.[6]

There will be times when a team's unity is severely tested, when adversity will pit one player against another or one squad against another. The UCLA Bruins football team experienced just this kind of adversity in 2008.

During that season, UCLA had the fourth-best defense in the Pac-10 and the eighth-best offense. The team finished the season with a decidedly lackluster 4-8 record. Head coach Rick Neuheisel empathized with the frustration felt by the players on the defensive squad. The defense put forth a strong effort, but that effort didn't result in wins.

"I think it's a very tough pill to swallow if you're a defensive football player," Coach Neuheisel said. "I think that they are proud of their own efforts, and they also understand that the offensive guys come to work every day and try as hard as they can. ... It's a tough thing to continue to come into the locker room and allow the team [spirit] to still flourish without a measure of divisiveness. And that's the biggest lesson and the biggest challenge for us."

Coach Neuheisel has worked hard to maintain a spirit of team unity even through adversity. That spirit is expressed by then-senior wide receiver Marcus Everett. "We are all one team," he said. "We practice separately, [but] we win or lose together, so we [have] to stick together."[7]

How do you encourage unity on your team and keep all of your players focused on the goal? Let me suggest to you five keys to building and maintaining team unity:

Keep your team focused on the team vision. Keep reminding your players of the purpose and the goals they share. Remind them that they are to set selfishness aside, sacrifice their egos, and work together to achieve one purpose: *winning*. Teams rattle apart when players lose sight of their purpose together. To keep your team unified, remind them again and again to keep their eyes on the prize.

Maintain healthy communication. Let your players know that your door is always open. Better yet, take the door off its hinges. Maintain good communications from coach to players, coach to coaches, and from players to players. Be transparent in all your communication with your team, and expect transparency from your players. Get to know your players, and find ways to encourage them to get to know, trust, and communicate well with one another. Clear, continual communication is essential to team unity.

Resolve conflict. Don't be afraid of conflict. Don't avoid it. Face it and resolve it. Conflict can be a positive force for change and growth on a team. When your coaching staff and players express strong opinions and strong disagreements with each other about important issues, it shows that everyone is intensely committed to winning. Let people air their opinions and contend strongly for them. If you are the coach in charge, then make sure that you have the final say and that everyone in your organization buys into your program, whether they agree or not.

Put an end to gossip and backbiting. Conflict must be resolved in an open and healthy way, not through back channels and undermining one another. Spreading rumors about coaches and players should be treated as a matter for discipline and even dismissal. You can't have a unified team if even one person is undermining others on the team.

Maintain team discipline. Don't allow star players to get away with behavior that you would not accept from a bench player. Treat all players alike in matters of discipline. When coaches show favoritism, players become demoralized and bitter. Their motivation sags. They lose interest in the shared goal, because they do not believe that the sacrifice is equally shared. Fairness helps produce team unity.

A Badge of Unity

In Chapter 2, we saw how Lou Holtz, when he took over as head coach of the Notre Dame fighting Irish in 1986, removed his players' names from their jerseys. He did this to get his players to stop focusing on their own egos and start thinking about the unity of the team.

But Mike Leach, former head coach of the Texas Tech Red Raiders football team, takes a different view. Widely considered one of the most creative and innovative offensive strategists in NCAA football, Leach spent nine seasons at Texas Tech—and all of his seasons were winning ones. Leach says:

> I don't know whether having or not having a name on the back of a jersey is going to solve any unity problems. If a player is self-absorbed to the point where having his name on the jersey is that big of a distraction, he probably has other problems he needs to address. Keeping players focused on the team is important. We have the names on the jerseys. We don't have any problem with it. But we don't just put the names on jerseys of the good players. We put the bad players' names on, too. The most important name to play for is the one on the front of the jersey.[8]

So there you have it, two very different perspectives from two very successful NCAA football coaches. Each view makes a lot of sense. Take your pick.

Normally, your goal as coach is to unify your team around your vision and shared purpose, your commitment to winning. But sometimes, teams unify around deeper issues, even matters of life and death. So it was with the University of Texas at Austin baseball team in 2007.

The Longhorns have a tradition as one of the best baseball programs in the nation, having made more trips to the College World Series than any other school in the nation. UT-Austin has won the College World Series in 1949, 1950, 1975, 1983, 2002, and 2005. Winning championships is important to the Longhorns.

But in 2007, when the mother of senior utility infielder Clay Van Hook was diagnosed with cancer and began undergoing chemotherapy, Clay and his teammates suddenly had an even more important cause to root for than winning baseball games.

One day, Clay showed up for practice with his head shaved. When his teammates asked him about it, he explained that he and his dad had gotten their heads shaved in support of his mom. Since she was losing her hair to chemotherapy, they adopted the cueball look themselves as a display of family solidarity.

Clay didn't plan to start a trend on the team. But when Clay explained the reason for his shiny dome to his two roommates, Todd Gilfillan and Randy Boone, they told him, "Tell your mom we're shaving our heads, too." As the week went by, more and more of Clay's teammates showed up at practice with shaved heads, until finally the entire team was shorn.

"It means a lot," Clay said, "for the guys on the team to do this for me because, as you probably know, they love their hair a lot. … We're a baseball team, but we're best friends too."

Watching his mother go through chemotherapy has changed Clay Van Hook's outlook on life and even his outlook on baseball. Once, when he was going through a slump and feeling down, he called his mom to complain about his problems. Then he asked how her day was—and she told him what it was like to go through chemotherapy.

That put Clay's problems into perspective. He realized, "Wow, this isn't that big of a deal. … If I go 0-for-4, I can just call her up and feel better. She's as positive as can be. It's a great thing to see how it has changed the lives of everyone connected to her."[9]

Clay's mother's battle with cancer has impacted the entire team. Clay and his teammates became bonded more tightly together by shaved heads and a shared purpose. What was initially a symbol of support for the mother of one teammate has become a bald badge of unity for the entire Longhorns team.

Everyone on your team is different. No two players are alike, and that's how it should be. Diversity of skills and abilities, diversity of personalities and strengths—these differences are vitally important to the making of a well-rounded team. There is a great strength in diversity—but that strength can only be harnessed when your team is unified, focused on one goal, committed to one purpose.

16

There's No Substitute for Talent

©Julian H. Gonzalez/Detroit Free Press/ZUMA Press

The 1984 NBA Draft was a jackpot of talent. It included four players later listed (by a blue ribbon panel of players, coaches, sports execs, and journalists) among the 50 Greatest Players in NBA History: Michael Jordan, Charles Barkley, Hakeem Olajuwon, and John Stockton. All four have been inducted into the Basketball Hall of Fame. And even the second tier of players in the 1984 draft represented an unusually strong roster of talent.

I was general manager of the Philadelphia 76ers then, and we were fortunate enough to land Charles Barkley, the self-proclaimed "Round Mound of Rebound." My friend Dr. Jack Ramsay, who gave me my start in the NBA, was coaching the Portland Trail Blazers at the time.

Everyone knew that Hakeem Olajuwon, a dominating 7'0" center from Nigeria, was going to be the number one pick, hands down. Dr. Jack and the Blazers' management group had either a number one or number two pick in the draft, depending on a coin toss. They needed a center. If Portland won the flip, they'd take Olajuwon. If they lost the flip, they'd take Sam Bowie, a 7'1" center from Kentucky.

The Houston Rockets won the coin toss and took Olajuwon. As planned, the Blazers took Bowie. The third pick went to the Chicago Bulls, who selected Michael Jordan—and the rest is NBA history. Years later, Dr. Jack ruefully reflected:

> Had I known how good Jordan was, I would have lobbied hard to select him. The coaches don't have a chance to see enough college and international competition to form solid opinions on player talent. They rely on the team's personnel director and scouts to apprise them of the ability of those in the draft. While NBA scouts all agreed that Jordan was a good player, I hadn't heard anyone say that he was going to be as great as he became. During our pre-draft meetings, none of the Blazers' scouting personnel recommended that we select him.
>
> Kevin Loughery, Jordan's first NBA coach, told me later that the Bulls would have done the same thing as Portland had the positions been reversed. Loughery said he was stunned to see how good Jordan was in the first workouts his team had that season. The basketball world was soon to discover the same thing. I often think about the pleasure it would have been to coach Michael and the impact he would have had on the Portland teams.[1]

Let's face it: The title I have selected for this chapter is an out-and-out cliché: "There's no substitute for talent." Shove a microphone in the face of a coach after a big game, and there's a good chance you'll hear him say, "There's no substitute for talent." If his team has just lost, that will be his excuse for losing: His star talent was sidelined, his bench couldn't get the job done, and (groan!) there's no substitute for talent.

But if his team has just won, he'll praise his star players, hug them and tousle their hair, and shout, "This is the best team I've ever coached! Man, there's no substitute for talent!" It's a cliché—but sayings turn into clichés by being true. And this cliché is as true as it gets.

The Art and Science of Recruiting Good Talent

Rollie Massimino is the men's basketball coach at Northwood University in West Palm Beach, Florida. He also coached the Villanova Wildcats to an NCAA championship in 1985, and is one of only 17 NCAA coaches with more than 500 career wins to his credit.

Massimino served his coaching apprenticeship in the early 1970s as an assistant to Chuck Daly at the University of Pennsylvania, and the two coaches have been friends ever since. After Rollie Massimino took command of the Northwood program in 2006, Chuck became one of his most faithful fans, attending all the Northwood games.

In March 2009, at age 78, Chuck Daly was diagnosed with pancreatic cancer. After Chuck was hospitalized, Rollie visited him every day. And even though Chuck knew that he was dying, and he was growing weaker every day, he would still needle his old friend and former assistant.

"Rollie," Chuck would say, "are you making any phone calls? Have you signed up any good players? Remember, Rollie, we want to be happy after the games."

And Rollie Massimino knew what Coach Daly meant. The only way to feel happy after a game is to win it. And in order to win it, you've got to have good talent on your team. Even on his deathbed, Chuck Daly was reminding Rollie Massimino what it takes to be successful as a coach. There's no substitute for talent.

North Carolina men's basketball coach Roy Williams was inducted into the Basketball Hall of Fame in 2007. As he met with the media two days before the induction ceremony, he stood alongside legendary mentor and predecessor (and fellow Hall of Famer) Dean Smith and briefly described his coaching philosophy. "I got this from Coach Smith," he said. "We both understand it's a game about the players. A Hall of Fame coach is a guy that's had great players. I'm not being humble, I'm just being truthful. Coach Smith told me the players are the most important thing."

The talent of the players is the foundation of any team. If you try to coach a team using all the other 20 principles in this book, but leave out talent, you are doomed to fail. Leadership is important, but it's no substitute for talent. Chemistry is important, but it's no substitute for talent. Character, discipline, preparation, and all the rest—they're all vitally important, but nothing is as fundamental as talent. Yogi Berra put it this way:

When people ask me what makes a good manager, I say two words: good players. More than anything, it's what makes a manager good, because without good players, your results won't be that good. In baseball, a manager can play percentages, play hunches, crunch numbers, and juggle lineups. He can be as good a strategist as a chess master and that's swell. Only he's not the one running, fielding, pitching, throwing, or hitting.

All that strategizing stuff is over-rated. Games are won or lost by how well the players play, not how the manager manages.[2]

And John Wooden, for all his emphasis on character, discipline, preparation, controlling the little things, and on and on, placed a very high premium on talent. He observed: "No matter how you total success in the coaching profession, it all comes down to a single factor: talent. Although not every coach can win consistently with talent, no coach can win without it."[3]

Mike Ditka coached the Chicago Bears and the New Orleans Saints. He took part in the Chicago Bears' last two NFL championships—as a player (tight end) in 1963 and as head coach in 1985 (Super Bowl XX). "Iron Mike" once said, "Don't ever fool yourself about coaches being geniuses. There is no such thing. As great as Bill Walsh was, he was a lot better when he had Joe Montana and Steve Young. The better the players, the better coach you are."[4]

Chuck Mills was head football coach at Wake Forest University from 1973 to 1977. He is noted as a human quote machine, and two of his best-known quotes have to do with the importance of talent. He once said, "Some pray for wisdom. My wisdom comes in praying for big, fast tackles." He also said, "I give the same half-time speech over and over. It works best when my players are better than the other coach's players."[5]

To assemble a winning team, you must choose your players well. You may be stuck with the decision you make for a long time to come, so make sure it's a decision you can live with. The players you choose will wear your uniforms and represent you as their coach. They could enhance your resumé—or sink your career. You have to do your homework, scout prospects thoroughly, watch them play under real-world conditions, and size up not only their talent but their willingness to dig deep and utilize their talent to the best of their ability. It's fine to put a prospect through a workout and check him with a stopwatch—but whenever possible, get some actual game film and watch him in action.

As you research a player, pay attention to warning signs. Listen to your intuition. Any player who throws off a bad vibe (such as a possibly uncoachable attitude or indications of drugs or other self-destructive behavior) could give you a season-long headache. Don't ignore that little voice that says, "Something's not quite right here."

Hiring—And Firing

In sports or in business, knowing whom to fire can be as important as knowing whom to hire. You not only need talented players, but talented coaches. Winning often requires that you make personnel changes on your staff and on your team. Firing staffers and players is the worst part of any coach's job, any leader's job. I've had to fire quite a few people myself, and nothing puts more knots in my stomach than having to tell someone, "We have to let you go."

After playing for the Bears and Eagles, Mike Ditka played four seasons with the Dallas Cowboys under Coach Tom Landry before going on to a coaching career of his own. He once talked about the pain of releasing players:

> When I released defensive lineman Mike Hartenstine after 1986, it broke my heart. But there is a time when it has to happen, and you're the only one who can do it. Nobody teaches you how. I watched Coach Landry do it, and I watched him break down. I'd hear him tell a coach, "I'm keeping this man because he's a better football player, but I'm cutting a man who has so much more character." Oh, it hurt him!
>
> I believe in loyalty. … But you can't move on unless better players replace lesser ones, and the guys you have replace the guys you don't have. Loyalty only goes so far. Character only goes so far. Football is played with talent and speed and mean.[6]

The task of recruiting talented assistants, trainers, and other staffers is almost as important as recruiting talented players. Some coaches, unfortunately, feel threatened by subordinates who are more talented in some area than they are. So they hire less talented assistants in order to make themselves look good by comparison. This is self-defeating behavior.

If you *really* want to look like a brilliant coach, hire brilliant assistants! Hire people who are smarter, more gifted, and more talented in some area than you are. Hire experience and expertise. Hire people who can ably give you advice so you can make better decisions. Lady Volunteers basketball coach Pat Summitt explains:

> The greatest strength a human being can have is to recognize his or her own weaknesses. … I hire people who have qualities I am deficient in. By evaluating my own strengths and weaknesses, I can put people in position to complement me. It means setting aside your ego. But it's a far more sensible way of doing business than to insist on being right all the time.[7]

Chuck Daly coached the Detroit Pistons to back-to-back NBA Championships in 1989 and 1990, and coached the 1992 USA Dream Team to a gold medal. He said, "I always tried to hire people for what I needed at that time. I rarely hired someone I knew very well. I wanted new ideas. I always felt I needed … different personalities at different places."[8]

Getting the Most Out of Your Players' Talent

While there is no substitute for talent, it's possible to rely too heavily on talent alone. Anyone can coach great talent, and get results—for a while. The truly great coaches know how to get results with even modestly talented players. Though you always try to get the most talented players you can, ultimately, you must play the hand you are dealt. You must coach the team you've got. You can't always get the caliber of talent you wish you had, but you have a schedule to play and you have to find a way to win.

Remember, too, that great talent often comes with big headaches. Highly talented players are often narcissistic, temperamental, and difficult to coach. They are typically accustomed to being pampered and fawned over. Again and again, I've seen talented prima donnas undermine their coaches—and even get coaches fired. I've seen coaches endanger their careers and their sanity by trying to coax and cajole a talented-but-undisciplined player to live up to his potential.

Raw talent is unrealized potential. It takes all the other qualities of great coaching and great teams—character, hard work, perseverance, passion—to turn the unrealized potential of raw talent into championships. As former Dolphins coach Don Shula warns, "A lot of coaches have a tendency to stay too long with people with potential. We call them coach killers. As soon as you find out who the coach killers are on your team, the better off you are. You go with the guys who may have lesser talent, but more dedication, more singleness of purpose. You spot them and stick with them because in a big game, they'll win it for you."[9]

Duke's Mike Krzyzewski says that coaches need to find that perfect balance between recruiting top talent and avoiding an overreliance on talent alone. "When you first assemble a group," he says, "it's not a team right off the bat. It is a collection of individuals, just like any other group. And there is some truth to the adage 'You're only as good as your talent.' As a matter of fact, I think everyone understands that you can't win championships without talent. So assembling skillful individuals as part of your team is a given. Then, of course, it becomes a matter of motivating those people to perform as a team."[10]

There's no substitute for talent—but talent without discipline won't win games. Talent without teamwork won't win championships. Talent without preparation can never be successful in the long run. It takes qualities like discipline, teamwork, and preparation to bring talent to the fore, to enable talent to realize its fullest potential. Sometimes, it even takes a blast from the coach's lungs to bring out a player's talent.

The late Al McGuire coached basketball at Marquette University in Wisconsin from 1964 to 1977. He was inducted into the Basketball Hall of Fame in 1992. He once said:

> The only reason I yell at a player is because he has talent. If I didn't think he had talent, I wouldn't yell at him. It would be a mortal sin if I didn't get the talent out of a person. I had a player who was the nicest man I had ever met in my life. I had to hurt him. I had to hurt him because the guy played without knowing the score. To him everything was beautiful. He was so nice that all he wanted to do was play. That's all right if a player doesn't have talent, but when a player has talent, it was my obligation to get him to produce. Just because you have ability doesn't mean that you are going to produce or reach a certain level. You must study your players to know what is best for each particular person so that you can get the most out of his talent.[11]

The great coaches know: There's no substitute for talent—but as Lou Holtz warns, "Winning is difficult on all levels, and talent does not win games on its own."[12] And Vince Lombardi put it this way: "I'd rather have a player with 50 percent ability and 100 percent desire because the guy with 100 percent desire is going to play every day, so you can make a system to fit what he can do. The other guy—the guy with 100 percent ability and 50 percent desire—can screw up your whole system because one day he will be out there waltzing around."[13]

Every structure needs a foundation, and talent is the foundation of the structure of your team. But a strong foundation of the talent is the starting point of your team, not the be-all and end-all. Once you have your foundation in place, keep building!

We All Have More to Give

Bill Musselman was an amazing human being and an intensely competitive coach. He coached basketball in the NCAA, the CBA, the NBA, and a couple of other leagues. Somehow, he managed to pack all of that passion for coaching into an abbreviated lifespan of 59 years. Bill died all too soon of cancer.

When I was editing *Chicken Soup for the Soul: Inside Basketball* with Jack Canfield and Mark Victor Hansen, Bill's daughter, Nicole Musselman Boykin, gave me a tribute she had written to her dad. Nicole wrote movingly about her father's closing days. He was wheelchair-bound, due to a stroke and advanced bone cancer. He had lost a lot of weight, his kidneys had stopped functioning, and his voice was raspy and nearly inaudible at times.

One day, Nicole and her brother, Eric Musselman (who was then an NBA coach) went to visit their dad at the hospital. During the visit, Bill asked to go to the hospital chapel, so Nicole and Eric took him there in his wheelchair. He sat in his wheelchair in the middle of the aisle, head bowed, praying. Nicole prayed with him. Then Bill asked his daughter to put his sunglasses on him and wheel him outside. So she and Eric took their dad outside. It was a beautiful, bright day.

Once outside, Bill turned to Eric and asked for a cell phone. Eric handed his father a phone and, Nicole recalled, her father "dialed with more energy than we had seen in weeks."

Whom did he call? Damon "Biggie" Stoudamire—the Portland Trail Blazers' 5'10" point guard. The moment Bill began speaking into the phone, the wheezing and gasping left his voice. Suddenly, he sounded like the intense Coach Musselman of old, the man whose voice used to rattle the rafters at arenas around the country.

"Biggie," Bill said, "it's Bill Musselman. … What's going on with you? … You've got to dig deep! You have more inside you! Don't let anyone keep you down!"

Eric and Nicole were amazed at the strength of his voice, and the intensity of his words. He waved his arms as he spoke.

"Dig deeper, Biggie!" Bill said. "Get in there, fight, be strong, be tough! We all have more to give than we think! Push yourself! Use every ounce of your potential! I know you have more, I know you can find more inside! We all can."

Nicole recalls, "His words were crisp and clear for a man who had lost all of his speech six months earlier from a stroke. Eric and I stood there a bit shocked but smiling and grasping on to each of my father's words. On that day, in the glorious sunshine, my father gave us our last life lesson—one last bit of advice."

The message Bill Musselman gave to Damon Stoudamire, and to Eric and Nicole, and to you, is a powerful, transformative message: We all have talent and ability within us. We've all been given gifts. We all have more within us than we know, more than we imagine. We all can dig deeper and summon more of our talent—and when we do that, we can accomplish audacious, seemingly "impossible" goals.

Bill Musselman once told Nicole, "Two percent of basketball players are born with endless talent, the kind of talent that would take a complete fool to mess up. The other 98 percent are going to succeed because of how much they put into it and how deep they dig into their soul."[14]

Coach Musselman wasn't content to let talented players rest on their laurels. He was committed to getting players to use every ounce of talent they possessed. That is his legacy, his last will and testament for every coach, every leader, and every player reading these words. Dig deep. Fulfill your potential. Never surrender your will to win. Spend every ounce of energy and talent within you—and you will prevail.

17

Learn to Handle the Media and the Critics

©Allen Eyestone/Palm Beach Post/ZUMA Press

After coaching UTEP and Texas A&M to dramatic turnarounds, Billy Gillispie earned a reputation as a basketball genius. His A&M Aggies achieved three consecutive 20-win seasons for the first time in the school's history. So when Billy Gillispie replaced Tubby Smith at the University of Kentucky in 2007, expectations were high.

Gillispie's stock plummeted, however, when the UK Wildcats racked up a 40-27 record in two seasons under his leadership (worse than the prior two seasons under Tubby Smith), and missed the NCAA tourney for the first time since 1991. In March 2009, Gillispie was fired from his $2.3 million-a-year coaching job.

Sportscaster Josh Little of KOLO-TV blamed Gillispie's woes on both "the losses and Gillispie's somewhat sarcastic demeanor." He added, "A sometimes prickly relationship with the media didn't help matters. A couple of run-ins with a female TV reporter during brief halftime interviews this year struck some as inappropriate, and Gillispie could be contentious at times. He claimed he wasn't hired to be a celebrity, but to win games. He struggled at both, at least by Kentucky standards."[1]

The TV reporter in question was ESPN's Jeannine Edwards. During a road game against Ole Miss, January 27, 2009, Ole Miss prevented Kentucky's star guard Jodie Meeks—the number one scorer in the SEC, and number three in the nation—from making any field goals in the first half. So, at halftime, Edwards got Coach Gillispie on-camera and asked him a perfectly reasonable question: "With Ole Miss keeping Jodie Meeks covered, what adjustments do you need to make for the second half?"

"This is Kentucky, it's not Jodie Meeks," Gillispie replied. "He's a very good player. What difference does it make? Our team's ahead by two. Ole Miss is playing very good. This is not a one-man team. *And that's really a bad question."*[2]

Ouch! Yet Edwards ignored the coach's insult, maintained her professionalism, and continued the questioning in a respectful manner. Indeed, her questioning was validated by the end of the evening when Ole Miss upended the Wildcats 85-80.

Two weeks later, during a home game against Florida, Gillispie again responded abrasively to a seemingly innocuous Jeannine Edwards question, prompting some in the media to wonder if Coach Gillispie harbored some personal animus toward the ESPN broadcaster.

Wrote NCAA Basketball Fanhouse blogger Michael David Smith: "It's time for Gillispie to just start answering Edwards' questions, and stop critiquing Edwards' questions. No head coach likes dealing with sideline reporters, but … dealing with sideline reporters is part of the job. As long as you're going to deal with sideline reporters, you might as well deal with them politely."[3] And Louisville *Courier-Journal* columnist Eric Crawford observed:

When Billy is rude to Jeannine Edwards … it becomes news. Now this should be said: I think you have to accept as a reporter … that sometimes coaches are going to react that way. Some are just more artful at it than others.

Let's take former UK coach and current U of L head man Rick Pitino. He can be just as evasive as football coach Steve Kragthorpe, who is taking a world of criticism for his less than detailed answers, and as pointed as Gillispie, who is taking his own heat. The difference is that while Kragthorpe may talk around a question with generalities, Pitino will launch into an entertaining story that, more often than not, becomes the next sound bite on the news.

If Pitino really wants to correct a reporter, and I've heard him do this, he'll say, "You're really too good of a reporter to ask that question." And if he doesn't want to answer a question, sometimes he'll ignore it entirely and say whatever he wants. Bob Valvano, who does color commentary for U of L radio broadcasts, has the definitive quote: "He gives you fantastic answers to questions you did not ask."[4]

Coaches need to know how to communicate with the news media and get their message out, while maintaining a good working relationship with reporters. That means keeping your cool even when reporters publish negative, unfair, and even untrue stories. To be in leadership is to be in the eye of the storm—and the most successful coaches are those who have learned how to maintain calm while the media storm rages around them.

Some Talking Points

You're a coach. Your job is to prepare and motivate your players for winning. The news media, unfortunately, has a very different agenda from yours. Reporters and columnists don't care about you or the success of your organization. Anything you say to the press can and will be used against you—so you have to be careful what you say and how you say it.

At the same time, it pays to make friends with the press. It can be enormously helpful to give good interviews and provide good sound bites to the media. You can't afford to bristle when criticized or interrogated. Instead of trying to defeat your media critics, you must win them over.

Leaders who know how to give an articulate, relaxed interview will build a good reputation—not only for themselves, but for their organization and their players. Good interviewees always get more opportunities to sell their teams to the public. As ESPN producer and sideline reporter Suzy Kolber says, "We're always going to put on the guys who express themselves the best."[5] The following are some tips for maintaining a successful relationship with the media:

Plan ahead what you want to say. Come up with three strong points that will convey yourself, your team, and your message in a powerful, positive way. Limit your answers to those three points. Your message will be succinct and memorable, and you'll come across as a thoughtful and organized leader.

Become a storyteller. Build a repertoire of interesting stories about your team, your players, and yourself—stories that portray your organization in a positive light. Norm Charlton, a former MLB relief pitcher and bullpen coach for the Mariners, recommends having a few short, pithy stories you can tell at the drop of a hat to illustrate the point you are making. "Stories create interest, which attracts fans," he said. "Our job is not just to play ball."[6]

Never stonewall the press. Always give reporters something good to report. There's a hilarious YouTube video of an NCAA coach approaching a gaggle of reporters and cameramen. The coach has a cell phone pressed to his ear. "Respect me," he says, "I'm on the phone, okay?" But it's hard to tell if he's actually talking on the phone or if he's using the phone as a prop to get him past the media gantlet.

The reporters shout questions, and the coach keeps walking. The cameras follow him into a building and down a hallway. The coach walks faster … and faster … and soon he is running down the hallway, trying to get away from the reporters.

One reporter calls out, "Coach, you're not really gonna run away from me, are ya?"

The coach replies, "You need to get in shape, don't ya?"

The reporter fires back, "I can run all day with you."

And the truth is, they can run all day with you. The advice of media experts is: You can't outrun the media, so don't even try. Face reporters, give them a good quote or sound bite, and shape your message for maximum effect. Turn your media encounters to your own advantage.

Andrea Kirby is a former TV sportscaster and founder of the media coaching firm Andrea Kirby Coaches, Inc. She specializes in training sports execs, coaches, managers, and players in dealing effectively with the media. She encourages sports personalities to always face the cameras, even when dealing with bad news. "If you give [reporters] something interesting," she says, "they'll go away and leave you alone. And they'll also write something that makes you look good."[7]

Get rid of bad speaking habits. One of the best ways to rid ourselves of distracting mannerisms and annoying habits is "video feedback." Simply practice speaking in front of a video camera, or have a friend record you whenever you give a talk to a group or to your team. When you watch the playback, you will probably notice mannerisms you are not even aware of.

Terry Donahue is a former college football coach (UCLA) and NFL general manager (San Francisco 49ers), and is currently a network TV football analyst. "Whenever you view yourself on film," he says, "you're horrified."[8] But that initial sense of horror, of course, is what illuminates your drawbacks as a speaker, so that you can correct them. Just as game film shows you what needs to be fixed in the game, video feedback shows what *you* need to fix in *you*.

Communicate with energy and enthusiasm. Put passion and enthusiasm in your voice as you speak, and use gestures and movement to add octane to your message. When you speak, you should radiate authority and a sense of being in command.

Always maintain good eye contact. When you look your interviewer in the eye, you convey confidence, and you make a connection with the reporter and with your audience. If your gaze is downcast or constantly shifting from side to side, you look evasive, as if you have something to hide. Don't allow nervous mannerisms to undermine your message. Look 'em in the eye and speak with self-assurance.

Watch your temper. When the situation warrants—for example, when you are defending a player or your organization against unfair treatment—measured, controlled anger can sometimes be effective in interviews. A good coach is expected to be passionate in defending his team.

On the other hand, you must stay in control of your temper. Uncontrolled rage, irrationality, defensiveness, and insults only serve to undermine your image and your message. The public and the media will accept your anger in defense of your team, but will be less accepting if you are simply defending yourself, making excuses, or blaming others. Never berate your own team or your individual players in the media. Don't use the media to get even with management and owners. In all your public dealings, maintain your dignity and self-control.

Keep it clean. Nothing makes a coach look worse on TV than a video clip full of bleeps. Following a tough loss in 1997, Toronto Raptors rookie coach Darrell Walker got into an embarrassing encounter with a TV reporter. With the camera rolling, the reporter asked Walker why his point guard shot so much and didn't distribute the ball. Instead of answering the reporter's question, Walker responded with a profane tirade.

After the heavily bleeped footage aired, Andrea Kirby was brought in to train Walker in dealing with the media. She had seen this scenario before with other coaches she had trained. "You ask a negative question," she said, "and these guys don't know how to handle it. They take it personally." Her job was to teach Coach Walker how to take it professionally, not personally.

"Darrell was embarrassed when I showed him himself on tape," Kirby recalled. "We spent two days with him. Finally, he figured it all out. When I asked him, 'Why does he shoot so much?' he said, 'Well, the guy just likes to shoot.'" Not the most exciting answer in the world, but it was truthful—and it didn't have to be bleeped.

Admit mistakes and take responsibility. Unfortunately, many coaches feel it's a sign of weakness to admit, "I messed up." Yet, reporters and the public respect leaders who take responsibility—and they will punish leaders who duck responsibility and shift the blame.

"I've had some athletes that have gotten themselves in big trouble," Andrea Kirby recalls. "A team will call and say, 'So-and-so did this or said this and everybody is up in arms.' My first and foremost advice is, 'If you've made a mistake, you must say that.'"[9]

When it's time to own up to a mistake, do so boldly and forthrightly. Avoid weaselly, impersonal, pseudo-apologies like, "Mistakes were made." Instead, accept personal responsibility. Say, "I blew it. The buck stops with me. I take full responsibility." You'll be amazed at how people will respect you for owning up to it. The best advice I've ever heard on this subject comes from Washington insider Lanny Davis, who said, "Tell it early, tell it all, tell it yourself." That's good counsel when you're facing a bad situation.

Consider taking training from a professional media coach. Before he went into the college football broadcast booth, Terry Donahue went through media training with Pygmalion, Inc., in Los Angeles. "It was like Speech 101 that I never attended when I was in college," he said. "It's all about your presentation, how you look, how you stand, how you position yourself, what kind of image you present in coming across to others, what you should try to avoid doing, what you should try to do."[10]

If you are considering taking training from a media coach, you may want to contact Andrea Kirby of Andrea Kirby Coaches, Inc., Palo Alto, California, Pygmalion, Inc., of Los Angeles, Decker Communications, Inc., of San Francisco, or The LeMaster Group of Dallas.

Practice! Keep coming back to these communicating tips, practice them again and again, and soon you'll be communicating like a pro.

Poise in the Face of Criticism

In 2002, the Tampa Bay Buccaneers hired Jon Gruden as head coach. Gruden retooled the Bucs' offense (the team already had the best defense in the NFL) and the Buccaneers went all the way to Super Bowl XXXVII. In Qualcomm Stadium, San Diego, on January 26, 2003, Gruden's new team beat his former team, the Oakland Raiders, 48-21.

The following year, salary cap limits, personnel problems, and injuries (including fullback Mike Alstott and wide receiver Joe Jurevicius) combined to cripple the Buccaneers' hopes for a winning season, much less a championship season. They finished with a 7-9 record. The following season was even worse, 5-11.

Fans were impatient. Media critics were cruelly derisive. Jon Gruden, who had been heralded by *USA Today* as the NFL's "boy wonder," quickly became a whipping boy.

Gruden and his wife Cindy have three sons, and his boys had a difficult time watching their famous dad go from being idolized in the media to undergoing intense and negative scrutiny. Jon Gruden took it as an opportunity to teach his sons about the importance of persevering through adversity and media controversy.

As he told Skip Wood of *USA Today*, "My kids have got to learn that their dad's probably going to be criticized, just as anybody in this position will be at one time or another. I don't think they're real sensitive about it, but it's important they know that Dad's doing the best he can. To me, that's the greatest thing I can leave with my kids. If I can teach them to be the best they can, I'll be one proud father."[11]

The late Alex Agase coached football at Northwestern and Purdue, and was named National Coach of the Year in 1970 by the Football Writers Association. He had a thick hide with respect to criticism. When media critics challenged his game strategy and decision-making, he replied, "If you really want to advise me, do it on Saturday afternoon between 1 and 4 o'clock. And you've got 25 seconds to do it, between plays. Not on Monday. I know the right thing to do on Monday."[12]

Penn State head football coach Joe Paterno holds the record for most victories by a Division IA-FBS coach, based on NCAA criteria. He has coached more undefeated seasons and more bowl game victories than any other coach in NCAA football history. In spite of these impressive accomplishments, Joe Paterno has received his share of criticism from the fans and media over the years. He takes it all in stride and offers good advice for his fellow coaches.

"I really don't care what people say," he says. "I try to tell young coaches, the minute you start reacting to criticism, forget it. It affects your judgment and ability to make tough decisions. You lose your courage. I never paid much attention to it."[13]

One of my mentors in the pro sports business, Dr. Jack Ramsay, put it this way: "Character traits such as maintaining poise in the face of criticism, accepting both victory and defeat with equanimity, remembering those who were with you on the road to success, and giving full effort at all times (and demanding the same of others) are all applicable to anyone in authority ... Coaches are right up there in the front lines."[14]

As a coach, you are accustomed to doing your job in an arena against tough opponents and adversity. Whatever game you coach, whether it's football, basketball, baseball, lacrosse, or the game of running a business or organization, you live and work in an arena. You face tough opponents every day, and the grandstands are filled with critics. You are subject to scrutiny and criticism. You'd better be ready to handle it. If you can't, it's time to get out of the arena.

In the Eye of the Media Storm

Not only will you, as the coach and leader of your organization, be the focus of media attention (and criticism) from time to time, so will your players. Part of your job as coach is to prepare your team for the scrutiny they will receive—for both the criticism and the praise (which can be just as disruptive as the criticism).

Coach John Wooden was constantly in the media spotlight during his time as UCLA Bruins basketball coach—and so were his players. He recalls that he taught his players to bulletproof themselves against both criticism and praise:

> I took criticism from outsiders with a grain of salt. I told my players each year, "Fellows, you're going to receive some criticism. Some of it will be deserved and some of it will be undeserved. Either way, deserved or undeserved, you're not going to like it.
>
> "You're also going to receive some praise on occasion. Some of it will be deserved and some of it will be undeserved. Either way, deserved or undeserved, you're going to like it. However, your strength as an individual depends on how you respond to both criticism and praise. If you let either one have any special effect on you, it's going to hurt us. Whether it is criticism or praise, deserved or undeserved, makes no difference. If we let it affect us, it hurts us." ...
>
> You have little control over what criticism or praise outsiders send your way. Take it all with a grain of salt. Let your opponent get all caught up in other people's opinions. But don't you do it.[15]

Phil Jackson understood the importance of preparing his players for dealing with the media. He set down clear rules and boundary lines. He built a wall of protection around his team and defended it fiercely. In his book *Sacred Hoops*, he explained:

When I took over the Bulls in 1989, I told the players that, as far as I was concerned, the only people who really mattered were the team's inner circle: the twelve players, the four coaches, the trainer, and the equipment manager. Everyone else was an outsider, even [Bulls general manager] Jerry Krause. The idea was to heighten the feeling of intimacy, the sense that we were engaged in something sacred and inviolate. To protect the sanctity of the group, I keep the media out of practices and restrict the number of people who travel with the team. I also instruct the players not to blab to the press about everything we do. In order to build trust, the players need to know that they can be open and honest with each other, without seeing their words in the paper the next day.[16]

Pat Summitt, head coach of the Tennessee Lady Volunteers basketball team, is a pro at dealing with reporters—and preparing her players for media encounters. During the Lady Vols 1997-1998 season, her team was electrifying the nation, cutting through one of the toughest schedules in the nation like a chain saw. As the Lady Vols continued undefeated past the midway point of the season, media scrutiny became intense. Any utterance from Summitt or one of her players was a potential headline—and a potential controversy. Amid this media circus, her job was to keep her players focused on the business of winning, one game at a time.

Following a home game against the third-ranked UConn Huskies before a record crowd of nearly 25,000 fans, the Lady Vols won a resounding, emotional 84-69 victory. After the game, one of Summitt's players was interviewed on a postgame radio show. The interviewer asked her if the noisy Tennessee fans were a factor in the win. The player, wanting to send a compliment to the fans, replied, "Oh, yeah, I think Connecticut about ran off the floor, they were so scared."

It was a joke, a bit of hyperbole, intended to thank Volunteer fans for raising an intimidating ruckus. But when the quote was repeated out of context in the news for the next few days, it was portrayed as an insult to the Huskies team, an accusation of cowardice.

When Huskies coach Geno Auriemma heard the player's out-of-context remark, he fired back some disparaging remarks about the Volunteers. "A controversy was born," Summitt recalls. Her phone rang continually as both local and national sports reporters demanded interviews, quotes, and soundbites. Summitt refused to "throw fuel on the fire," and declined to comment. She continued:

A day later, we drove to South Carolina to begin a four-game road swing. Before practice, I gathered our team in a circle and told them I wasn't crazy about the comments made on either side. I realized [the player who made the comment] was only a college freshman, but this was an opportunity for the entire team to learn from the situation. ...

One thing was clear: no women's team had gotten this much media attention before. We were receiving daily calls from the national press, and cameras and microphones were at courtside every night.

"All eyes are on this team," I told the Lady Vols. "You have to handle success. We win with class."[17]

In a few days, the firestorm burned itself out. Pat Summitt kept herself and her players disciplined and focused. The Lady Vols went on to a 39-0 record, and their third consecutive national title. They started the season ranked number one, and they didn't budge from that pinnacle for even a moment. Media scrutiny remained intense throughout, but Pat Summitt adroitly managed her dealings with the press and kept her players insulated from the cameras and reporters.

She created a safe place in the eye of the media storm so that her players could focus on winning. That's what great coaches do.

18

It's Always About the Team

The year 1960 was a momentous year in the NFL. That was the year the NFL expanded to 13 teams with the addition of the Dallas Cowboys. Also that year, the Cardinals relocated from Chicago to St. Louis. Pete Rozelle was elected NFL commissioner in 1960, a job he would hold for the next three decades. And the Philadelphia Eagles won the NFL championship for the third (and thus far, last) time in franchise history.

There were other teams in the league with a greater aggregate of talent than the 1960 Eagles. There were teams that were more ably coached. There were teams that were younger and quicker and stronger than the aging, battle-scarred Eagles. Yet for one magical season, the Eagles banded together, reached deep within themselves, and became known as "the Team with Nothing but a Title."

The Eagles were quarterbacked by 34-year-old Norm Van Brocklin, who had already declared the 1960 season to be his last. Eagles coach Buck Shaw put Van Brocklin in control of the Eagles offense, essentially making him offensive coordinator as well as quarterback.

Norm Van Brocklin's favorite target, especially on deep routes, was wide receiver Tommy McDonald. McDonald seemed to elevate his abilities during that season. In 1960, he led the league in touchdown receptions and receiving yards.

Van Brocklin took the snaps from Chuck Bednarik, a 35-year-old block of human concrete often called "the last of the 60-minute players." Bednarik played center on offense, then at change of possession, he'd stay on the field and play the linebacker position. Bednarik was about as old-school as they come—a hard-nosed, blue-collar guy from the steel mills of Bethlehem, Pennsylvania. The son of hard-working Slovak émigrés, Bednarik enlisted during World War II and flew 30 combat missions over Germany as a waist gunner in a B-24—a job that requires nerves of steel. In his entire 14-season career, the hardworking Bednarik missed only three games. During the 1960's 12-game season, he was on the field for roughly 600 of a possible 720 minutes.

The rest of the Eagles lineup included offensive lineman Howard Keys (who had played every position on the offensive line at one time or another), running back and kick returner Timmy Brown, halfback Billy Ray Barnes, nimble running back Theron Sapp, and Pete Retzlaff, who could switch from running back to wide receiver to tight end as needed. In addition to Bednarik, the Eagles' defensive squad included starting left corner Jimmy Carr, All-Pro linebacker Maxie Baughan, and defensive back Tom Brookshier.

After dropping the season opener at home to the Cleveland Browns, the Eagles took off on a nine-game winning streak. They played two consecutive games against the New York Giants, November 20 and 27. In the second of those two games, Chuck Bednarik put a hit on Giants halfback Frank Gifford that forced a fumble, knocked Gifford unconscious, and nearly ended his career (Gifford missed the entire 1961 season because of that hit).

Giants kicker Pat Summerall recalled, "They carried Frank off the field on a stretcher. Unknown to us, some fan that day had had a heart attack in the stands. The man unfortunately died in our locker room. They were taking him out with a sheet over his face, just as we started to walk in, and we all thought that Bednarik had killed Gifford."[1]

"It's a Whole Team Concept"

But, of course, the most important game of the 1960 season was the final game for the NFL championship, the Philadelphia Eagles vs. the Green Bay Packers. In Chapter 14, we looked at that game from the point of view of Vince Lombardi and the Packers. But from the Eagles' side of the ball, it's a whole different ballgame.

The 10-2 Eagles of the Eastern Conference were making their first appearance in a title game since 1949. They faced the 8-4 Packers of the Western Conference, who were just two years removed from a shame-faced 1-10-1 season, the Packers' last season before the arrival of Vince Lombardi. The game was played the day after Christmas, on Franklin Field at the University of Pennsylvania.

Throughout the first three quarters, it was a battle in the trenches, a low-scoring contest dominated by defense on both sides. Finally, with 5:21 remaining in the fourth quarter, the Eagles took a 17-13 lead with a touchdown on the five-yard run. The Packers' next drive ended with frustration and a punt. The Eagles went three and out, leaving the Packers 1:22 for a final drive.

Packers quarterback Bart Starr patiently marched his team down the field with a series of short passes. As the clock was winding down, Starr dumped one off to Jim Taylor in the left flat. Taylor, a quick and nimble runner with powerful legs, used his upper body like a battering ram, charging right into the Eagles secondary. He twisted and turned, shaking off Eagles defensive back Bobby Jackson at the 10.

But Jackson got just enough of a grip on Taylor to slow him down. Right in Taylor's path stood "Concrete Charlie" Bednarik. The Eagles linebacker wrapped Taylor up in a bear hug, wrestled him to the ground, and pounced on him. While the Packers hurried back to the line, unable to stop the clock, Taylor struggled futilely to throw Bednarik off his back.

But "Concrete Charlie" wouldn't budge. He pinned Jim Taylor to the ground while the clock ticked down to zero. The gun sounded—and Bednarik climbed to his feet. "You can get up now, Jim," he said. "The game's over."

After the game, Chuck Bednarik put his arms around both Jim Taylor and Packers halfback Paul Hornung. "You guys will be back in the championship game next year," Bednarik told his defeated opponents (and those words proved prophetic).[2]

Bednarik had played 58 of the game's 60 regulation minutes. Of the 142 plays in the game, he was on the field for 139 of them. For playing both sides of the ball all season long, he received a bonus—the princely sum of $250.

Wide receiver Tommy McDonald remembers that the 1960s Eagles were totally focused on playing together as a team—and focused on winning. "We would bite, scratch, kick, gouge, anything we could do to win a game," he said. And win they did. "It just seemed like we had a guardian angel over us or something."[3]

While Chuck Bednarik dominated defensively, quarterback Norm Van Brocklin kept the offense fired up throughout the game. Philadelphia sports columnist Larry Merchant observed, "If ever a single player lifted a team that was average into winning a championship, it was [Van Brocklin], and he did it by the sheer force of his personality, his will, and his skill."[4] And that, of course, is what leaders do: They fire up the entire team to overachieve and outdo themselves.

Tight end Pete Retzlaff remembers the 1960 Eagles as a team totally united by a single purpose: "It was just a strange, unique group of guys," he said, "that suddenly decided that the most important thing in the world to them was to win a championship."[5]

Defensive back Bobby Freeman recalled the 1960 Eagles as possessing a kind of Gestalt synergy, in which the whole team was greater than the sum of its parts. "We had a bunch of misfits," he said. "You mix them together and a team personality comes out. Sometimes it works. Sometimes it just doesn't click. It worked with the Eagles. We had an outstanding team personality. … We were loose, but we had a sort of deadly sense of seriousness when it counted."[6]

And defensive end Riley Gunnels remembers the 1960 Eagles as a team that soared above its collective level of talent, achieving far more than they had any right to achieve—and they did it with teamwork. "Football is a *team* sport," Gunnels says. "Position by position, we may not have had the best personnel, but it's a whole team concept out there on the field. That's what wins. What matters is how well each guy covers for the next guy and how well a team plays together as a unit. There wasn't a team around that could compare to the Eagles as a whole team."[7]

Teamwork Wins Championships

As coaches and leaders, we must always remind ourselves and our players that it's always about the team. Ask retired soccer star Mia Hamm. She has scored more career goals (158) than any other soccer player, male or female, and is the author of *Go for the Goal: A Champion's Guide to Winning in Soccer and Life*. Despite her amazing personal accomplishments, she prefers to see herself not as an individual achiever but as part of a larger whole. "I am a member of a team," she once said, "and I rely on the team, I defer to it and sacrifice for it, because the team, not the individual, is the ultimate champion."[8] Or, as she has so often (and so succinctly) put it, "There's no 'me' in Mia."[9]

My friend Chuck Daly always stressed the one quality all players need in order to function together as a complete and unified team: Unselfishness. "Having coached at all the levels," he said, "I know one thing: teams win championships, not individuals. The players must have ability, but it's essential that they perform as a team. They have to be unselfish, and it's hard to find unselfish players."[10]

The paradox of teamwork is that unselfish team play always pays dividends to individual players. Coach Jim Calhoun of the University of Connecticut put it this way: "At UConn, we work diligently every year at building the concept of team. One idea that I constantly emphasize is this: *When we benefit, I benefit.* In other words, when the team performs well, everyone on the team will share in its success. I want the players, as a group, to take ownership of the team."[11]

Anyone who has ever been part of a championship team, whether as a player or coach, knows that teams win championships, not individuals. Terry Bradshaw quarterbacked the Pittsburgh Steelers through 14 seasons. Over six seasons, from 1974 through 1979, he won an unprecedented four Super Bowl titles—Super Bowls IX, X, XIII, and XIV. He said, "We are all in this together. One way or another we're all dependent on each other. I could have been the greatest passer in the history of the world, but no one would ever know it if I didn't have receivers like Lynn Swan and John Stallworth catching them, or an offensive line to protect me."[12]

One of the greatest teamwork innovations in basketball is the triangle offense—a strategy originally devised by USC's head coach Sam Barry, then refined by Tex Winter, who played for Barry in the 1940s. Tex Winter was on the coaching staff of the Chicago Bulls when Phil Jackson came aboard, and Tex taught the triangle offense to Phil Jackson. It was exactly what Jackson was looking for. He called it "a system that emphasizes cooperation and freedom, the very values I'd spent my life pursuing off the court and dreamed of applying to the game."

What's more, Phil added, he would have a chance to implement the triangle offense in a total team environment with "the most creative player in basketball," Michael Jordan.[13] In *Sacred Hoops,* Phil describes his philosophy of teamwork:

> Most leaders tend to view teamwork as a social engineering problem: take *x* group, add *y* motivational technique and get *z* result. But working with the Bulls I've learned that the most effective way to forge a winning team is to call on the players' need to connect with something larger than themselves. Even for those who don't consider themselves "spiritual" in a conventional sense, creating a successful team—whether it's an NBA

champion or a record-setting sales force—is essentially a spiritual act. It requires the individuals involved to surrender their self-interest for the greater good so that the whole adds up to more than the sum of its parts. …

I've discovered that when you free players to use *all* their resources—mental, physical, and spiritual—an interesting shift in awareness occurs. … Not only do they play better and win more, they also become more attuned with each other. And the joy they experience working in harmony is a powerful motivating force that comes from deep within, not from some frenzied coach pacing along the sidelines, shouting obscenities into the air.

No team understood better than the championship Chicago Bulls that selflessness is the sole of teamwork.[14]

When Phil Jackson introduced Michael Jordan to the triangle offense, Jordan was skeptical, referring to it as "Tex's equal opportunity offense." Phil Jackson explained, "You've got to share the spotlight with your teammates because if you don't, they won't grow."

Jordan said, "I think we're going to have trouble when the ball gets to certain people, because they can't pass and they can't make decisions with the ball."

"I understand that," Jackson replied. "But I think if you give the system a chance, they'll learn to be playmakers. The important thing is to let everybody touch the ball, so they won't feel like spectators. You can't beat a good defensive team with one man. It's got to be a team effort."

"Okay," Jordan said. "Whatever you want to do, I'm behind you."

So, Phil Jackson and Tex Winter taught the triangle offense to the Bulls—and Michael Jordan was surprised to discover how much of a threat he became to opposing teams when he *didn't* have the ball. As Jordan constantly moved around the floor, defenders had to account for him, even though the ball was elsewhere. The mere fact that the ball might go to Jordan at any moment created wide-open opportunities for Jordan's teammates.

Even though the triangle offense was designed to involve the entire team, it actually freed Michael Jordan to unleash his phenomenal talent. "Every now and then," Phil Jackson recalled, "Michael would break loose and take over a game. But that didn't bother me as long as it didn't become a habit. I knew he needed bursts of creativity to keep from getting bored, and that his solo performances would strike terror in the hearts of our enemies, not to mention help win some key games."[15]

Years later, Michael Jordan looked back and reflected, "There are plenty of teams in every sport that have great players and never win titles. Most of the time, those players aren't willing to sacrifice for the greater good of the team. The funny thing is, in the end, their unwillingness to sacrifice only makes individual goals more difficult to achieve. One thing I believe to the fullest is that if you think and achieve as a team, the individual accolades will take care of themselves. Talent wins games, but teamwork and intelligence win championships."[16]

Turning a Bunch of Players Into a Team

The engine of teamwork is a process called synergy (from the Greek syn-ergos, meaning "working together"). When players mesh together and work together cooperatively, they produce a dynamic effect that is greater than the sum of the individual parts. In his book *The Winner Within*, former NBA coach Pat Riley (now president of the Miami Heat) described the synergistic power of teamwork:

Teamwork is the essence of life.

If there's one thing on which I am an authority, it's how to blend the talents and strengths of individuals into a force that becomes greater than the sum of its parts. My driving belief is this: great teamwork is the only way to reach our ultimate moments, to create breakthroughs that define our careers, to fulfill our lives with a sense of lasting significance. ...

When our teams excel, we win. Our best efforts, combined with those of our teammates, grow into something far greater and far more satisfying than anything we could have achieved on our own. Teams make us part of something that matters.[17]

You can't just throw a group of people together—even highly talented people—and declare them to be a team. They may be a group, a committee, a bunch of people wearing identical uniforms, but they are not a team, not yet. They don't yet possess that synergistic magic that transforms a bunch of individuals into a genuine *team*. Mike Krzyzewski put it this way in his book *The Gold Standard: Building a World-Class Team*: "You do not select a team, you select a group of people and then work together to develop into a team. In other words, teams don't instantaneously *become*, they *evolve*."[18]

One important way you help your players evolve into a cohesive team is by making sure they acknowledge one another's contributions and share the glory of accomplishment with one another. Coach John Wooden recalls:

Back in the 1930s when I was coaching at South Bend Central High School, I began requiring that a player who scored a basket gave a nod of acknowledgment—a "thank you"—to his teammate who made the assist: "Let him know you appreciate his help, and maybe he'll do it again. Give him a nod, a thumbs-up, a wink."

Jimmy Powers, one of my top players, asked, "Coach Wooden, won't that take up too much time?" I told him, "Jimmy, I'm not asking you to run over there and give him a big hug. A nod will do."

Members of the team can be taught they're a team and not just a bunch of independent operators. Everyone contributes to the success of everyone else. This is called *cooperation*, and it is a value fundamental to my philosophy of competitive greatness. It is a trademark of a real team.

I accomplished this, in part, by instituting my "thank you" rule. I timed it out. It takes less than one second to say thank you. The rewards last much longer.[19]

Another important way you encourage your players to evolve into a team is by allowing the natural leaders on the team to emerge. On every team, there are personalities who display natural leadership qualities, and there are other personalities who are looking for leaders to rally around.

On the 1960 Eagles, head coach Buck Shaw recognized the natural leadership of quarterback Norm Van Brocklin and placed him in control of the Eagles offense. Buck Shaw also saw how the Eagles defense rallied around the natural leadership of linebacker Chuck Bednarik. Though Shaw was the master strategist of both the Eagles offense and defense, he gave Van Brocklin and Bednarik a great deal of latitude in overseeing and motivating their respective squads.

Coach Mike Krzyzewski believes in the importance of identifying and empowering player-leaders as a means of solidifying a team. In *The Gold Standard*, he writes:

I think one of the primary mistakes that leaders make in team building is in believing that they have to be the sole provider of leadership. *Great teams have multiple leaders, multiple voices.* A major part of building a team is discovering who those voices will be in cultivating them, making sure that their leadership is established within your group. In order to do this, the team leader must first make certain that he or she has a solid relationship with those leaders. All members of the team should be bonded to one another but a leader must be connected, most of all, with his internal leadership.[20]

Tom Donnelly, the track and cross country coach at Haverford College, told me a story that illustrates the true nature of a team. "I graduated from Villanova in 1969," he said, "and was hired by Archbishop Wood Academy in Warminster, Pennsylvania. In addition to teaching duties, I also coached the track and cross-country teams. In my first year, I took my nine runners out to a remote training center for an intense training session. On the first day, I took the youngsters out on a five-mile run and realized they were not in very good shape. We had a lot of work to do.

"That night I took them out on a trail run. I was leading the way with my flashlight, when a thought struck me. What would happen if I turned the flashlight off?

"So I flicked off the light for about 10 seconds—then I switched it back on and looked behind me. There, on the trail, I saw a remarkable sight: Nine teenage boys were all huddled together, holding on to each other for dear life. They were scared to death, trying to find some strength and courage by sticking together as tightly as possible.

"What a great teaching moment for me, a 22-year-old coach in his first day on the job! I told them, 'This is how a team works. To be a great team, you have to come together and trust each other and stick together through the tough times when you really need each other. You nine guys have to become like one.'

"We went on to win our league championship that fall. That was a great lesson on building a unified team and I've tried to apply that principle each year in my 40 years of coaching."

That's as true and insightful picture of authentic teamwork as you'll ever find. Mold your players into a bonded huddle of players who hold on to each other for dear life. Teach them to rely on each other through the tough times, the dark times. Encourage them to weld themselves to one another and become as one.

Talent is crucial, but talent alone doesn't win championships. To truly be the best, remember: it's always about the team.

19

Communicate!

©Mike McGinnis/Cal Sport Media/ZUMA Press

Ask anyone, "Who was The Gipper?" Odds are, they'll reply, "Ronald Reagan."

But the original Gipper, portrayed by Ronald Reagan in the 1940 biopic *Knute Rockne, All American*, was the Notre Dame quarterback-halfback-punter George Gipp. He led the Fighting Irish in rushing and passing in 1918, 1919, and 1920, and his career rushing record (2,341 yards) stood unbroken for more than half a century.

Gipp played his final game on November 20, 1920, against Northwestern. Afterwards, he stayed on the field in the bitter cold, giving punting lessons to other players. A few days later, Gipp came down with strep throat and pneumonia.

He was confined to a hospital bed at Saint Joseph Hospital in South Bend, where he grew steadily weaker. His coach, Knute Rockne, visited him on the night of December 13. A few hours after Rockne left the hospital, early in the morning on December 14, George Gipp died. He was 25 years old. For years after Gipp's death, Rockne would not talk about that last conversation between himself and "The Gipper."

Eight years passed. The 1928 season was the worst of Rockne's coaching career. Struggling to avoid the disgrace of a losing season, his 4-2 Irish went to Yankee Stadium to square off against an undefeated Army team with six consecutive wins under their belts. Looking down his schedule, Rockne knew that, after Army, his embattled Irish faced almost certain losses to Carnegie Tech and USC. If they didn't beat the Cadets, the Irish would likely end up 4-5 for the season.

He called in former heavyweight boxing champion Jack Dempsey to give his team a pre-game pep talk. Then, he sent his team out on the field, knowing he still had one ace in the hole—the ghost of George Gipp.

The Irish battled the Cadets to a 0-0 standstill in the first two quarters. At halftime, Rockne took his team back to the locker room. He could see that his players looked spent. Their will to fight was sinking. It was time for that ace in the hole.

"Well, boys," he said, "I'm going to tell you something I've kept to myself for years."

Instantly, all eyes were riveted on Coach Rockne.

"None of you ever knew George Gipp," the coach began. "He was long before your time. But you know what a tradition he is at Notre Dame. And the last thing he said to me—'Rock,' he said, 'sometime, when the team is up against it, and the breaks are beating the boys, tell them to go out there with all they've got and win just one for the Gipper. I don't know where I'll be then, Rock, but I'll know about it, and I'll be happy.' That's what he said. And this is the day. And you are the team."

One of Rockne's assistant coaches later recalled, "There was a moment of silence, and then all of a sudden those players ran out of the dressing room and almost tore the hinges off the door. There were all ready to kill someone."

But as the third quarter began, disaster struck. Army quarterback Billy Nave handed off to halfback Chris Cagle, who eluded Irish defenders and launched a 41-yard pass. That gain set up a touchdown—and a 6-0 Army lead.

Notre Dame halfback Jack Chevigny retaliated with a game-tying touchdown on fourth-and-goal from the one-yard line. Plunging into the end zone, he shouted, "That's one for the Gipper!"

Later, Notre Dame left halfback Butch Niemiec passed to tight end Johnny O'Brien, who caught it at the 10, shook off two tacklers, and trotted into the end zone for the go-ahead TD. From the sidelines, Chevigny shouted, "That's *another* one for the Gipper!"

Clinging to their lead, the Irish watched the Cadets make one final desperate drive. It came down to a fourth-and-goal from the one-foot line as the final seconds ticked away. Army tried to punch the ball through the Notre Dame defensive front—and though Army's Dick Hutchinson carried the ball within inches of the goal line, the Irish stopped the Cadets cold. Game over.

Aided by the ghost of George Gipp, the Fighting Irish staved off disaster, and (after losing to Carnegie Tech and USC) Knute Rockne ended the most painful season of his career with a 5-4-0 (.555) record. The 1928 season may not have been the stuff that football legends are made of, but his halftime speech certainly was.[1]

Communicate to Motivate and Inspire

Knute Rockne knew that motivation is the key to winning—and communication is the key to motivation. His team was struggling, and he had to find words that would reach the hearts of his men and fire them up for an epic struggle. In the end, the game was decided by inches and seconds—and the story of George Gipp, which Rockne told simply but powerfully at halftime—was the difference between victory and defeat.

The level of emotional intensity Notre Dame needed to beat Army is something coaches rarely achieve. In fact, such emotional intensity is simply unsustainable over an entire season. As Ray Robinson observed in *Rockne of Notre Dame: The Making of a Football Legend*, "Rockne was aware that the emotional pitch his men had reached against Army would be hard to sustain. 'If there are two games that you have to win you can point for those, especially if one is the final game of the schedule,' he said. 'But you've got to try to take the others in stride.'"[2]

Knute Rockne was a master communicator, partly because he communicated so eloquently and could reach the emotions of his listeners, and partly because he knew that words should be used strategically and sparingly. He understood that if the coach talks too much, his words could lose their power.

On one occasion, before a home game against Princeton, Rockne let Princeton's head coach, William W. Roper, do all the talking. In those days, the Notre Dame locker room was next to the visiting team's locker room, and if you were quiet and you were close to the adjoining wall, you could hear everything that was said in the other locker room.

Minutes before the 1924 game against Princeton, Coach Rockne stood before his team in the locker room—and said nothing. The players were puzzled—then they realized that their coach was listening to a voice from the other side of the wall.

"They tell me that this fellow Bill Roper is a terrific orator," Rockne said at last. "You fellows just lay on the floor and listen to him, while I save my voice. Maybe you'll learn something."

The Notre Dame team listened, then went out on the field fired up by the opposing coach's pep talk. Notre Dame beat Princeton 25-2 that day.[3]

Frank Robinson worked as a manager in Major League Baseball from 1975 to 2006, following a stellar 21-season career as an outfielder with the Reds and Orioles. He is the only player to be honored as league MVP in both the American and National Leagues. Effective communication was an integral part of Robinson's managing philosophy. He once said:

> What does it take to be a good manager? . . .
>
> It's very important to communicate with your players on a daily basis. ... Everybody says, "I want to know my role." In the old days, there was no such thing. If you weren't a starter, you were on the bench. If you weren't a starting pitcher, you were in the bullpen. Nowadays, you have to spell it out in spring training. ... And during the first month of the season, you have to spell it out again. ...
>
> I was low maintenance throughout my career. You didn't have to talk to me. Today you almost have to talk to the players every day. I might talk to a player about last night's game. ... Some of the other ones you've got to go and pump up a little bit because he had a tough night or whatever. You have to know who needs that hands-on type of thing. But you have to do a little bit each day. And I make sure that I walk through the clubhouse each day just to say hello to some of the guys.[4]

ESPN baseball analyst Tim Kurkjian cites Jim Leyland and Bobby Cox as baseball managers who are successful in large part because of their communication skills. He writes:

> Tigers manager Jim Leyland, who has managed four teams, including the 1997 World Series Champion Florida Marlins, is a great communicator. "I was the twenty-fifth guy on the team; I was terrible," said ex-Pirate Dave Hostetler. "Every day, Jim would come up to me, and say something positive, anything, like 'good at-bat last night.' That made me feel good." Leyland's Tigers 2006 went to the World Series in part because of his tremendous relationship with his players. …
>
> That's how Bobby Cox works, which is one reason why, by any statistical measure, he is one of the five greatest managers of all time. Every day, he says hello to every player on his team, one reason why his players love him. He treats them like men. He never trashes them. He's intensely loyal to them, and respectful of them and their ability. "Look up 'players manager' in the dictionary, and his smiling face is right there," says Braves third baseman Chipper Jones. "I've never heard any player say anything bad about him. He is the reason why players who leave here want to come back."[5]

Jack McKeon, who was National League Manager of the Year in 1999 and 2003, used the bulletin board to communicate team values to his players. He recalls:

> I had to put a little reminder on the board the last week of May during the second game of the series against the Reds. I put up this note: "To whom it may concern: Check your egos at the door. We won last year with 25 guys playing as a team."
>
> That's it.
>
> It was just a gentle reminder. I wanted to reinforce what we are. We're a team, we're not a bunch of selfish players. It was aimed at just a couple of guys. They are good kids, but sometimes they have to be reminded that it's a team game and not to show up anyone.[6]

Even while McKeon was telling his players to check their egos at the door, he was careful not to bruise their egos by issuing reprimands in front of the whole team. If there was a behavior or attitude problem that needed to be addressed in a team meeting, he would gather his players and say, "Now look, there is a lot of stuff I'm going to say. It doesn't apply to everybody, but if the shoe fits you, wear it. And I hate for some of you guys in this room to have to hear this stuff, it doesn't apply to you, but for the ones it does, listen up and take care of it." McKeon would avoid pointing fingers at individuals, and in this way he kept players from becoming defensive or resentful when he had to challenge or reprimand them.[7]

Some Coaching on Communicating

Communication skills are essential to coaching greatness. As a leader, you must inspire, motivate, teach, confront, and energize your team. You must know when to speak and when to bite your tongue. Above all, you must communicate your vision and your passion for winning to your players. The following are some tips from great coaches on how to communicate effectively to motivate and inspire your team.

First, one Super Bowl-winning coach, Jon Gruden, relates what he learned about coaching and communicating from his Super Bowl-winning mentor, Mike Holmgren. In his book *Do you Love Football?!*, Gruden credits Holmgren's background as a high school teacher for making him "so comfortable in his ability to communicate with players."

Holmgren would take complicated tasks and break them down to a set of simple, step-by-step instructions. "It wasn't a 45-minute lecture," Gruden said. "He had a knack for conveying his thoughts in 25 words or less. He didn't start rambling and talking about things that were irrelevant to the question that you had just asked. He was always to the point."

Gruden said that Holmgren was at his best when installing plays in the game plan. Everything was presented in black and white, no shades of gray. Every player knew exactly where he was supposed to be and what he was supposed to do in every play. Most important of all, when Holmgren spoke, he instilled confidence in his coaches and players. Gruden wrote:

> When he installs a game plan, showing each play and its corresponding number on the overhead projector, he always exudes confidence.
>
> "Picture Number 73 is going to be a touchdown Sunday," he'd say matter-of-factly, about a pass play designed to have Joe [Montana] throw to Jerry Rice, who would just blow past some poor DB trying to cover him one-on-one over the middle. "Pay attention, men. It's 76 X Shallow Cross. Roger's going in motion to the weak side. The free safety is going to jump the tight end on the hook route, and Jerry Rice is going to be there for a touchdown. It's going to happen, man. Circle it now. Star it. It's a touchdown."
>
> I would sit there and go, "Man, it's seven to nothing already. What's the next picture?"

But that's how you install plays. Confident. Concise. Crystal-clear. No one does it better than Mike Holmgren.[8]

Great communicators know how to keep it simple. Cal Ripken, Jr., recalls how, when he moved up to the majors from the Triple-A Rochester Red Wings, Orioles manager Earl Weaver made the decision to switch him from third base to shortstop. At 6'4", Ripken was considerably taller than the prototypical shortstop, and Weaver took some heat from the front office and the fans for moving Ripken to that position. Just before Ripken's first game at shortstop, Weaver called him into his office. Ripken had the impression that Weaver was uneasy with the decision he'd made, so he wanted to impart a few last-minute instructions. Ripken recalls Weaver's words:

> "Look, just make the routine plays," he said. "Don't try to go beyond yourself. If the ball is hit to you, make sure you catch it. Take it out of your glove, get a good grip on it, and make a good throw to first base."
>
> I nodded and smiled as my manager spoke to me as if I were a Little Leaguer. But I think that was one of Earl's gifts. He usually spoke in a sincere tone and used simple words. As a result, people clearly understood the message he was trying to convey.
>
> "If the runner is safe, at least he'll only be at first base," continued Earl. "But if you catch the ball and throw it over Murray's head, then not only will the runner be safe, he'll also be on second base. And we can't have that. Do you understand?"
>
> "Yes, sir, I understand."
>
> "Okay, then get out there and give us a good game."
>
> When I took the field that day, I was under the impression that this stint at shortstop was only temporary. But it lasted fifteen years.[9]

John Madden, former Raiders coach and network football analyst, has a gift for painting highly visual mental images with words alone. When he was inducted into the Pro Football Hall of Fame in 2006, he vividly described what he imagined took place in the Hall of Champions every night when they turn out the lights.

"I believe that the busts talk to each other," he said. "I can't wait for that conversation, I really can't. Vince Lombardi, Knute Rockne, Reggie White, Walter Payton, all my ex-players, we'll be there forever and ever talking about whatever. That's what I believe. That's what I think is going to happen, and no one's ever going to talk me out of that."[10]

These are just a few important insights into the communication side of coaching: Be confident. Keep it simple. And communicate vividly, using word-pictures that make your words memorable.

Two-Way Communication

Dawn Staley is a three-time Olympian basketball player (who was chosen to carry the American flag at the opening ceremonies for the 2004 Summer Olympics), and is currently the head women's basketball coach at the University of South Carolina. According to Anne Donovan, former head coach of the Seattle Storm, Staley is a great coach largely because of her communication skills. "She can communicate with anybody," Donovan says, "whether it's the recruit, the parent, the coach or a teammate. ... You respect her, and you would never cross a line with her. I don't know if coaching has this anymore, where players want to win for somebody, but players want to win for Dawn."

Before Dawn Staley took her present position at South Carolina, she coached women's basketball for eight years at Temple University, beginning in 2000. Before her arrival, Temple suffered through 10 consecutive losing seasons. During her first year as head coach, Temple advanced to the Women's National Invitation Tournament. During her eight-year tenure, Temple made six trips to the NCAA Tournament.

One of Dawn Staley's most effective communicating tools is a quick sense of humor, which she uses as a counterweight to the authoritarian demeanor the coaching role requires. In a USA Today profile of Dawn Staley, writer Reid Cherner observed, "Staley is less worried about impressing her players than impressing upon them. ... [She] sees every day as an opportunity to teach, and she'll use any means possible to reach her players." Staley's Olympic teammate Sue Bird described her as "one funny chick"—yet, as Cherner noted, she does not hesitate to be stern with the team. And former Temple University basketball player Candice Dupree recalled, "Even though she is hard on us a lot of the time, she makes it fun."

Dawn Staley recalls that she tried "screaming all the time," but screaming didn't get results. She added, "I think when you use humor the right way, it's healthy, it's useful and the kids get it. They can laugh and they can have fun while I'm kicking their butts. It's a beautiful thing."[11]

Another important communication skill all coaches need is the ability to listen to emotional warning signs—and the wisdom to know when to press an issue or disengage. Emotions often run high on the athletic field, and that's as it should be.

But leaders need to maintain control of their emotions at all times—even when a player is out of control. The way coaches maintain control of themselves and the situation is through effective communication.

In the late 1960s, Bum Phillips was defensive coordinator of the San Diego Chargers under head coach Sid Gillman. Phillips recalls a day during practice when one of Gillman's players got mad and unleashed a barrage of vile language. Gillman didn't like what the player had to say about him (and his ancestry), so strong words were exchanged on both sides. It looked to Phillips as if the two men might even come to blows.

Then Gillman said, "Wait, wait, hold it! Don't you say anything more, and I won't say anything more. I'm going over to this group here and you go work with the group on the other side of the field. We'll talk about it tomorrow."

Gillman was a wise coach. He saw where this conflict was headed, and he had the sense to pull back and defuse the situation. He would have been within his rights to suspend the insubordinate player—but that would not have helped the team. It might have even escalated the crisis.

Bum Phillips concluded, "Sid was a big man that way. He was a disciplinarian but there also are times when you must call a halt. The alternative is to force the issue and just make it worse. A school superintendent I once worked for told me, 'Don't ever force a guy to tell you no.' If it's important to you and you can see you might get a 'no,' don't force the issue. Walk away. Sid, in that instance, forced the issue but he was man enough not to penalize himself and the player."[12]

Many times, I heard Chuck Daly say, "The most important asset an NBA coach has is 'selective hearing.' You could have a confrontation every minute of the day with somebody in this business. You've got to pick your battles." In other words, coaches shouldn't respond to everything players do wrong. If a player talks back to you in the heat of a game, when emotions are running high, let it go. You didn't hear it.

Phil Jackson underscores the importance of *listening* in dealing with players. In *Sacred Hoops*, he observes that he has learned (often through painful experience) that he gets better performance from his players by backing off and listening to them than by forcing his own agenda on them. "Over the years," he wrote, "I've learned to listen closely to players—not just to what they say, but also to their body language and the silence between the words."[13] This story from Jackson's tenure with the Bulls illustrates his point:

> During the 1991 playoffs … Horace [Grant] was having trouble guarding Armon Gilliam in a series against the Philadelphia 76ers, and he pleaded for some help with a double-team. But even though the strategy I was using wasn't working, I was adamant: I insisted that Horace play Gilliam straight up. Late in the third quarter of Game 3, Gilliam elbowed Horace, and Horace turned and hit him back. The refs called a foul on Horace, and, in a rage, I pulled him out of the game. …

All of a sudden, Horace, who is devoutly religious, was cursing at me and shouting "I'm tired of being your whipping boy." Eventually, after a few more outbursts, he calmed down, but the game was lost. Clinging to a misguided notion of how things should be, I ended up alienating Horace and making a bad judgment that ultimately cost us the game.[14]

The moral of the story: Good coaching requires good two-way communication. Coaches need to listen as well as talk. Leaders tend to think they know best, but sometimes, they need to listen to the people in the trenches—and heed what they say.

Communication—
The Key to Coach-Player Relationships

Like Phil Jackson, Tennessee's Pat Summitt believes that one of a coach's most important tasks is to listen to the players. "I meet four times a year with each player on our team, individually," she says. "We look eyeball to eyeball and talk about everything from her fears to her ambitions. I spell out what her role is and what's expected of her, but more important, I asked what *she* wants. After those talks, I feel more in tune with her. I know what she needs to hear to help her performance. And I have heard *her*. … Listening has allowed me to be a better coach."[15]

It's important to listen not only to what a player says, but what he doesn't say, to his nonverbal cues. When you talk and talk to a player, yet nothing gets through, talking louder isn't the answer. It's time to listen.

Summitt tells the story of the 1989 Lady Volunteers, led by a phenomenal player named Bridgette Gordon. During an NCAA championship game against Auburn, the Lady Vols had built a big lead. When Auburn came roaring back in the second half and cut Tennessee's lead to six, Summitt called a time-out.

While Coach Summitt was talking to her team, she could see that Bridgette seemed dazed and unresponsive, and she held her hand over her mouth. Though Summitt didn't know it, Bridgette Gordon had taken an elbow in the mouth, damaging her front teeth. She was in extreme pain, but didn't want anyone to know about her injury.

All Coach Summitt knew was that her star player seemed inattentive, and she had to find a way to reach her. "She was our leading scorer, our go-to player," Summit recalled. "We needed her to take the game over."

So, Summitt got right in Bridgette Gordon's face, just inches from her nose, and yelled over the crowd noise, "Bridgette, are you listening to me?"

Bridgette nodded vaguely, but still seemed detached.

"Bridgette Gordon," Summitt shouted, "what's wrong? You can't tell me Auburn wants this game more than you do!"

The player said nothing, just shook her head. Coach Summitt pulled her hand from her mouth and told her she had to get back in the game and *do* something—she couldn't hide behind her hand. The girl nodded—and Summitt hoped she had managed to reach her.

The game resumed—and Bridgette, dazed and hurting, went out and made four consecutive shots. In no time at all, the Lady Vols had padded their lead to 18. But Coach Summitt's rough treatment of Bridgette had hurt the coach-player relationship. After sinking those shots, Bridgette glared at Summitt with a look of resentment.

After the game, Pat Summitt learned about Bridgette's injury and sent her to a dentist for emergency treatment. The girl had a loose tooth and required a root canal to save it.

"I felt awful," Summit recalled. "Did I say the right thing, or the wrong thing? I still don't know. But I had to trust that Bridgette and I understood each other."

As it turned out, the coach-player relationship, though strained, was not broken. Summitt reflected, "The only reason I could speak to Bridgette that way and still maintain a relationship with her was because we had done so much communicating over the years. … A lot of conversations had led up to that moment against Auburn."[16]

Great coaches are great communicators. They motivate and inspire. They teach and listen. They are accessible and available. They communicate with confidence and simplicity. They communicate to build relationships—and the strength of those relationships will get both player and coach through the tough times.

20

Develop Your Leadership Abilities Every Day

©Bob Leverone/Sporting News/ZUMA Press

At the funeral for veteran basketball coach Bill Musselman in 2000, an older man approached Bill's son Eric and told him the following story of a boy he had met some four decades earlier:

> I was driving down the two-lane highway on the way to Orville, Ohio, and saw a boy about 11 or 12 years old. He was dribbling a basketball along the side of the road, using his right hand. I pulled over and said, "Son, where are you going?"
>
> He kept dribbling and replied, "Orville."
>
> "Do you know Orville is 10 miles away?"
>
> "Yes."
>
> "What are you going to do when you get there?"
>
> "Dribble back home with my left hand."

"Eric," the man concluded, "That boy was your father."[1]

The key to Bill Musselman's greatness as a coach was that, from the time he was a boy in rural Ohio, he worked diligently and persistently to develop his basketball abilities every day.

Bill Musselman set a great example for every coach and leader who reads these words: The key to leadership greatness is to develop your leadership abilities every day. Whether you are coaching a sports team, running a business, or commanding a military unit, you must take time every day to develop and improve your leadership skills.

No one remains static from day to day. You are either sharpening your skills—or getting rusty. You are either moving forward—or moving backward. Every day, you can find at least one thing to do to improve your leadership ability.

You can continually improve your coaching skills by physical conditioning, reading, getting input and feedback from others, mentoring and being mentored, and taking courses or private training. Whatever you do, make sure you let your entire team see that you are intensely focused on continuous improvement. If your people see you compromising, they will compromise. If they see you sprinting flat-out for ever-higher goals, they will follow your example and redouble their own efforts.

Vince Lombardi once said, "Contrary to the opinion of many, leaders are not born. Leaders are made, and they are made by effort and hard work."[2] So make sure you put in the effort and hard work, day by day, to become more skilled and effective as a leader and a coach.

Steps to Improving Your Leadership Skills

You are a coach under construction. Sure, you've already got the job. You're already a leader and people look up to you. But the great coaches will tell you that, no matter how good you are, there's always room for improvement.

You were born with some natural leadership skills, yet you can always improve them. You were born lacking other skills, yet you can always learn them. The following are some practical suggestions for becoming even more skilled and effective as a leader and coach.

Ask people to critique you. It takes a tough coach to invite criticism. But I know that, since you are reading this book, you are already committed to self-improvement. You're ready and willing to accept constructive criticism from your bosses, from fellow coaches, and even from your players. Put out a suggestion box and invite people to offer their ideas for improvement, signed or anonymous, as they prefer.

Great leaders are thick-skinned, and constantly striving for excellence, reaching for perfection. The sting of criticism lasts for a moment. The benefits of criticism last a lifetime.

Accept tough new challenges. We learn best by experience—and especially by experiences that stretch us and move us out of our comfort zone. Challenging situations force us to reach deep within ourselves and draw upon resources we didn't know we had. You may fall flat on your face—but so what? In the process, you'll discover what works and what doesn't—and you'll grow stronger and more resilient as a leader.

Network. Attend all the coaching clinics and leadership seminars you can. Establish relationships with other leaders and coaches, and practice two-way sharing of ideas and techniques. When you run up against a specific problem in your day-to-day work, contact your colleagues and ask for their insight.

Embrace change. Don't get stuck in a rut. Eagerly accept new assignments and seek out new professional experiences. When change comes at you, don't avoid it—accept it as an adventure. Shake up the status quo. Try out new ideas, propose new strategies, and rearrange the organizational chart. Let people try their hand at new sets of duties. Constantly look for new approaches and new ways of doing things.

When decisions must be made, pass them through an ethical filter. Never compromise your integrity. Never do something wrong, hoping to get a right result. Do the right thing, even if it hurts you.

Purify your motives. Why did you go into the coaching profession? Is it because you want fame or wealth? Is it because you enjoy bossing people around? If so, you got into coaching for all the wrong reasons. Sure, leaders need to have a healthy sense of self-confidence, and you should be adequately rewarded for your work. But great leaders are always great servants. The most beloved coaches are those who truly care about their players and help them to succeed—even at great personal sacrifice.

As a coach, you ask your players to leave their egos at the door and commit themselves to the team. You should ask no less of yourself. Coaching is not about the coach. It's about the team. It's about a commitment to excellence. Above all, it's about being a servant—not being served.

Don Meyer, head men's basketball coach at Northern State University in South Dakota, says, "We should all study Wooden." That's good advice. When *The Sporting News* ranked the 50 greatest coaches of all time, John Wooden was ranked number one—and rightly so.

Yet the greatest coach of all time is also the most humble, selfless servant of others I have ever met. He coached because he was a teacher at heart, and coaching is teaching. He coached because he wanted to shape minds and influence lives in a positive direction. He wasn't in it for the fame. And he certainly wasn't in it for the money. As ESPN sportswriter Rick Reilly noted, Coach never asked for a raise and never made more than $35,000 a year.

Willie Naulls played basketball under Coach John Wooden from 1953 to 1956. He once said, "John Wooden is a servant. You almost feel uncomfortable, you have so much respect for him, yet he wants to serve you all the time. … I consider Wooden like my father."

In his book *Practical Modern Basketball*, Coach Wooden quotes from the essay "The Art of Leadership" by American advertising man and inspirational author Wilferd Arlan Peterson:

- The leader is a servant.
- The leader sees through the eyes of his followers.
- The leader says, "Let's go!" and leads the way rather than, "Get going!"
- The leader assumes his followers are working with him, not for him.
- The leader is a man builder.
- The leader has faith in people. He believes in them, and thus draws out the best in them.
- The leader uses his heart as well as his head. After he has considered the facts with his head, he lets his heart take a look too. He is a friend.[3]

So, as a coach, ask yourself, "Why am I doing this? What are my motives? What am I in it for?" If you can honestly say, "I am a leader because I am a servant," then you're coaching for the right reasons. Make sure, as you daily improve your leadership skills, that you continually examine and refine your motives for coaching.

Read. This is so important a concept that I am going to devote an entire section to it.

Leaders Are Readers

Not all readers are leaders, but I'm convinced that all great leaders are readers. This is certainly true of Coach Wooden. I have been in his Encino, California, home several times, and each time I pause to admire the many books that line the walls of his home. He is a student of history, poetry, and classic literature.

When I was researching my book *How to Be Like Coach Wooden*, I interviewed many of Coach's former players. Most were impressed by Coach Wooden's love for good books. One of Coach Wooden's former players, Brett Vroman, told me that Coach's love of reading even helped him recruit a player. "I was one of the few players Coach Wooden ever came to personally recruit," Vroman told me. "We lived in Provo, Utah, and my mother was an English teacher. They really hit it off, talking about English literature, reciting lines of poetry, and so forth." Before Coach left the Vroman home, Brett's parents told him that they couldn't imagine their son playing for any other coach.

Another former UCLA player, Bill Johnson, recalled, "One year at Christmas we took a road trip to Michigan State and Bradley. A couple of us had to take an English Lit exam at the hotel and Coach Wooden served as the proctor. I'll never forget how he talked with us about poetry and his love for the written and spoken word. He could have taught the course."[4]

Vince Lombardi holds the number two slot on *The Sporting News* list of the 50 greatest coaches of all time. He, too, was a devoted reader and a student of history and literature. Coach Lombardi's son, Vince, Jr., described his famous father this way:

> He was a thoughtful person with a quick mind, trained mostly by Jesuits. He thought and worried about deep issues, including the sometimes conflicting demands that were imposed upon him by his faith and his career. (Faith called upon him to be patient and forgiving; football required him to be impatient, tough, and relentless.) He was fond of the classics and enjoyed playing Latin word games with his old parochial school buddies. He read voraciously.[5]

Notre Dame's Knute Rockne, who was number 10 on the *Sporting News* list of greatest coaches, was an ardent reader, both as a Notre Dame student and as Notre Dame's most illustrious coach. Ray Robinson, in his biography of Knute Rockne, wrote:

He was an exemplary student. He worked diligently at his studies and also became involved in a number of extracurricular activities. He was one of the editors of *The Dome*, the school's yearbook. ...

He got a 98 in English in 1913, a course that emphasized oration, an early sign that Knute was warming up for his role as one of the most eloquent football coaches of all time. ... Rockne's intense participation in sports, including the captaincy of the football team in his senior year, plus a load of outside jobs and extracurricular activities, failed to deter him from achieving near-perfection as a student, and magna cum laude honors. ...

Father Cavanaugh paid an extraordinary tribute to Rockne, saying that Knute was never unprepared in the classroom. ... "In addition to his scientific studies, he was deeply interested in cultural things and read broadly in general literature. His was a case of brain hunger. It remained so until the end of his life," said Father Cavanaugh.[6]

I love Father Cavanaugh's statement that Rockne had "a case of brain hunger." What a vivid description of the mindset of a voracious reader. All the great coaches I've ever known have had hungry brains. They hunger for knowledge. They thirst for the wisdom of history. They crave new ideas.

As a coach, you never know where the next great insight will come from. You may discover a whole new approach to coaching your team from the memoirs of a great general, or from a history of the battle at Thermopylae, or from a science fiction novel. As a reader, you should not only be voracious, but omnivorous. Don't just read books on coaching. Read on a wide variety of subjects. You'll discover coaching insights in books on history, science, psychology, sociology, literature, politics, and on and on.

Reading not only informs you, it sharpens your thought processes, broadens your experience and understanding, and increases your wisdom. As you read and acquire stories and thought-provoking quotations, you will become a more captivating speaker, able to convey your vision to your team more persuasively and powerfully.

Tony Romo is almost as famous for his dating life (country singer Carrie Underwood, actress Sophia Bush, and singer Jessica Simpson) as he is for quarterbacking the Dallas Cowboys. What is less well known is that Tony Romo is not only a leader on the field, he is a reader on the sidelines.

A graduate of Eastern Illinois University, Romo joined the Cowboys in 2003 as an undrafted free agent. During his early years with Dallas, he remained second or third on the depth chart behind starting quarterbacks Vinny Testaverde and Drew Bledsoe.

In 2006, Dallas head coach Bill Parcells elevated him to starting quarterback. In games, Romo has displayed confidence, awareness, and streaks of brilliance, plus the ability to bounce back from adversity. He's a leader on the field.

A profile of Romo in *The Dallas Morning News* called him "a fan of sports history. He'll read books to learn what makes somebody great and incorporate that into what he does."[7] And *New York Times* reporter Juliet Macur described him as "the geek who devours motivational books." She went on to say:

> Romo sat on the bench for three years, watching and learning. And he read books. During downtime, he curled up on a blue leather couch in the locker room and studied motivational books about sports. He read about Larry Bird and Pat Riley and Jordan. He read about Johnny Unitas and Vince Lombardi, and twice read the same book about Secretariat.
>
> "I just tried to learn little things that helped me out as a player," Romo said. "All those little things really do help you, just like I might put on 'Rocky' music because it makes you say, 'Now I want to go out and run.' That stuff gets you going."[8]

All great leaders are eager, hungry readers. As a coach, nurture a brain that is hungry for good books, and then nourish your hungry brain every day of your life.

Make Room for Your Mentors

A final word of advice, coach: If you want to improve your leadership ability on a daily basis, make room in your life for your mentors.

I have been in the college and pro sports business for more than 50 years. And from my earliest days as a Minor League Baseball executive to the present day, I have continually gone back to my mentors for advice. Every time I've faced a tough decision, or have gone through adversity and opposition, or have simply needed a reality check, I've consulted my mentors for an extra helping of their experience and wisdom.

I can't count the times I have gone to Andy Seminick or Bill Durney, my mentors in the Phillies farm club system, or Mr. R. E. Littlejohn, who owned the first team I ever operated. Many times, I drove to Bill Veeck's home for another infusion of his leadership wisdom. I have often turned for advice to Dr. Jack Ramsay, who gave me my first job in the NBA, and to my friend Rich DeVos, owner of the Orlando Magic, and these men have steered me through difficult passages in my career and personal life.

Here I am, at a stage when many people are coming to me for advice, looking to me as their mentor, yet I still make room in my life for my own mentors. Many of them have passed away, but their wise words still resonate in my memory. Those who are living continue to hear from me on a regular basis. You may outlive your mentors, but you will never outgrow the need for their insight.

Kellie Jolly Harper is a coach who understands the value of mentors. She played on Pat Summitt's Tennessee women's basketball team in the late 1990s, and helped power the Lady Vols to three consecutive championships, including the undefeated season in 1998-1999. During Kellie Harper's four years with the Lady Vols, the team compiled a 131-17 record. As point guard, she was the leader on the floor, so it was only natural that she would eventually become a coach in her own right.

In fact, Harper is a proud "branch" of Pat Summitt's far-flung coaching tree, which includes more than 70 former players and assistants. As successor to the late and legendary North Carolina coach Kay Yow, Kellie Harper has taken on a daunting challenge. Yow coached the women's Wolfpack for 34 years before succumbing to cancer in January 2009. Harper has accepted that mantle after coaching the Catamounts of Western Carolina for five seasons.[9]

The relationship between Pat Summitt and Kellie Harper is not just one of coach and former player, but a continuing relationship of mentor and protégé. Kellie Harper's respect for her mentor knows no bounds. "Pat Summitt is huge for the game of women's basketball," Harper says. "She is a pioneer, a legacy, a legend and all of those adjectives."[10]

Her respect for her mentor has only grown after coaching against her. "Sometimes it's a little surreal and you look down at the other end of the court and you realize your coach is down there," she says.[11] Pat Summitt, meanwhile, has become accustomed to hearing from Harper and from other former players and assistants on a continuing basis. "They'll call," she says, "and they want to say, 'Okay, here's a situation and I want to get your opinion on it.'"[12]

Kellie Harper has not only gone back to Summitt for advice and insight, but she has arranged for her own players to interview and question Summitt via an Internet connection. Pat Summitt is glad to be a mentor even to players she may have to coach against in future games.

Though Harper is content to be herself and to coach her teams her own way, she acknowledges that much of who she is and what she does as a coach was instilled in her by Pat Summitt. In fact, Harper identifies with her mentor in many ways. "Pat and I grew up very similarly," she says. "She came from a very close-knit family. Her parents expected her to be a good person and always do things the right way. She had to work on her family farm. In those regards, we're very, very similar. We both are very proud of where we come from and will never forget that." In an interview with the *Sparta Expositor*, Harper listed some of the Summitt qualities she seeks to emulate:

- *Poise*: "I know I'm not Pat Summitt as a coach," Kellie Harper says. "I can't be her. I wish I could be, but I do try to emulate her poise on the sidelines. That was one of my favorite things as a player. No matter what the situation, no matter how much time was on the clock, she always made our team settle down just with her tone and her confidence. She knew how to pass that along with her body language and what she said."
- *Genuineness*: "She is what she is. When you see Pat on television, that's the way she really is. … She's really tough in practice, but the part you don't see is she's very funny and very genuine."
- *Class*: "Pat runs a classy program first and foremost. When I say classy, I mean from the way the pictures are hung on the wall to the way your players dress to the way they act in a restaurant to how they treat guests on campus. Everything we do, I want it to be with the utmost of class."
- *High recruiting standards*: "She doesn't settle when she recruits. She wants the whole package. She wants good people, good players, good students and, at the same time, she wants her players to develop in all those aspects while they are in her program."
- *A focus on good character*: "We try to recruit … good character because I have seen you can be successful doing it the right way. We try to teach them more than basketball while they are a part of our program. Pat always told us we were in a fish bowl. She said people know who you are and are always watching. You never know when you'll make an impact on somebody."
- *Adaptability*: "Year after year, she is always at or near the top. Some coaches will be successful for a while, then fall off and maybe rise again. She's always there. No matter what goes on in the regular season, she seems to always be contending for a championship. That is a testament to her adapting. She has won over the years with all different types of teams and players. She adapts to the different style of kids she coaches and to the way basketball has changed. … She is always trying to learn something new from anybody at any level."
- *Intensity*: "She never walked into a practice slow. It was always full speed walking—a very 'let's-get-in-here-and-get-this-done' walk. … Every drill was intense. … We always went full speed in every single drill."
- *Teachability*: "I will never forget being on the sidelines and her turning to her assistants and saying, 'Help me. What do we need to do?' She utilizes her staff and their strengths. That taught me an invaluable lesson. If you are going to have good people around you, use them. When you talk to her, she's like a sponge. She processes everything you say and you just know she's filing it away and, at some point, she might want to use it one day in her program. It's amazing. That is one thing that makes her successful—her drive to get better."[13]

Kellie Harper couldn't have chosen a better role model to emulate, or a more accomplished mentor to learn from. Though Harper is a talented and accomplished coach and mentor in her own right, she wisely makes room for her own mentor—and she stays focused on developing and improving her leadership abilities every day. That's how a good coach becomes great, and how a great coach spreads the branches of her coaching tree.

Don't settle for "good." Become a *great* coach. Develop your leadership abilities every day.

21

Win!

I once heard Steve Spurrier tell a story from his boyhood. He was 13 and playing on his first team, a Babe Ruth league baseball team. His father, a Presbyterian minister, was the coach.

The first day of practice, Steve's father asked all the boys on the team a question: "How many of you boys believe in the old saying, 'It's not whether you win or lose, but how you play the game that counts'?"

Half the boys raised their hands—but not Steve. He knew that was the wrong answer. He recalled, "My dad told the team, 'The game is played to win. And we're going to try our best to win the game.' That really spoke to me. Winning was a big part of what my dad was all about, and that intensity about winning is a big part of what I'm all about today."

In late May and early June 1944, General George S. Patton toured U.S. Army bases in England, giving a stirring speech to fire up the troops just prior to the D-Day invasion of Europe. He said, "Americans love a winner and cannot tolerate a loser. Americans play to win—all the time. I wouldn't give a hoot for a man who lost and laughed. … The very thought of losing is hateful to an American."[1]

Another prominent World War II general, Bernard Montgomery of Great Britain, had this outlook, "You can't be a great general and have defeats."

Mike Martin, head baseball coach at Florida State University, told me a story from his earliest days as coach of the Seminoles. "It was 1980," he said, "and my first game as coach at Florida State was sheer misery. We were shut out 10 to nothing by the University of Miami. We were so bad, we didn't even get a runner to third base. Then we lost the second game on an error in the bottom of the ninth.

"After that, we came back to win the third game in the top of the ninth, and I felt really good about that win. We got on the bus and were driving away from the Miami campus, and we saw the U.M. coach punishing his players with extra wind sprints. My assistant coach, Jim Morris (who's now head coach at U.M.) turned to me and said, 'Are we really this bad? We beat them one game out of three, and their coach punishes them!'

"Those wind sprints were designed to teach those players about being competitive—and it reinforced a lesson in my own mind as well. Great leaders aren't content with two wins out of three. They want to win it all."

When former Giants quarterback Phil Simms appeared on my sports talk radio show, I asked him the most important lesson he learned from his old coach, Bill Parcells. Simms replied, "Bill taught us that the only thing that matters is winning. No one cares who was injured or what went wrong during the game or any of the other circumstances. All people want to know is, 'Did you win or not?'"

That's what this coaching life is all about: Winning. Your job is to get your players to care enough about winning that they will do whatever it takes, make any sacrifice, endure any pain, and go through walls for you—all for the sake of winning.

A Coach's Product: Winning

What is winning? Often it can be boiled down to this: Make sure the other guy loses, and make sure you don't. In other words, games are *lost* as often as they are *won*.

Games are lost by mental mistakes, missed free throws, blown coverages, missed assignments, impatience, inattention, and sheer frustration. Games are lost when a quarterback tries to force a pass into heavy traffic—and turns a TD into an INT. Games are lost when a point guard loses focus and forgets there are only two seconds left in the fourth quarter. Games are lost in the bottom of the ninth, when a batter grounds into a double play with bases loaded and one away.

As former Steelers head coach Chuck Noll has said, "Before you can win a game, you must first not lose it."[2] Or as Bobby Knight put it, "Victory favors the team making the fewest mistakes."[3]

Sometimes, in order to win, you've got to find a way to make the other guy lose. You do that by studying your opponent, finding out what works for him—then depriving him of it. As Woody Hayes used to say, "We've always taken great pride in taking away an opponent's best play. For many years we've had an expression: 'Make them beat us left-handed.'"[4]

Farmers produce crops. Bakers produce cakes. A coach's product is wins, pure and simple. If a coach doesn't deliver that product often enough, he ends up collecting unemployment. The late head coach of the San Francisco 49ers, Bill Walsh, put it this way:

> The bottom line in professional sports is winning. Everything has to focus on that product: winning football games. Other offshoots—the public relations, the merchandising, the high-sounding philosophical approach—mean little compared with being successful on the playing field. But winning does not necessarily mean being a victor in every game. It's not winning every game at any cost. We have to remind ourselves that it's not just a single game that we are trying to win. It is a season and a series of seasons in which the team wins more games than it loses and each team member plays up to his potential. If you are continually developing your skills and refining your approach, then winning will be the final result.[5]

True words. Winning must be honest and honorable, but winning is the goal. Good character is not only about being honest, hard-working, humble, and disciplined. Good character is also expressed in being competitive and focused on excellence. The desire to compete hard and win is at the heart of what you seek to teach your players. If you're not coaching to win, you're in the wrong profession.

The Most Exciting Thing to Watch Is Winning

Great coaches are intensely competitive. Two of the most competitive coaches I've ever known are the Van Gundy brothers, Jeff and Stan.

Jeff Van Gundy has served as head coach of the NBA's New York Knicks and the Houston Rockets. He coached the Knicks to the playoffs six times—most famously, during the Knicks' "Cinderella season," which took them to the 1999 NBA Finals. How intense was Jeff when he was coaching? During an ESPN broadcast interview on March 6, 2009, he admitted getting only three or four hours of sleep per night during the season. That's *intense*.

What drove Jeff Van Gundy? He hated to lose! "There's a lot more misery in losing than joy in winning," he once said. "What you do as a coach is move on to the next game. Great road wins stick with you a little bit more, but certainly the losses stick with you more than the wins."

A profile of Jeff Van Gundy in the *New York Times* noted that his "almost maniacal attention to detail has made Van Gundy's teams among the most prepared in the league. And when the playoffs come around, when Van Gundy has more time to focus on one opponent, the Knicks' preparedness is what gives them their edge. … If Van Gundy ever lets go of his obsession, even a little bit, he may let go of his excellence as a coach as well."

"I think Jeff is going to burn himself out," said Brendan Malone, a former Van Gundy assistant. "He could last a long time if he would relax, but that's not his nature. He doesn't exhale. That's his edge. If he exhales, it's over. Everybody exhales except for Jeff Van Gundy."[6] Now that Jeff has traded the sidelines for the broadcast booth, perhaps he is getting more sleep—and taking time to exhale now and then.

Jeff's brother Stan is every bit as intense. He was head coach of the Miami Heat from 2003 to 2005, and joined our Orlando Magic organization as head coach in 2007. In his first season with the Magic, Stan Van Gundy coached the team to a 52-win season and the first division championship in more than a decade. The Magic beat the Toronto Raptors 4–1 in round one of the playoffs, then lost the Eastern Semifinals to the Detroit Pistons 4–1.

In Stan's second year, the 2008-2009 season, the Magic won 59 games—the second most regular season wins in franchise history. The Magic again won the division, then went on to beat the Cleveland Cavaliers (who had the best record in the NBA) in the Eastern Conference Finals 4-2. Next, Stan led the Magic into the NBA Finals for the first time since 1995; the Magic lost to Kobe Bryant and the Los Angeles Lakers in five games.

"He's one of those coaches," said Lakers coach Phil Jackson, "whose teams always seem to produce more than the sum of their parts. I'd describe him as resilient, resourceful and relentless."[7] And *The Sporting News* described Stan's intensity this way:

> [Stan Van Gundy] doesn't wear a tie with his jacket. His face is often unshaved and scruffy. He seems to live and die with each play. He'll cover his face, pull his hair, stomp his foot and scream at players in that high-pitched tone—which [Magic center Dwight] Howard loves to mock—for even the smallest detail. Sometimes he'll do it all on the same play.

Stan's players find his manic intensity to be annoying, motivating, and inspiring, all at the same time. Dwight Howard says, "Me and Stan have had our ups and downs, but he is a great motivator. Even when he's yelling and screaming, throughout all that, he finds a way to put in just an ounce of something to get us fired up."

Point guard Rafer Alston played for Stan Van Gundy in both Miami and Orlando. Alston recalled a moment during the Eastern Conference Finals against Cleveland when he committed a late turnover. Immediately, Stan started blasting Alston from the sideline. As Alston ran past his apoplectic coach, he replied, "What could you possibly be yelling about? We're up by 40!" Even so, Alston adds, he admires Stan Van Gundy's passion for winning.

So does Magic general manager Otis Smith. "He talks about winning a championship every day," Smith told the Associated Press. "He deserves the credit for raising the bar, [for an attitude which says] that just getting to the playoffs is not good enough." The AP article concludes:

Van Gundy gets it done with one gear. The coach is rarely outworked.

> There have been nights when Van Gundy has gone straight from the airport after a road trip to the Magic's practice facility to watch film until the team meeting the next morning. He was so engulfed by work this season that he had to buy a new car after he went about 30,000 miles without changing the oil in the old one.

The NBA Finals are only causing that stress to swell.

"At 3 in the morning, I can't sleep because I'm worrying about how to stop Kobe Bryant," Van Gundy said.[8]

For Stan Van Gundy, it's all about winning. At his 2007 news conference when he arrived as head coach of the Magic, he said that he intended to introduce "a style of play that is fun for players to play and exciting for the fans to watch. But the most exciting thing to watch is when you are winning, and I don't think we want to forget that. There are some teams out there, and I'm not going to name names, that scored a lot of points this year and it wasn't too exciting because they weren't winning games. So the number one thing is that we want to win."[9]

The Thrill of Victory

As starting quarterback of the San Francisco 49ers, Steve Young won league MVP awards in 1992 and 1994. He led the 49ers to three Super Bowl championships (Super Bowls XXIII, XXIV, and XXIX). He has known the thrill of standing with his teammates at the absolute pinnacle of his profession. He once described what that moment feels like:

My favorite moment still was the five minutes after the Super Bowl when we were alone in the locker room. Just the fifty players and coaches kneeling in the Lord's Prayer, then looking up at each other and realizing that, yes, we're world champions. No media, no one, just us. That feeling when you do something great together is like no other.[10]

Jon Gruden expresses that feeling in these words: "The thrill of victory at the highest, man, that's what we're in it for. That's what it's all about. We're not here for the Liberty Bowl watches and Peach Bowl rings. Every year there is a game you got to get to—and you got to win it."[11]

And my friend Bobby Bowden, longtime head football coach at Florida State, once told me, "I still believe that winning is the greatest feeling there is in coaching." Bobby should know. He experienced the feeling of winning almost three times as often as he experienced defeat. After Bowden retired in January 2010, I heard him say, "If I had won some more ball games I would have signed another five-year contract. That's how good I feel. But I didn't win enough dadgum games."

Dr. Rosabeth Moss Kanter holds the Ernest L. Arbuckle Professorship at Harvard Business School. She is an expert on employee performance and managing change in competitive environments. In her 2004 book *Confidence: How Winning and Losing Streaks Begin and End*, she writes:

Winning creates a positive aura around everything, a "halo" effect that encourages positive team behavior that makes further wins more likely. Winning makes it easier to attract the best talent, the most loyal fans, the biggest revenues to reinvest in perpetuating victory. Losing has a repellent effect. It is harder for the team to bond, harder for it to attract new talent, easier for it to fall behind. Winners get the benefit of the doubt. Losing breeds qualms. In the midst of a winning streak, winners are assumed to have made brilliant moves when perhaps they were just lucky. In the midst of a losing streak, if losers eke out a victory, sometimes they are assumed to have cheated.

In short, confidence grows in winning streaks and helps propel a tradition of success. Confidence erodes in losing streaks, and its absence makes it hard to stop losing.[12]

In short, winning begets more winning. Losing begets more losing. The thrill of victory produces the habits of victory. The agony of defeat creates its own downward-tending spiral. As former Notre Dame football coach Lou Holtz once told me, "I don't want to win all the games—only the next one."

So, as a coach, you must find ways to make that first victory happen. Then the next. And the next. The thrill of victory will become habit-forming, and lead to more and more wins.

The Agony of Defeat

Sports is not just about the thrill of victory. It's often about the agony of defeat. No true competitor can ever be content to lose. Yet, every coach must face the fact that losing is a fact of life. Undefeated seasons are rare.

So how do you reconcile the inevitability of an eventual loss with an intense desire to win every game? Losing is totally unacceptable—but when you lose, you must find a way to endure what you cannot accept. After Vince Lombardi left Green Bay to coach the Washington Redskins, he explained how he dealt with the paradox:

I used to run the Green Bay Packers. At first, we didn't win. Later on, we won our fair share. Still never as many as I wanted. Which was all of them. ... Second place is meaningless. You can't always be first, but you have to believe that you should have been—that you were never beaten—that time just ran out on you.[13]

Winning is never final—but neither is defeat. Don Shula, the only NFL coach to lead a team through an undefeated season, had this to say about winning and losing: "When we win, we know it's not final. We know we've got to line up next week and prove ourselves all over again. If we lose, we also know we're not dead and we must get off the floor and have a chance to change the score the next time we play."[14]

In a 2002 article in *Capitalism Magazine*, former General Electric CEO Jack Welch tells a story from his high school years about the agony of defeat, and how his first and toughest coach—his mother—taught him to get over it.

Young Jack Welch was co-captain of his high school hockey team. After getting off to a good start and winning the first three games of the season, Welch's team lost the next six games, five of them by just one goal.

In the 10th game of the season, Welch's teammates had battled their way to a 2-2 tie (Welch himself had scored both team goals), and they felt revved up and optimistic as they went into sudden-death overtime. But only a few minutes into the overtime period, their opponents scored. It was their seventh loss in a row—and all the more devastating because they had come so close to winning.

Angry and frustrated, Welch flung his hockey stick across the ice, then he skated after it, picked up the stick, and headed to the locker room. While Welch was in the locker room, commiserating with his teammates, the locker room door crashed open. His mother strode into the locker room, her Irish eyes blazing.

All eyes were on the middle-aged woman in the flowered-print dress who stalked past the wooden benches, oblivious of Welch's half-dressed teammates. She headed straight for Jack and yanked him up by the fabric of his uniform.

"You punk!" she said. "If you don't know how to lose, you'll never know how to win! If you don't know this, you shouldn't be playing!"

Welch was mortified and humiliated—yet he knew his mother was right, and the embarrassing lesson of that moment stayed with him throughout his life. He concluded:

> Grace Welch taught me the value of competition, just as she taught me the pleasure of winning and the need to take defeat in stride.
>
> If I have any leadership style, a way of getting the best out of people, I owe it to her. ... Many of my basic management beliefs—things like competing hard to win, facing reality, motivating people by alternately hugging and kicking them, setting stretch goals, and relentlessly following up on people to make sure things get done—can be traced to her as well. ...

It was over the kitchen table, playing gin rummy with her, that I learned the fun and joy of competition. I remember racing across the street from the schoolyard for lunch when I was in the first grade, itching for the chance to play gin rummy with her. When she beat me, which was often, she'd put the winning cards on the table and shout, "Gin!" I'd get so mad, but I couldn't wait to come home again and get the chance to beat her.

That was probably the start of my competitiveness, on the baseball diamond, the hockey rink, the golf course, and business.[15]

Some of the best insights on losing come from the winningest coach of all time, John Wooden. In his book *Wooden On Leadership*, he says:

When you give your total effort—everything you have—the score can never make you a loser. And when you do less, it can't somehow magically turn you into a winner. …

Sometimes the competition you and your organization face will be bigger or stronger, more experienced or better financed. … Teach those under your leadership that success is theirs when together you summon the will to put forth everything you have. …

We live in a society obsessed with winning and being number one. Don't follow the pack. Rather, focus on the process instead of the prize. Even during the height of UCLA's best seasons, I never fixated on winning—didn't even mention it. Rather, I did everything I could to make sure that all our players gave everything they had to give, both in practice and in games. The score will take care of itself when you take care of the effort that precedes the score.[16]

Or, as Coach Mike Krzyzewski put it so succinctly, "Our goal is not to win. It's to play together and play hard. Then winning takes care of itself."[17]

Maybe it seems like I'm contradicting myself. Earlier, I said that coaching is all about winning. I said that winning is a coach's product, and that a coach must mass-produce that product or face unemployment. Winning is the goal, and if you're not coaching to win, you're in the wrong business.

But now we hear Coach Wooden and Coach Krzyzewski both saying that we shouldn't fixate on winning. Isn't that a contradiction?

No. It's a paradox, not a contradiction. A paradox is where two statements seem to contradict each other, yet both are true. The paradox here is that our goal is to win, but we achieve that goal by focusing not on winning, but by *doing the things that lead to winning*. We win not by being obsessed with winning, but by being focused on the process, on the preparation, on the intangible qualities like character and loyalty, on playing together and playing hard.

If we focus on that process, John Wooden says, "The score will take care of itself." If the team plays together and plays hard, Coach Krzyzewski says, "Then winning takes care of itself." That is the profound and paradoxical truth of the coaching profession.

The 21 Keys to Coaching—And *Winning*

How do you set your team on the pathway to winning? In the first 20 chapters, we've identified the following key points:

- *Be yourself*. Find out who you are as a coach. Discover what you do best—then do it. Don't try to be something you're not.
- *Build character*. It's not just talent that wins. It's also integrity, diligence, courage, perseverance, and all the other traits that make up good character.
- *Build a strong work ethic*. There is no winning without hard work.
- *Build perseverance*. Winners never quit and quitters never win.
- *Build a disciplined team*. Discipline is the willingness to sacrifice something you want right now in order to gain something far greater.
- *Focus on preparation*. Games are usually won or lost on the practice field, long before the team steps onto the playing field. The team that wins is usually the team that is better prepared.
- *Maintain balance in your life*. Balance is the key to staying power. If you don't have a life, get one.
- *Be bold and confident*. A certain amount of risk-taking is essential to winning. Before taking a risk, do your homework and study the facts, but also listen to your intuition. Calculated risks pay off more often than not. When presented with two evenly balanced courses of action, always choose the bolder.
- *Be a teacher and a learner*. If you focus on teaching your players what they need to be successful in life, winning will be a byproduct. If you also focus on becoming a life-long learner, you set a winning example for your players.
- *Care for your players as people*. Your team is made up of human beings, not X's and O's. Care for them, respect them, and they will come through for you.
- *Maintain passion, enthusiasm, and fun*. If you aren't passionate about coaching, why do it? If the game isn't fun, why play it?
- *Take care of the little things*. If you do, then the big things, such as winning, will take care of themselves.

- *Surround yourself with loyal people.* Be loyal to your players and staff, and they will repay your loyalty many times over.
- *Empower your players.* Make them believe they are winners, and they will go out and win for you.
- *Maintain a unity of purpose with a diversity of skills.* Recruit a diverse group of players representing a variety of personalities and skills. Point them to a common goal. Imbue them with a single purpose. The result: Winning chemistry.
- *There's no substitute for talent.* Make sure you get the most out of the talent you've got.
- *Learn to handle the media and the critics.* Coaches live in a media fishbowl. A prickly relationship with your critics will only distract your team from the goal of winning.
- *It's always about the team.* When the team excels, we all win.
- *Communicate!* Great coaches can inspire and motivate teams with words alone. Persuade your players that winning is their destiny, and they will work harder to fulfill their destiny.
- *Develop your leadership abilities every day.* Set an example to your team of continuous personal improvement.
- These are the first 20 principles of great coaching, as outlined throughout this book. Add them all together, and they equal the 21st principle: *Win!*

Epilogue: "His Last Words Were About Winning"

Finally, let me tell you a story about a man who was intensely competitive until his dying day. That man was Wellington T. "Duke" Mara, co-owner of the NFL's New York Giants from 1959 until his death in October 2005, and son of Giants founder Tim Mara.

Duke was known as a man who cared about his staff and players as much as he cared about winning. Even after people left his organization, if they fell on hard times or became ill, Duke would pay for their housing and medical treatment. He sometimes kept old-timers on his payroll out of personal loyalty, even though he could not always justify the cost. He operated on the premise: Once a Giant, *always* a Giant.

Former Giants linebacker Harry Carson loved Mr. Mara. "Even though he was the owner, he was like a player," Carson said. "After every game, he was the first one to come into the locker room. After a win, you'd see a big, broad smile on his face and [he would] congratulate every player. After a loss, he'd come around and tell the players to hold their heads up. He was one of us."

On Sunday, October 23, 2005, the Giants hosted the Denver Broncos in New York. The morning of the game, Mara's son told him, "Dad, we're playing Denver today." Duke Mara smiled weakly and said, "I don't want to lose."

The Giants trailed the Broncos through most of the game. Eli Manning, in his first year as starting quarterback, led his team back from a fourth-quarter deficit on a last-chance drive. On the final play, he eluded the grasp of a Broncos defender and scored on a two-yard touchdown pass to Amani Toomer with five seconds remaining. The Giants won 24-23, snapping Denver's five-game winning streak.

It was an intensely emotional win for the Giants because Coach Tom Coughlin had informed the team that the 89-year-old owner was at his home in Rye, New York, dying of cancer. The players wanted to win this game for Duke Mara. As the team filed into the locker room following the big win, they chanted, "Duke, Duke, Duke!"

Sometime after the game, news reached the team that Mr. Mara had watched much of the game from his sick bed, though he had been too weak to stay awake for the entire game. However, he had awakened in time to see Eli Manning's game-winning touchdown pass. The report was that he smiled, then drifted back to sleep.

The day after the game, two of the Giants' star players, Tiki Barber and Jeremy Shockey, visited Mr. Mara at his home. "We were able to say a prayer and say goodbye, and that meant a lot to me," Barber said later.[1]

On Tuesday, October 25, 2005, Duke Mara passed away. My friend Ernie Accorsi, who was the Giants' general manager at that time, summed up the passion of Wellington T. Mara's life: "The last words he spoke were about winning."

So, it's fitting that the last words of this book should be about winning. No matter what game you coach, you are in it to win. You are in it to instill a winning attitude within your players. As Vince Lombardi said, "If winning isn't everything, why do they keep score?"[2]

Earl Weaver, the Baltimore Orioles' Hall of Fame manager, once told former baseball commissioner Fay Vincent, "I was always worried about my next win...always...because if you didn't have enough of them, you were going to get fired, and I didn't want to get fired...not after five years, not after 10 years, not after 15 years. So, I was proud of the fact that that never happened to me."

That's my final word, coach. That's the 21st principle, and I can't make it any simpler than this: Go out and *win!*

Notes

1. Be Yourself

1. Quoted by Donald T. Phillips, *Run to Win: Vince Lombardi on Coaching and Leadership* (New York: St. Martin's Press, 2001), p. 244.
2. Quoted by Vince Lombardi, Jr., *What It Takes to Be #1: Vince Lombardi on Leadership* (New York: McGraw-Hill, 2003), p. 56.
3. Ira Berkow, "Army Head Women's Basketball Coach Maggie Dixon," originally printed in the *New York Times*, reprinted at PatriotLeague.org, March 16, 2006, retrieved at http://www.patriotleague.org/genrel/031606aaa.html; Associated Press, "Autopsy Shows Dixon had Enlarged Heart," ESPN Online, April 14, 2006, retrieved at http://sports.espn.go.com/ncw/news/story?id=2400335.
4. Jay Bilas, "Learn From the Best, But Be Yourself," ESPN.com, December 21, 2003, retrieved at http://sports.espn.go.com/ncb/columns/story?columnist=bilas_jay&id=1691694.
5. Quoted by Terry Pluto, *Falling From Grace* (New York: Simon & Schuster, 1995), p. 187.
6. Quoted by Charles Bennett, "Stallings High on Swinney," *The Post and Courier*, October 17, 2008, retrieved at http://www.postandcourier.com/news/2008/oct/17/stallings_high_on_swinney58184/.
7. David Asman interview with Tony Dungy, "Coach Dungy Moves On," January 27, 2009, retrieved at http://www.foxbusiness.com/search-results/m/21803601/coach-dungy-moves-on.htm.
8. Paul "Bear" Bryant, quoted by Coach's Office, "Selected Lectures from the Past: Paul Bear Bryant—1958-1982 University of Alabama," retrieved at http://www.coachsoffice.com/lectures_from_the_past.htm.
9. Quoted by Larry Chang, *Wisdom for the Soul* (Washington, DC: Gnosophia Publishers, 2006), p. 423.
10. Joe Posnanski, "Talkin' Pitch Counts and Nolan Ryan's Crusade, with Bill James," *Sports Illustrated* Online, June 15, 2009, retrieved at http://m.si.com/news/sp/wr_mlb_sports/detail/1673139/full%3Bjsessionid=76ACD87D27EA36A7B1CFF3B22D4EACA8.cnnsilive9i.
11. Willy Stern and Elias Levenson, "Secrets of the Survivors," *BusinessWeek*, October 9, 1995, retrieved at http://www.businessweek.com/archives/1995/b344582.arc.htm.

12. Quoted by Pat Williams with Michael Weinreb, *Marketing Your Dreams* (Champaign, IL: Sports Publishing, 2001), p. 88.

13. Adam de Jong, "The Soul of UCLA, On- and Off-Court," *The Daily Bruin*, October 19, 2005, retrieved at http://dailybruin.ucla.edu/stories/2005/oct/19/ithe-soul-of-ucla-on-and-off-c/.

2. Build Character

1. John R. Wooden with Steve Jamison, *The Essential Wooden* (New York: McGraw-Hill, 2006), p. 192.

2. John Wooden with Steve Jamison, *Wooden: A Lifetime of Observations and Reflections On and Off the Court* (New York: McGraw-Hill, 1997), p. 93.

3. Quoted by Coach Hugh Wyatt, "Coach Hugh Wyatt's Football Coaching News You Can Use," retrieved at http://coachwyatt.com/May02.html.

4. Whitey Herzog, *You're Missin' a Great Game* (New York: Berkley, 2000), p. 172.

5. Bob LaMonte with Robert L. Shook, *Winning the NFL Way* (New York: HarperBusiness, 2004), pp. 77-78.

6. Dean Smith with Gerald D. Bell, *The Carolina Way: Leadership Lessons from a Life in Coaching* (New York: Penguin, 2004), p. 88.

7. Quoted by David Chadwick, *The 12 Leadership Principles of Dean Smith* (Kingston, NY: Total Sports, 1999), p. 129.

8. Head Football Coach Lou Holtz, "Philosophies on Coaching," Lou Holtz Online, retrieved at http://louholtzonline.tripod.com/holtzism.html.

9. Lou Holtz with John Heisler, *The Fighting Spirit: a Championship Season at Notre Dame* (New York: Pocket Books, 1989), p. 53.

10. Eva Wolever, "Idlewild Baptist Church Member Super Bowl XLI Head Coach," *Florida Baptist Witness*, February 1, 2007, retrieved at http://www.floridabaptistwitness.com/692 8.article.

3. Build a Strong Work Ethic

1. Encyclopedia of World Biography: Notable Biographies, Sh-Z, "Patricia Head Summitt Biography," retrieved at http://www.notablebiographies.com/news/Sh-Z/Summitt-Patricia-Head.html.

2. Al Browning, *I Remember Paul "Bear" Bryant* (Nashville: Cumberland House Publishing, 2001), p. xxii.

3. Ibid., p. 157.

4. Henry T. Blackaby, *Spiritual Leadership: Moving People on to God's Agenda* (Nashville: B&H Publishing Group, 2001), pp. 153-154.

5. Quoted by John A. Byrne, *Fast Company: The Rules of Business—55 Essential Ideas to Help Smart People (and Organizations) Perform at Their Best* (New York: Broadway, 2008), p. 102.

6. Kenneth H. Blanchard and Don Shula, *The Little Book of Coaching: Motivating People to Be Winners* (New York: HarperBusiness, 2001), p. 33.

7. Jack Gallagher, "Vermeil: the Epitome of Coaching and Class," original publication date unknown, retrieved at http://search.japantimes.co.jp/cgi-bin/sp20000127jg.html.

8. Alison Rostankowski, interviewer, and Rex Kern, interviewee, "Beyond the Gridiron— The Life and Times of Woody Hayes," Crouse Entertainment Group and WOSU-Columbus, Ohio, October 2002, retrieved at http://www.duncanentertainment.com/interview_kern.php.

9. Vince Lombardi, Jr., *The Lombardi Rules: 26 Lessons From Vince Lombardi, the World's Greatest Coach* (New York: McGraw-Hill, 2004), p. 30.

10. Ibid.

11. Paul De La Garza, "A Man and His Mission: Gen. Tommy Franks Shares His Thoughts on Life, Religion and War in a Question-And-Answer Session," *St. Petersburg Times*, December 12, 2001, retrieved at http://www.sptimes.com/News/121201/news_pf/Worldandnation/A_man_and_his_mission.shtml.

12. Ibid.

4. Build Perseverance

1. Brent Zwerneman, *Game of My Life: 25 Stories of Aggies Football* (Champaign, IL: Sports Publishing, 2003), pp. 47-49.

2. Dinesh D'Souza, *Ronald Reagan* (New York: Free Press, 1999), p. 239.

3. Donald T. Phillips, *The Founding Fathers on Leadership* (New York: Grand Central Publishing, 1998), p. 244.

4. Quoted by Bruce Allar, "Currying No Favors," *The Sporting News*, November 21, 1994, retrieved at http://findarticles.com/p/articles/mi_m1208/is_n21_v218/ai_15903796/.

5. Quoted by Benjamin J. Stein, "Mistakes Winners Don't Make," *Reader's Digest*, November 1994, p. 205.

6. Author unknown, "Kay Yow," NC State Wolfpack website, retrieved at http://www.gopack.com/ViewArticle.dbml?DB_OEM_ID=9200&ATCLID=522025.

7. Shera Everette, "NC State Coach Yow Succumbs to Cancer," *Rocky Mount Telegram*, January 24, 2009, retrieved at http://www.rockymounttelegram.com/news/nc-state-coach-yow-succumbs-to-cancer-392836.html.

8. Addison Ore, "A Former Player Reveres Kay Yow's Legacy," The Associated Press, February 19, 2009, retrieved at http://www.gotriad.com/content/2009/02/18/article/a_former_player_reveres_kay_yows_legacy.

5. Build a Disciplined Team

1. George W. Sinquefield, "Running the Christian Race," retrieved at http://www.our.homewithgod.com/sinque/Sermon64.html.

2. Quoted by Steve Chandler (with Scott Richardson), *100 Ways to Motivate Others: How Great Leaders Can Produce Insane Results Without Driving People Crazy* (Franklin Lakes, NJ: Career Press, 2008), p. 152.

3. Randy Howe, *Coachisms* (Guilford, CT: Lyons Press 2005), p. 40.

4. Quotation Collection, "Bobby Bowden Quotes" webpage, retrieved at http://www.quotationcollection.com/author/Bobby_Bowden/quotes.

5. "Previous Daily Quotes, Page 7," Lady Mustangs webpage, retrieved at http://www.ladymustangs.com/dailyquotespage7.htm.

6. Lao-Tzu, quoted by James J. Mapes, *Quantum Leap Thinking: An Owner's Guide to the Mind* (Naperville, IL: Sourcebooks, Inc., 2003), p. 113.

7. Proverbs 12:1 (New International Version).

8. Jack Ramsay, *Dr. Jack's Leadership Lessons Learned From a Lifetime in Basketball* (Hoboken, NJ: Wiley & Sons, 2004), p. 171.

9. Ibid., p. 171-172.

10. Ray Didinger, *Game Plans for Success* (New York: McGraw-Hill, 1996), p. 17-18.

11. Pat Summitt, "The Coaching Toolbox" webpage, excerpts from *Reach for the Summit*, retrieved at http://www.coachingtoolbox.net/filingcabinet/pat-summitt.html.

12. Quoted by Donald T. Phillips, *Run to Win: Vince Lombardi on Coaching and Leadership* (New York: St. Martin's Press, 2001), p. 26.

13. Vince Lombardi, Jr., *What It Takes to Be #1: Vince Lombardi on Leadership* (New York: McGraw-Hill, 2003), p. 116.

14. Lou Holtz, *Winning Every Day: The Game Plan for Success* (New York: HarperBusiness, 1998), pp. 169-170.

15. Ibid., 170-171.

16. Alexander Wolff, "They're raising stars in the Sunshine State," *Sports Illustrated*, September 5, 1988, retrieved at http://vault.sportsillustrated.cnn.com/vault/article/magazine/MAG1067701/1/index.htm.

6. Focus on Preparation

1. Author uncredited, "Miami's Unmiraculous Miracle Worker," *Time Magazine*, December 11, 1972, retrieved at http://www.time.com/time/magazine/article/0,9171,878119-2,00.html.

2. Bob Griese and Brian Griese, *Undefeated: How Father and Son Triumphed Over Unbelievable Odds Both On and Off the Field* (Nashville: Nelson, 2000), pp. 44-45, 55.

3. Fred Kerber, "The End is Approaching," Nets Blog, NYPost.com, April 1, 2009, retrieved at http://blogs.nypost.com/sports/nets/archives/2009/04/the_end_is_appr.html.

4. David Fleming, "Ssshhh! Coach at Work," ESPN website, November 11, 2008, retrieved at http://sports.espn.go.com/espnmag/story?id=3696221.

5. Pat Williams with David Wimbish, *How to Be like Coach Wooden* (Deerfield Beach, FL: HCI Books, 2006), p. 254.

6. John C. Maxwell, *Talent Is Never Enough* (Nashville: Thomas Nelson, 2007), p. 95-96.

7. Quoted by Brad Winters, "Basketball Inspirational and Motivational Quotes," Basketball Coaching Quotes, retrieved at http://www.coachlikeapro.com/basketball-coaching-quotes.html.

8. Quoted by Bruce Jenner with Mark Seal, *Finding the Champion Within* (New York: Simon & Schuster, 1998), p. 34.

9. Andrew Hill and John Wooden, *Be Quick—But Don't Hurry!: Finding Success in the Teachings of a Lifetime* (New York: Simon & Schuster, 2001), pp. 69- 71.

10. Quoted by Pat Williams with Dave Wimbish in *How to Be like Coach Wooden* (Deerfield Beach, FL: HCI Books, 2006), p. 64.

11. Author uncredited, "The Bowden Story," Florida State University Athletics website, retrieved at http://www.seminoles.com/sports/m-footbl/mtt/fsu-m-footbl-s-bowden.html.

12. Author uncredited, "University of the Cumberlands Women's Soccer 2006 Wrap-Up," Women's Soccer webpage, retrieved at http://www.ucumberlands.edu/athletics/soccer/womens/wrapup/2006wrapup.html.

13. Alison Rostankowski, interviewer, and Rex Kern, interviewee, "Beyond the Gridiron—The Life and Times of Woody Hayes," Crouse Entertainment Group and WOSU-Columbus, Ohio, October 2002, retrieved at http://www.duncanentertainment.com/interview_kern.php.

14. Author uncredited, "Preparing for Competition," EJ Clair Sports webpage, June 2003, retrieved at http://ejclairsports.com/index.php?option=com_content&task=view&id=38&Itemid=40.

15. Coach Tom Coughlin, Press Conference, July 23, 2008, transcript retrieved at http://www.giants.com/news/transcripts/story.asp?story_id=27215.

16. Michael Mink, "George Allen's Urgency to Win," originally published in *Investor's Business Daily*, reprinted in Bay Ledger News Zone, January 10, 2008, retrieved at http://www.blnz.com/news/2008/02/19/George_Allens_Urgency_3153.html.

17. Quoted by Mirza Zukic, "Former UCLA Coach Addresses Athletes, Coaches," *Indiana Gazette*, February 14, 2009, retrieved at http://www.indianagazette.com/articles/2009/02/16/sports/iup_crimson_hawks/10010831.prt.

18. Quoted By Jack Canfield and Janet Switzer, *The Success Principles: How to Get From Where You Are to Where You Want to Be* (New York: William Morrow, 2004), p. 132.

19. Rick Weinberg, "ESPN Counts down the 100 Most Memorable Moments of the Past 25 Years—17: Laettner's Buzzer-Beater Sinks Kentucky," ESPN.com, retrieved at http://sports.espn.go.com/espn/espn25/story?page=moments/17; Author uncredited, "Laettner's Buzzer-Beater Ended '92 Classic," ESPN.com, November 19, 2003, retrieved at http://espn.go.com/classic/s/game_of_week_duke_uk.html.

20. Quoted by Mike Krzyzewski with Donald T. Phillips, *Leading with the Heart: Coach K's Successful Strategies for Basketball, Business, and Life* (New York: Warner, 2000), p. 85.

7. Maintain Balance in Your Life

1. Jill Ewert, "Dayton Moore: A Royal Risk," *Sharing the Victory* online, retrieved at http://www.sharingthevictory.com/vsPrintPage.lsp?OriginalPageOID=B2A8DB4D-0F3E-45D4-9B79C98A0F15CEB8&OBJECTID=0B6089DD-07C1-4E41-AEE59F2F35B1C94F&METHOD=display.
2. Gregory K. Morris, Ph.D., *In Pursuit of Leadership: Principles and Practices from the Life of Moses* (Camarillo, CA: Xulon Press, 2006), pp. 192-193.
3. Monica L. Wofford, *Lessons in Leadership! Newsletter* Number 4, retrieved at http://www.monicawofford.com/newsletters/newsletter-004.pdf.
4. Don Yaeger, "Tony Dungy's Championship Life," *Success*, October 2008, retrieved at http://www.donyaeger.com/uploads/success/Championship_Life_OCT.pdf.
5. John R. Wooden with Steve Jamison, *The Essential Wooden* (New York: McGraw-Hill, 2006), p. 121.
6. John Wooden with Steve Jamison, *Wooden on Leadership* (New York: McGraw-Hill Professional, 2005), p. 131-134.
7. Curt Schleier, "He Passed His Way to the Top," originally published in *Investor's Business Daily*, reprinted by Bay Ledger News Zone, May 13, 2008, retrieved at http://www.blnz.com/news/2008/05/14/Passed_2470.html.
8. Jack Ramsay, *Dr. Jack's Leadership Lessons Learned From a Lifetime in Basketball* (Hoboken, NJ: Wiley & Sons, 2004), p. 165.
9. Mike Krzyzewski with Jamie K. Spatola, *Beyond Basketball: Coach K's Keywords for Success* (New York: Warner Business Books, 2006), p. 126.
10. John Hareas, "Inspired by Holzman, Jackson Arrives in Springfield," NBA.com, September 7, 2007, retrieved at http://www.nba.com/news/jackson_070907.html; Ken Peters—Associated Press, "Lakers Think 'Happy Thoughts,'" *The Augusta Chronicle* (Georgia), June 8, 2002, retrieved at http://chat.augustachronicle.com/stories/2002/06/08/nba_343040.shtml.

8. Be Bold and Confident

1. David Claerbaut, *Bart Starr: When Leadership Mattered* (Lanham, MD: Taylor, 2004), pp. 25-29.
2. Pat Williams, *The Paradox of Power* (Nashville: FaithWords: 2004), pp. 171-172.
3. "Amanda Butler, Head Coach," 2007-2008 Florida Gator Basketball, retrieved at http://www.gatorzone.com/basketball/women/media/2007/pdf/staff/Amanda Butler.pdf; "Amanda Butler," Florida Gator Basketball, retrieved at http://www.coachamandabutler.com/index2.php?page=yes.

4. "#15 Kim Critton," 2007-2008 Florida Gator Basketball, retrieved at http://www.gatorzone.com/basketball/women/media/2007/pdf/gators/CrittonKim.pdf.

5. Alexander Wolff, "Dean Smith: Fanfare for an Uncommon Man," *Sports Illustrated*, December 22, 1997, retrieved at http://vault.sportsillustrated.cnn.com/vault/article/magazine/MAG1011686/1/index.htm.

6. Ibid.

7. "Coach K Quotes," Coach K—The Official Website of Coach Mike Krzyzewski, September 2006, retrieved at http://www.coachk.com/quotes.php.

8. Dr. Homer Rice, "Attitude Technique and Leadership Principles," *The Sport Digest*, United States Sports Academy, retrieved at http://thesportdigest.com/article/attitude-technique-and-leadership-principles.

9. Bob Griese and Brian Griese, *Undefeated: How Father and Son Triumphed Over Unbelievable Odds Both On and Off the Field* (Nashville: Nelson, 2000), pp. 93.

10. Mike Krzyzewski with Donald T. Phillips, *Leading with the Heart: Coach K's Successful Strategies for Basketball, Business, and Life* (New York: Warner, 2000), p. 10.

11. Phil Jackson with Hugh Delehanty, *Sacred Hoops: Spiritual Lessons of a Hardwood Warrior* (New York: Hyperion, 2006), pp. 72-74.

12. Jack McKeon with Kevin Kernan, *I'm Just Getting Started: Baseball's Best Storyteller on Old School Baseball, Defying the Odds, and Good Cigars* (Chicago: Triumph Books, 2005), pp. 3, 15, 18.

13. Quoted by Joe Garagiola, *It's Anybody's Ballgame* (New York: Jove, 1989), p. 197.

14. Quoted by Keith Johnson, *The Confidence Makeover* (Shippensburg, PA: Destiny Image, 2006), p. 61.

15. Lou Holtz, *Winning Every Day* (New York: HarperCollins, 1998), pp. 87-88.

9. Be a Teacher and a Learner

1. Jim Calhoun with Richard Ernsberger, Jr., *A Passion to Lead: Seven Leadership Secrets for Success in Business, Sports, and Life* (New York: Macmillan, 2007), p. 7.

2. Richie Brand, "Jim Calhoun Shows You Can," *Investors Business Daily*, January 23, 2008, retrieved at http://www.thefreelibrary.com/Jim+Calhoun+Shows+You+Can-a01611461883; Ian O'Connor, "Calhoun: A Builder and Now a Survivor," *The Journal News* (Westchester NY), March 25, 2003, reprinted by *The Enquirer* (Cincinnati), retrieved at http://www.enquirer.com/editions/2003/03/25/spt_wwwncaa3i25.html.

3. Wendy Soderburg, "The Wizard and The Miracle Worker," *UCLA Magazine*, April 1, 2006, retrieved at http://www.magazine.ucla.edu/features/wooden_kondos/.

4. Rick Reilly, "Life of Reilly: One Coach Still Knows More Than All the Others Combined; and He's Been Retired for Three Decades," *ESPN Magazine*, October 29, 2008, retrieved at http://sports.espn.go.com/espnmag/story?section=magazine&id=3669154.

5. Pat Williams with David Wimbish, *How to Be like Coach Wooden* (Deerfield Beach, FL: HCI Books, 2006), pp. 16-17.

6. Bill Walton, "John Wooden, Like UCLA, Simply the Best," BillWalton.com, retrieved at http://www.billwalton.com/wooden.html.

7. Rick Reilly, ibid.

8. John Wooden with Steve Jamison, *Wooden: A Lifetime of Observations and Reflections On and Off the Court* (New York: McGraw-Hill, 1997), pp. 61-62.

9. Valorie Kondos Field, "Ask the Bruins – Valorie Kondos Field," UCLABruins.com, February 23, 2007, retrieved at http://www.uclabruins.com/sports/w-gym/spec-rel/022307aaa.html.

10. Scott Fowler, *North Carolina Tar Heels: Where Have You Gone?* (Champaign, IL: Sports Publishing, 2005), p. xii.

11. Quoted by Shane M. Murphy, *The Sport Psych Handbook* (Champaign, IL: Human Kinetics, 2004), p. 191.

12. Quoted by Roscoe Nance, "Jackson Makes Hall of Fame on Principle," *USA Today*, September 7, 2007, retrieved at http://www.usatoday.com/sports/basketball/2007-09-06-jackson-hall-of-fame_N.htm.

13. Bill Russell, *Second Wind: The Memoirs of an Opinionated Man* (New York: Simon and Schuster, 1991), p. 91.

14. Quoted by John Ralston, *Coaching Today's Athlete* (Palo Alto, CA: National Press Books, 1971), p. 13.

15. Quoted in "Beyond X's and O's," *American Football Monthly* online, July 2000, retrieved at http://www.americanfootballmonthly.com/Subaccess/articles.php?category=beyondxsandos&article_id=3587&output=article&s=.

16. John Baldoni, *Great Communication Secrets of Great Leaders* (New York: McGraw-Hill Professional, 2003), p. 148.

17. Ibid., pp. 156-157.

18. Michael Richman, "Football Coach Chuck Noll: Commitment To Teaching Made Him One Of The Best," *Investor's Business Daily*, September 10, 2001, retrieved at http://www.accessmylibrary.com/coms2/summary_0286-7347839_ITM.

19. Michael P. Geffner, "Can Mike D'Antoni Save the Knicks?," The New York Post, October 12, 2008, retrieved at http://www.nypost.com/pagesixmag/issues/20081012/Can+Mike+DAntoni+Save+Knicks.

20. Timothy Nolan, "An 'E' for Excellence and a 'Kay' for Class: Interview with North Carolina State University Basketball Coach Kay Yow," *Coach and Athletic Director*, March 1, 1997, retrieved at http://www.thefreelibrary.com/An+%22E%22+for+excellence+and+a+%22Kay%22+for+class-a019325416

21. Bud Bilanich, "Kay Yow: Successful Coach, Positive Person," FastCompany.com, January 26, 2009, retrieved at http://www.fastcompany.com/blog/bud-bilanich/success-common-sense/kay-yow-successful-coach-positive-person.

22. Quoted by Jack T. Clary, *The Gamemakers* (River Grove, IL: Follett Publishing, 1976), p. 228.
23. John Wooden with Steve Jamison, *Wooden: A Lifetime of Observations and Reflections On And Off The Court* (New York: McGraw-Hill, 1997), p. 30.
24. Yogi Berra with Dave Kaplan, *When You Come to a Fork in the Road, Take It!: Inspiration and Wisdom from One of Baseball's Greatest Heroes* (New York: Hyperion, 2002), p. 35.
25. Vincent J. Dooley with Tony Barnhart, *Dooley: My Forty Years at Georgia* (Chicago: Triumph Books, 2005), pp. 3-4.

10. Care for Your Players as People

1. Red Auerbach and John Feinstein, *Let Me Tell You a Story: A Lifetime in the Game* (New York: Little, Brown & Co., 2004), p. 28.
2. Wayne Embry, "Boston Celtics: Statements on Red Auerbach," NBA.com, retrieved at http://www.nba.com/celtics/news/AuerbachStatements.html.
3. Bobby Murcer with Glen Waggoner, *Yankee for Life: My 40-Year Journey in Pinstripes* (New York: HarperCollins, 2008), p. 59.
4. Quoted by Michael R. Steele, *Knute Rockne: A Portrait of a Notre Dame Legend* (Champaign, IL: Sports Publishing, 1998), p. 116.
5. Ed Gubman, Ph.D., *The Engaging Leader: Winning with Today's Free Agent Workforce* (Chicago: Dearborn Trade Publishing, 2003), p. 18.
6. Quoted by Brad Winters, "Basketball Inspirational and Motivational Quotes," Basketball Coaching Quotes, retrieved at http://www.coachlikeapro.com/basketball-coaching-quotes.html.
7. Karen Crouse, "With Edwards Gone, Bradway Is in the Spotlight," *The New York Times*, January 8, 2006 retrieved at http://www.nytimes.com/2006/01/08/sports/football/08jets1.html.
8. Author uncredited, "R.E.S.P.E.C.T.," *Mentor*, Summer 2003, The Leadership Challenge, Inc., retrieved at http://www.tlcinc.com/mentor/mentor_summer_2003.html.
9. Quoted by Vince Lombardi, Jr., *What It Takes to Be #1: Vince Lombardi on Leadership* (New York: McGraw-Hill, 2003), p. 132.
10. Vince Lombardi, Jr., *What It Takes to Be #1: Vince Lombardi on Leadership* (New York: McGraw-Hill, 2003), p. 153-154; some additional information, as noted, comes from a personal conversation with Ernie Accorsi.
11. Dick Vermeil, "Q&A with Dick Vermeil," Jacksonville Conference Call Transcript, October 13, 2004, retrieved at http://www.chiefsplanet.com/BB/archive/index.php/t-101178.html.
12. Michael Mink, "Walter Alston's Winning Resolve," *Investor's Business Daily*, June 20 4, 2008, reprinted by Bay Ledger News Zone, retrieved at http://www.blnz.com/news/2008/06/25/Walter_Alstons_Winning_Resolve_9042.html.

13. Marcia C. Smith, "UCLA's Enquist Goes Out Quietly," *Orange County Register*, September 27, 2006, retrieved at http://sueenquist.com/articles/; Gilbert Quiñonez, "Coach's Aid Extended Beyond the Dugout," *Daily Bruin*, September 28, 2006, retrieved at http://dailybruin.ucla.edu/stories/2006/sep/28/icoachs-aid-extended-beyond-th/.

14. Vytas Mazeika, "Coach inspires squad with 'Sueisms'," Daily Bruin, May 2, 2001, retrieved at http://dailybruin.ucla.edu/stories/2001/may/2/coach-inspires-squad-with-suei/; Mirza Zukic, "Former UCLA Coach Addresses Athletes, Coaches," *Indiana Gazette*, February 14, 2009, retrieved at http://www.indianagazette.com/articles/2009/02/16/sports/iup_crimson_hawks/10010831.prt.

15. Eddie Robinson with Richard Edward Lapchick, *Never Before, Never Again* (New York: St. Martin's Press, 1999), P. 114.

16. Bill Plaschke with Tommy Lasorda, *I Live for This: Baseball's Last True Believer* (New York: Houghton Mifflin Books, 2007), pp. 12, 106, 123.

17. "Dean Smith Leadership Principle 1," Leadership in Perspective, July 12, 2006, retrieved at http://theleadership.wordpress.com/2006/07/12/dean-smith-leadership-principle-1/.

18. Ron Thomas, *They Cleared the Lane: The NBA's Black Pioneers* (Lincoln, NE: University of Nebraska Press, 2004), pp. 219-220.

19. Peter Horan, "Bear Bryant: A Lesson About Dealing With People," December 5, 2006, AllBusiness.com, retrieved at http://www.allbusiness.com/management/3876594-1.html.

11. Maintain Passion, Enthusiasm, and Fun

1. Bob Valvano, "Jimmy V and Me," excerpt from *The Gifts of Jimmy V*, retrieved at http://www.jimmyv.org/jimmy-v-and-me/259-volume-2number-1-by-bob-valvano.html.

2. Robert D. Ramsey, *Don't Teach the Canaries Not to Sing* (Thousand Oaks, CA: Corwin Press, 2007), p. 21.

3. Dean Smith with Gerald D. Bell, *The Carolina Way: Leadership Lessons from a Life in Coaching* (New York: Penguin, 2004), pp. 28-29.

4. Jon Spoelstra, *Ice to the Eskimos: How to Market a Product Nobody Wants* (New York: HarperCollins, 1997), pp. 164-165

5. Marv Levy, "Words of Wisdom," Coach Ellis' Home Page, retrieved at http://www.amug.org/~nlellis/teams/page76.html.

6. Larry Weisman, "Rams Coach Loves to Throw Ball, Caution to Wind," *USA Today*, February 1, 2002, retrieved at http://www.usatoday.com/sports/nfl/super/2002-02-01-martz-cover.htm.

7. Jim Calhoun with Richard Ernsberger, Jr., *A Passion to Lead: Seven Leadership Secrets for Success in Business, Sports, and Life* (New York: Macmillan, 2007), pp. 21-22.

8. Philip Seib, *The Player: Christy Mathewson, Baseball, and the American Century* (New York: Four Walls Eight Windows, 2004), p. 83.

9. Cal Ripken, Sr., with Larry Burke, The Ripken Way: A Manual for Baseball and Life (New York: Atria, 1999), p. xxii.

10. Quoted by Ray Didinger and Robert S. Lyons, *The Eagles Encyclopedia* (Philadelphia Temple University Press, 2005) p. 40.

11. O Shiri, "John Madden's Possible Return to the Oakland Raiders," Bleacher Report, April 23, 2009, retrieved at http://bleacherreport.com/articles/160953-john-madden-possible-return-to-the-silver-and-black.

12. Quoted at "Nelson Mandela Quotes," ThinkExist.com, retrieved at http://thinkexist.com/quotation/there-is-no-passion-to-be-found-playing-small-in/348626.html.

13. Jon Gruden with Vic Carucci, *Do You Love Football?!: Winning with Heart, Passion, and Not Much Sleep* (New York: HarperCollins, 2003), p. 3.

14. Mike Freeman, *Bloody Sundays: Inside the Rough-and-Tumble World of the NFL* (New York: HarperCollins, 2003), p. 65.

15. Quoted by Steve Newhouse, "Jamie and Maggie Dixon," CollegeHoopsNet.com, June 21, 2004, retrieved at http://www.collegehoopsnet.com/conferenceusa/depaul/062104.htm.

16. Ira Berkow, "Army Head Women's Basketball Coach Maggie Dixon," originally printed in the *New York Times*, reprinted at PatriotLeague.org, March 16, 2006, retrieved at http://www.patriotleague.org/genrel/031606aaa.html.

17. Ken McMillan, "Army Women's Basketball: Dixon Legacy Lives in Garden Classic," Times Herald-Record, December 9, 2007, retrieved at http://www.recordonline.com/apps/pbcs.dll/article?AID=/20071209/SPORTS/712090342.

12. Take Care of the Little Things

1. "History: Louisville Slugger Anecdotes," Louisville Slugger Museum, retrieved at http://www.slugger.com/museum/anec.htm.

2. Quoted by David Cataneo, *I Remember Ted Williams: Anecdotes and Memories of Baseball's Splendid Splinter by the Players and People Who Knew Him* (Nashville: Cumberland House Publishing, 2002), p. 46.

3. Quoted by Pat Williams, *The Pursuit: Wisdom for the Adventure of Your Life* (Ventura, CA: Regal, 2008), p. 141.

4. Whitey Herzog, *You're Missin' a Great Game* (New York: Berkley, 2000), p. 8-9.

5. Quoted by Jack Canfield, Mark Victor Hansen, and Chrissy Donnelly, *Chicken Soup for the Baseball Fan's Soul* (Deerfield Beach, FL: HCI Books, 2001), p. 17.

6. Quoted by Vince Lombardi, Jr., *What It Takes to Be #1: Vince Lombardi on Leadership* (New York: McGraw-Hill, 2003), p. 244.

7. Lou Holtz with John Heisler, *The Fighting Spirit: A Championship Season at Notre Dame* (New York: Pocket Books, 1989), p. 48.

8. Harvey Mackay, *Swim With the Sharks Without Being Eaten Alive* (New York: Ballantine, 1999), pp. 152-153.

9. Jim Calhoun with Richard Ernsberger, Jr., *A Passion to Lead: Seven Leadership Secrets for Success in Business, Sports, and Life* (New York: Macmillan, 2007), pp. 27.

10. Alyson Footer, "Notes: Astros Prefer to Look Ahead," MLB.com, February 17, 2006, retrieved at http://mlb.mlb.com/news/article.jsp?ymd=20060217&content_id=1314091&vkey=spt2006news&fext=.jsp&c_id=mlb.

11. Kevin Newell, "The Joe Torre Story," *Coach and Athletic Director*, November 1, 2005, retrieved at http://content.scholastic.com/browse/article.jsp?id=7081.

12. Phil Simms with Vic Carucci, *Sunday Morning Quarterback: Going Deep on the Strategies, Myths, and Mayhem of Football* (New York: HarperCollins, 2004), p. 150.

13. Ibid., p. 53.

14. Alan Hobson, *From Everest to Enlightenment: An Adventure of the Soul* (Calgary: Inner Everests, Inc., 1999), pp. 92-94.

15. Ibid.

16. Alan Hobson and Cecelia Hobson, *Climb Back from Cancer: A Survivor and Caregivers Inspirational Journey* (Canmore, Alberta, Canada: Climb Back, Inc., 2004), p. 51-52.

13. Surround Yourself With Loyal People

1. Yogi Berra, *You Can Observe a Lot by Watching: What I've Learned About Teamwork from the Yankees and Life* (Hoboken, NJ: Wiley & Sons, 2004), p. 7.

2. William C. Kashatus, Almost a Dynasty: The Rise and Fall of the 1980 Phillies (Philadelphia: University of Pennsylvania Press: 2008), pp. 90-91.

3. Ibid., p. 91.

4. Jeff D'Alessio, "Sporting News' 50 Greatest Coaches of All Time," *The Sporting News*, Wednesday, July 29, 2009, retrieved at http://www.sportingnews.com/college-basketball/article/2009-07-29/sporting-news-50-greatest-coaches-all-time.

5. Pat Summitt with Sally Jenkins, *Reach For the Summit* (Broadway Books, New York, 1999), p. 46, 51-52.

6. Oren Harari, *The Leadership Secrets of Colin Powell* (New York: McGraw-Hill Professional, 2003), pp. 172-173.

7. Michael Mink, "George Allen's Urgency to Win," *Investor's Business Daily*, January 10, 2008, reprinted by Bay Ledger News Zone, retrieved at http://www.blnz.com/news/2008/02/19/George_Allens_Urgency_3153.html.

8. Ibid.

9. Quoted by Bernard Postal, Jesse Silver, and Roy Silver, *Encyclopedia of Jews in Sports* (New York: Bloch, 1965), p. 41.

10. Bob Starkey, "Hoop Thoughts," LSU Lady Tiger Basketball, May 3, 2009, retrieved at http://hoopthoughts.blogspot.com/2009/05/ultimate-coaches-clinic.html.

11. Donald W. Patterson, "The Legacy," Dean Smith, News & Record Online, retrieved at http://ss002.infi.net/triad/nronline/projects/dean/legacy.htm.

14. Empower Your Players

1. Terry Pluto, "Browns Town 1964: Jim Brown," The Official Website of the Cleveland Browns, September 8, 2004, retrieved at http://www.clevelandbrowns.com/print_page.php?id=3021.

2. Quoted by Dan Spainhour, *Coach Yourself: A Motivational Guide For Coaches and Leaders* (Winston Salem, NC: Educational Coaching Business Communications, 2007), p. 70.

3. Ed Hinton, "Deep Into His Job: Jimmy Johnson Dived Headfirst Into Coaching the Cowboys ... ," *Sports Illustrated*, September 7, 1992, retrieved at http://vault.sportsillustrated.cnn.com/vault/article/magazine/MAG1004203/1/index.htm.

4. Ibid.

5. Dave Anderson: "Taylor's One-Arm Show," *New York Times*, November 29, 1988, retrieved at http://www.nytimes.com/1988/11/29/sports/sports-of-the-times-taylor-s-one-arm-show.html.

6. Larry Schwartz, "Taylor Redefined the Outside Linebacker Position," ESPN.com, November 19, 2003, retrieved at http://espn.go.com/classic/s/taylorlawrenceadd.html.

7. Steve Delsohn and Mark Heisler, *Bob Knight: The Unauthorized Biography* (New York: Simon and Schuster, 2006), pp. 7, 204.

8. Jon Gruden with Vic Carucci, *Do You Love Football?!* (New York: HarperCollins, 2003), p. 67-68.

9. Dale Carnegie and Associates, Stuart R. Levine, Michael A. Crom, *The Leader in You* (New York: Simon and Schuster, 1995), pp. 104-105.

10. John Wooden with Steve Jamison, *Wooden: A Lifetime of Observations and Reflections On and Off the Court* (New York: McGraw-Hill, 1997), p. 139-140.

11. Robert Evangelista, *The Business of Winning* (Atlanta: CEP Press, 2001), pp. 218-219.

15. Unity of Purpose, Diversity of Skills

1. Mike Wise, "What Good Old Ernie Required Was Vision," *New York Times*, April 20 2, 1999, retrieved at http://www.nytimes.com/1999/04/22/sports/on-pro-basketball-what-good-old-ernie-required-was-vision.html.

2. Bill Russell with William Francis McSweeney, *Go Up for Glory* (New York: Coward McCann, 1966), p. 119.

3. John Wooden with Steve Jamison, *Wooden: A Lifetime of Observations and Reflections On and Off the Court* (New York: McGraw-Hill, 1997), p. 74.

4. Brian Howell, "Marshall Choosing Wrong Path," *Longmont (CO) Times-Call*, August 30, 2009, retrieved at http://www.timescall.com/sports_story.asp?id=17827; additional material from the Associated Press, "Denver Broncos Suspend Receiver Brandon Marshall," Yahoo.com, August 28, 2009, retrieved at http://sports.yahoo.com/nfl/news?slug=ap-broncos-marshallsuspended&prov=ap&type=lgns.

5. Whitey Herzog, *You're Missin' a Great Game* (New York: Berkley, 2000), p. 166-167.

6. Joe Haefner, "Creating Team Unity With Coach K," Breakthrough Basketball website, retrieved at http://www.breakthroughbasketball.com/blog/index.php/creating-team-unity-with-coach-k/.

7. Sara Salam, "Football sees hope in strong team unity," UCLA *Daily Bruin*, December 1, 2008, retrieved at http://dailybruin.com/stories/2008/dec/1/football-sees-hope-strong-team-unity/.

8. Mike Leach, "How to Build Team Unity," *The Sporting News*, September 16, 2005 retrieved at http://findarticles.com/p/articles/mi_m1208/is_37_229/ai_n15386700/.

9. Brad Grey, "Baseball Players Honor Fellow Infielder's Mother with Touching Gesture," *The Daily Texan*, March 5, 2007, retrieved at http://www.dailytexanonline.com/sports/shorn-to-solidarity-1.960453.

16. There's No Substitute for Talent

1. Dr. Jack Ramsay, *Dr. Jack's Leadership Lessons Learned From a Lifetime in Basketball* (Hoboken, NJ: Wiley & Sons, 2004), pp. 207-208.

2. Yogi Berra, *You Can Observe a Lot by Watching: What I've Learned About Teamwork from the Yankees and Life* (Hoboken, NJ: Wiley & Sons, 2004), p. 201.

3. Dale Brown, *Basketball Coaches Organizational Handbook* (Monterey, CA: Coaches Choice, 2003), p. 251.

4. Quoted by Dick Weiss, Miami Tested Wright Away, *New York Daily News*, September 5, 2005, retrieved at http://www.nydailynews.com/archives/sports/2005/09/05/2005-09-05_miami_tested_wright_away.html.

5. "This May Sum Up the Importance of Coaching," CrowdPicks.com, June 29, 2009, retrieved at http://www.crowdpicks.com/TeamPage/tabid/61/ctl/ViewPost/mid/694/NEID/68753/Default.aspx.

6. Mike Ditka with Rick Telander, *In Life, First You Kick Ass: Reflections on the 1985 Bears and Wisdom from Da Coach* (Champaign, IL: Sports Publishing, 2005), p. 41-42.

7. Pat Summitt with Sally Jenkins, *Reach For the Summit* (Broadway Books, New York, 1999), p. 152.

8. Robert S. Lyons, *Palestra Pandemonium* (Philadelphia: Temple University Press, 2002), p. 193.

9. Mike Sando, "Around the NFC West: Rams, Raji and Risk," ESPN.com, April 22, 2009, retrieved at http://myespn.go.com/blogs/nflnation?tag=don%20shula.

10. Mike Krzyzewski with Donald T. Phillips, *Leading with the Heart: Coach K's Successful Strategies for Basketball, Business, and Life* (New York: Warner, 2000), p. 22.

11. Quoted in "Basketball and Life," Hoopshelp Blog: Better Yourself, Better the Game, April 16, 2009, retrieved at http://www.hoopshelp.com.au/blog/?p=199.

12. Quoted by Dale Brown, *Basketball Coaches Organizational Handbook* (Monterey, CA: Coaches Choice, 2003), p. 42.

13. Quoted by Vince Lombardi, Jr., *What It Takes to Be #1: Vince Lombardi on Leadership* (New York: McGraw-Hill, 2003), p. 109.

14. Jack Canfield, Mark Victor Hansen, and Pat Williams, *Chicken Soup for the Soul: Inside Basketball* (New York: Simon & Schuster, 2009), pp. 266-268.

17. Learn to Handle the Media and the Critics

1. Josh Little, "Kentucky Fires Billy Gillispie," KOLOTV website, March 27, 2009, retrieved at http://www.kolotv.com/sports/headlines/42025207.html.

2. YouTube video, "Billy Clyde Gillispie tells Jeannine Edwards she asked a dumb question," viewed at http://www.youtube.com/watch?v=xrXeBAoF3sM&feature=player_embedded.

3. Michael David Smith, "What Is Billy Gillispie's Problem With ESPN's Jeannine Edwards?," NCAA Basketball Fanhouse, February 16, 2009, retrieved at http://ncaabasketball.fanhouse.com/2009/02/16/what-is-billy-gillispies-problem-with-espns-jeannine-edwards/.

4. Eric Crawford, "Gillispie, Coaches and the Media," March 6, 2009, Courier-Journal.com (Louisville, KY), retrieved at http://www.courier-journal.com/blogs/crawford/2009/03/gillispie-coaches-and-media.html.

5. Quoted by Larry Weisman, "Image Suits Up, Too," *USA Today*, November 28, 2002, retrieved at http://www.usatoday.com/sports/ccovfri.htm.

6. Frank Fitzpatrick, "This Coach Gives Professional Athletes Help In Handling Reporters' Questions," *Philadelphia Inquirer*, August 10, 1997, retrieved at http://community.seattletimes.nwsource.com/archive/?date=19970810&slug=2554013.

7. Ibid.

8. Larry Weisman, "Image Suits Up, Too," *USA Today*, November 28, 2002, retrieved at http://www.usatoday.com/sports/ccovfri.htm.

9. Frank Fitzpatrick, ibid.

10. Larry Weisman, "Image Suits Up, Too," *USA Today*, November 28, 2002, retrieved at http://www.usatoday.com/sports/ccovfri.htm.

11. Skip Wood, "Bucs' Boy Wonder Gruden Has Folks Wondering," *USA Today*, July 28, 2005, retrieved at http://www.usatoday.com/sports/football/nfl/bucs/2005-07-28-gruden-wonder_x.htm.

12. Quoted at "Alex Agase Quotes," ThinkExist.com, retrieved at http://thinkexist.com/quotes/alex_agase/.

13. Jere Longman, "Signs Point to a Penn State Rebirth," *New York Times*, August 11, 2002, retrieved at http://www.nytimes.com/2002/08/11/sports/college-football-signs-point-to-a-penn-state-rebirth.html.

14. Jack Ramsay, *Dr. Jack's Leadership Lessons Learned from a Lifetime in Basketball* (Hoboken, NJ: Wiley & Sons, 2004), p. 215.

15. Quoted by Jim Tressel, *The Winner's Manual: For the Game of Life* (Carol Stream, IL: Tyndale, 2008), p. 157.

16. Phil Jackson with Hugh Delehanty, *Sacred Hoops: Spiritual Lessons of a Hardwood Warrior* (New York: Hyperion, 2006), pp. 122.

17. Pat Summitt, *Raise the Roof* (New York: Broadway Books, 1998), pp. 147-148.

18. It's Always About the Team

1. Bryn Swartz, "Do You Believe In Miracles? The Story Of The 1960 Philadelphia Eagles," *T.O. Sports Magazine*, May 24, 2009, retrieved at http://www.tosports.ca/?p=4786.

2. Jonathan Rand, *Run It! And Let's Get the Hell Out of Here!: The 100 Best Plays in Pro Football History* (Guilford, CT: Globe Pequot, 2007), p. 139-141.

3. Bryn Swartz, "Do You Believe In Miracles? The Story Of The 1960 Philadelphia Eagles," *T.O. Sports Magazine*, May 24, 2009, retrieved at http://www.tosports.ca/?p=4786.

4. Ibid.

5. Ibid.

6. Bob Gordon, *The 1960 Philadelphia Eagles: The Team That They Said Had Nothing but a Championship* (Champaign, IL: Sports Publishing, 2001), p. 183.

7. Ibid.

8. Quoted by John C. Maxwell, *The 17 Indisputable Laws of Teamwork* (Nashville: Thomas Nelson, 2001), p. 23.

9. Mia Hamm, "Author Essay by Mia Hamm," HarperCollins website, retrieved at http://www.harpercollins.com/author/authorExtra.aspx?authorID=14021&isbn13=9780060740504&displayType=bookessay.

10. Chuck Daly, "Winning in the NBA," HoopsU.com, retrieved at http://www.hoopsu.com/coachingtips/winning-nba-daly.html.

11. Jim Calhoun with Richard Ernsberger, Jr., *A Passion to Lead: Seven Leadership Secrets for Success in Business, Sports, and Life* (New York: Macmillan, 2007), p. 208.

12. Terry Bradshaw with David Fisher, *Keep It Simple* (New York: Simon and Schuster, 2003), p. 282.

13. Phil Jackson with Hugh Delehanty, *Sacred Hoops: Spiritual Lessons of a Hardwood Warrior* (New York: Hyperion, 2006), p. 5.

14. Ibid., pp. 5-6.

15. Ibid., pp. 101-102.

16. Quoted by John C. Maxwell, *Talent Is Never Enough* (Nashville: Thomas Nelson, 2007), p. 262.

17. Pat Riley, *The Winner Within: A Life Plan for Team Players* (New York: Berkley Trade, 1994), 15–16.

18. Mike Krzyzewski with Jamie K. Spatola, *The Gold Standard: Building a World-Class Team* (New York: Hachette, 2009), p. xvii.

19. John R. Wooden with Steve Jamison, *The Essential Wooden* (New York: McGraw-Hill, 2006), p. 77.

20. Mike Krzyzewski with Jamie K. Spatola, ibid., p. 85, emphasis in the original.

19. Communicate!

1. Story compiled from these sources: "George Gipp: The Gipper," University of Notre Dame: Official Site for Fighting Irish Athletics," retrieved at http://www.und.com/sports/m-footbl/archive/allambios/nd-m-footbl-gipp.html; Author uncredited, "Knute Rockne's 'Win One for the Gipper' Speech," University of Notre Dame Archives page, retrieved at http://archives.nd.edu/rockne/speech.html; Emily Howard, "Win One for the Gipper!," *Scene Observer Online*, January 17, 2003, retrieved at http://www.nd.edu/~observer/01172003/Scene/0.html; Ray Robinson, *Rockne of Notre Dame: The Making of a Football Legend* (New York: Oxford University Press, 1999), pp. 209-214; Michael R. Steele, *The Fighting Irish Football Encyclopedia* (Champaign, IL: Sports Publishing, 2003), pp. 63-64.

2. Ray Robinson, *Rockne of Notre Dame: The Making of a Football Legend* (New York: Oxford University Press, 1999), p. 215.

3. Ibid., pp. 139-140.

4. Quoted by Fay Vincent, *We Would Have Played for Nothing: Baseball Stars of the 1950s and 1960s Talk About the Game They Loved* (New York: Simon & Schuster, 2008), pp. 282-283.

5. Tim Kurkjian, *Is This a Great Game, or What?: From A-Rod's Heart to Zim's Head* (New York: St. Martin's, 2008), p. 85.

6. Jack McKeon with Kevin Kernan, *I'm Just Getting Started: Baseball's Best Storyteller on Old-School Baseball, Defying the Odds, and Good Cigars* (Chicago: Triumph Books, 2005), p. 208.

7. Ibid.

8. Jon Gruden with Vic Carucci, *Do You Love Football?!: Winning with Heart, Passion, and Not Much Sleep* (New York: HarperCollins, 2003), p. 89.

9. Cal Ripken, Jr., with Donald T. Phillips, *Get in the Game: 8 Elements of Perseverance That Make the Difference* (New York: Penguin, 2007), pp. 82-83.

10. Rich Eisen, *Total Access: A Journey to the Center of the NFL Universe* (New York: St. Martin's Press, 2008), p. 254.

11. Reid Cherner, "Staley: Dream Believer," *USA Today*, December 7, 2004, retrieved at http://www.usatoday.com/sports/college/womensbasketball/atlantic10/2004-12-06-staley-cover_x.htm.

12. Quoted by Jack T. Clary, *The Gamemakers* (New York: Follett, 1976), pp. 172-173.

13. Phil Jackson with Hugh Delehanty, *Sacred Hoops: Spiritual Lessons of a Hardwood Warrior* (New York: Hyperion, 2006), pp. 72-74.

14. Ibid., pp. 68-69.

15. Pat Summitt with Sally Jenkins, *Reach for the Summit* (Broadway Books, New York, 1999), pp. 69-70.

16. Pat Summitt with Sally Jenkins, *Reach for the Summit* (Broadway Books, New York, 1999), p. 75-77.

20. Develop Your Leadership Abilities Every Day

1. Jack Canfield, Mark Victor Hansen, and Pat Williams, *Chicken Soup for the Soul: Inside Basketball* (New York: Simon & Schuster, 2009), p. 268.

2. Quoted by Murray Johannsen, "Are Leaders Born or Made?," Knol: A Unit of Knowledge, retrieved at http://knol.google.com/k/murray-johannsen/how-to-develop-your-leadership-skills-a/17cj3dhp1bcj4/3#.

3. Quoted by John R. Wooden, *Practical Modern Basketball* (Upper Saddle River, NJ: Benjamin Cummings, 1998), p. 6.

4. Pat Williams with David Wimbish, *How to Be Like Coach Wooden* (Deerfield Beach, FL: HCI Books, 2006), p. 85.

5. Vince Lombardi, Jr., *What It Takes to Be #1: Vince Lombardi on Leadership* (New York: McGraw-Hill, 2003), p. 42.

6. Ray Robinson, *Rockne of Notre Dame: The Making of a Football Legend* (New York: Oxford University Press, 1999), pp. 32-33.

7. Todd Archer, "Doesn't Care? That's Not Dallas Cowboys QB Tony Romo," *The Dallas Morning News*, January 22, 2009, retrieved at http://www.dallasnews.com/sharedcontent/dws/spt/columnists/tarcher/stories/012309dnspoarcher.1c13c9ff.html.

8. Juliet Macur, "Romo Shows Resiliency to Overcome Mistakes and Criticism," *The New York Times*, October 14, 2007, retrieved at http://www.nytimes.com/2007/10/14/sports/football/14romo.html.

9. Associated Press, "Harper Has Leadership Written All Over Her," May 4, 2009, NC State Wolfpack website, retrieved at http://www.gopack.com/ViewArticle.dbml?DB_OEM_ID=9200&ATCLID=3732902.

10. Author uncredited, "Western Carolina Succumbs to Summitt, Zolman, & Lady Vol Onslaught, 94-43," College Sports TV website, March 21, 2005, retrieved at http://www.cstv.com/sports/w-baskbl/stories/032105aad.html.

11. Associated Press, "Summitt's Influence Is Deep and Wide," *New York Times*, December 27, 2008, retrieved at http://www.nytimes.com/2008/12/28/sports/ncaabasketball/28summitt.html.

12. Ibid.

13. Tammy Wilhite, "Former Warriorette a Member of Lady Vols for 131 of 1,000 Wins," *Sparta Expositor*, February 26, 2009, retrieved at http://www.spartaexpositor.com/articles/2009/02/28/sports/basketball/doc49a6547a9c69b927352218.txt.

21. Win!

1. Stanley P. Hirshson, *General Patton: A Soldier's Life* (New York: HarperCollins, 2002), p. 474.

2. Quoted by Brad Adler, *Coaching Matters: Leadership and Tactics of the NFL's Ten Greatest Coaches* (Dulles, VA: Brassey's, Inc., 2003), p. 169.

3. John Feinstein, *A Season on the Brink: A Year with Bob Knight and the Indiana Hoosiers* (New York: Simon & Schuster, 1989), p. 71.

4. Quoted by Hugh Wyatt, Coach Hugh Wyatt's Double Wing Football Coaching, retrieved at http://www.coachwyatt.com/aug07.htm.

5. Bill Walsh, interviewed by Richard Rapaport, "To Build a Winning Team: An Interview with Head Coach Bill Walsh," Harvard Business School Prod. #: 93108-PDF-ENG, January 1, 1993, retrieved at http://harvardbusiness.org/product/to-build-a-winning-team-an-interview-with-head-coa/an/93108-PDF-ENG.

6. Chris Broussard, "Van Gundy Refuses To Stop For a Breath," *New York Times*, March 11, 2001, retrieved at http://www.nytimes.com/2001/03/11/sports/pro-basketball-van-gundy-refuses-to-stop-for-a-breath.html?pagewanted=2.

7. Allen Barra, "The Magic's Coach Just Looks Ordinary," *The Wall Street Journal*, June 9, 2009, retrieved at http://online.wsj.com/article/SB124450030598195757.html.

8. Associated Press, "Stan Van Gundy working Magic toward first title," *The Sporting News*, June 2, 2009, retrieved at http://www.sportingnews.com/nba/article/2009-06-02/stan-van-gundy-working-magic-toward-first-title.

9. Stan Van Gundy, "Transcript of Stan Van Gundy's Introductory News Conference with Orlando Magic," *The Baltimore Sun*, June 7, 2007, retrieved at http://www.baltimoresun.com/topic/orl-vangundytranscript00707jun07,0,1993958.story.

10. Quoted by Adam Schefter, *The Class of Football: Words of Hard-Earned Wisdom from Legends of the Gridiron* (New York: HarperCollins, 2009), p. 188.

11. Quoted by Chris Harry and Joey Johnston, *Tales From The Bucs Sideline* (Champaign, IL: Sports Publishing, 2004), p. 27.

12. Rosabeth Moss Kanter, Excerpt from *Confidence: How Winning and Losing Streaks Begin and End* (New York: Random House: 2004), retrieved at http://www.randomhouse.com/catalog/display.pperl?isbn=9780739314043&view=excerpt.

13. Quoted by Vince Lombardi, Jr., *What It Takes to Be #1: Vince Lombardi on Leadership* (New York: McGraw-Hill, 2003), p. 234-235.

14. Quoted by Jack T. Clary, *The Gamemakers* (New York: Follett, 1976), p. 253.

15. Jack Welch, "Building Self Confidence," *Capitalism Magazine*, February 20 8, 2002, retrieved at http://www.capitalismmagazine.com/article.asp?ID=1454.

16. John R. Wooden, Steve Jamison, *Wooden On Leadership* (New York: McGraw-Hill Professional 2005), pp. 9-10.

17. Mike Krzyzewski, "Previous Daily Quotes, Page 7," Lady Mustangs website, retrieved at http://www.ladymustangs.com/dailyquotespage7.htm.

Epilogue: "His Last Words Were About Winning"

1. Sam Farmer, "Wellington Mara, 89; N.Y. Giants Owner Was NFL's 'Heart and Soul'," *Los Angeles Times*, October 26, 2005, retrieved at http://articles.latimes.com/2005/oct/26/local/me-mara26.

2. Quoted by George J. Seperich and Russell W. McCalley, *Managing Power and People* (Armonk, NY: M.E. Sharpe, 2005), p. 212.

About the Author

Pat Williams is the senior vice president of the NBA's Orlando Magic. As one of America's top motivational, inspirational, and humorous speakers, he has addressed employees from many of the *Fortune 500* companies and the Million Dollar Round Table. He has been a featured speaker at two Billy Graham Crusades and two Peter Lowe Success Seminars. He has also spoken on many university campuses.

After serving for seven years in the United States Army, Pat spent seven years in the Philadelphia Phillies organization, two as a minor league catcher and five in the front office. He also spent three years in the Minnesota Twins organization. Since 1968, he has been affiliated with teams in Chicago, Atlanta, Philadelphia, including the 1983 World Champion 76ers, and now the Orlando Magic, which he co-founded in 1987 and helped lead to the NBA finals in 1995. Twenty-six of his teams have gone to the NBA playoffs and six have made the NBA finals. In 1996, Pat was named as one of the 50 most influential people in NBA history by a national publication.

In his NBA career, he has traded Pete Maravich, traded for Julius Erving, Moses Malone, and Penny Hardaway, and won four NBA draft lotteries, including back-to-back winners in 1992 and 1993 and most recently in 2004. He also drafted Charles Barkley, Shaquille O'Neal, Maurice Cheeks, Andrew Toney, and Darryl Dawkins, and signed Billy Cunningham, Chuck Daly, and Matt Guokas to their first professional coaching contracts. Thirteen of his former players have become NBA head coaches, while 17 have become assistant coaches.

Pat and his wife, Ruth, are the parents of 19 children, including 14 adopted from four nations, ranging in age from 24 to 38. For one year, 16 of his children were all teenagers at the same time. Pat and his family have been featured in *Sports Illustrated, Readers Digest, Good Housekeeping, Family Circle, The Wall Street Journal, Focus on the Family, New Man Magazine*, plus all of the major television networks, *The Maury Povich Show*, and Dr. Robert Schuller's *Hour of Power.*

Pat helps teach an adult Sunday school class at First Baptist Church of Orlando and hosts three weekly radio shows. In the last 14 years, he has completed 55 marathons, including the Boston Marathon 13 times, and also climbed Mt. Rainier. He is a weightlifter, Civil War buff, and serious baseball fan. Every winter, he plays in Major League Fantasy Camps and has caught for Hall of Famers Bob Feller, Bob Gibson, Fergie Jenkins, Rollie Fingers, Gaylord Perry, Phil Niekro, Tom Seaver, and Goose Gossage.

Pat was raised in Wilmington, Delaware, earned his bachelor's degree at Wake Forest University, and his master's degree at Indiana University. He has a doctorate in Humane Letters from Flagler University. He is a member of the Wake Forest Sports Hall of Fame after catching for the Deacon baseball team, including the 1962 Atlantic Coast Conference Championship team. He is also a member of the Delaware Sports Hall of Fame.

We would love to hear from you. Please send your comments about this book to Pat Williams at: c/o Orlando Magic; 8701 Maitland Summit Boulevard, Orlando, FL 32810; 407-916-2404; pwilliams@orlandomagic.com Visit his website at: www. PatWilliamsMotivate.com.

If you would like to set up a speaking engagement for Pat Williams, please write his assistant, Andrew Herdliska, at the Orlando Magic address, or call him at 407-916-2401. Requests can also be faxed to 407-916-2986 or e-mailed to aherdliska@orlandomagic. com.